ALL OF WHICH I SAW,
PART OF WHICH I WAS

ALL OF WHICH I SAW, PART OF WHICH I WAS

THE AUTOBIOGRAPHY OF GEORGE K. HUNTON

AS TOLD TO

Gary MacEoin

INTRODUCTION BY ROY WILKINS

1967

DOUBLEDAY & COMPANY, INC.

GARDEN CITY, NEW YORK

To my beloved parents,
George and Elizabeth Hunton

INTRODUCTION

No more convincing testimony to the life work of George Hunton could be found than the full-blown participation of the Catholic Church August 28, 1963, in the March on Washington for Civil Rights and Jobs. Not that George Hunton dictated that participation. He did not. But his quiet work, in support of the dedicated Father John LaFarge, S.J., and his "child," the Catholic Interracial Council, led to the Catholic interracial movement and its effective instrument, the broadened National Catholic Conference for Interracial Justice.

In the early days Father LaFarge and his faithful helper, George Hunton, proceeded ofttimes on faith alone, for the enrollment of the whole Church in the open and heavily secular crusade against discrimination on account of color was a slow business. The Protestant churches and denominations were not knocking down any fences in their haste toward non-discrimination. The Jewish faith was understanding and active, but could go only so far and so fast, because some of its clergy and laity leaned to local interpretations. The world of politics responded only spasmodically and expediently. The business community maintained its exclusions and limitations as did organized labor.

But George Hunton knew about discrimination and about the search for dignity and for freedom of the spirit and the mind. One ancestor, Moses Fletcher, a Protestant, had signed the Mayflower Compact aboard that historic ship in 1620. Three of his grandparents were Irish immigrants who fled to America because of the potato famine of the 1840s. The immigrants came face to face with both foreign and religious discrimination. In New Hampshire Hunton's father was told his Catholicism would hurt his campaign for election to the state legislature.

It was not until after he met Father LaFarge in 1931, however, that George Hunton, a graduate of Fordham University and a practicing attorney, became interested specifically in the plight of the Negro. More and more he became convinced that the lack of information among Catholics was a major hurdle. He worked at this problem through his editorship of the *Interracial Review*.

In his work with other organizations and with leading personalities in the civil rights field Hunton was spurred to concerned activity by his contacts with the harsher realities of the problem.

The famous Scottsboro Case was an electric eye-opener. Then came the first of many campaigns for federal, state, and municipal fair employment legislation. Activity in these drives spread the whole sorry story of racial employment discrimination and indicated plainly the need for wider and wider mobilization of supporters of equal opportunity.

George Hunton proceeded on that mobilization, enlisting increasing response from his own Church. In 1961 he received the St. Francis Peace Medal and in 1962 he and Father LaFarge were honored at a testimonial dinner, whose highlight was a warm congratulatory message from President John F. Kennedy.

No one pretends that the effort against racial discrimination is finished just because some advances have been made. It is safe to assert, however, that a very long and a very significant stride toward the goal here in the United States was taken in 1964 with the enactment of the comprehensive and unprecedented Civil Rights Act of 1964.

That enactment was made possible by a new and powerful element among the usual lobbying groups: the one composed of the three great religious faiths who displayed a thrilling, *working* unity (not a mere joint declaration) in support of the legislative guarantee of human rights. Nothing is taken away from the immensely valuable dedication and activity of the Protestant and

Jewish faiths by stating that the new and very persuasive ingredient was the committed Catholic Church. It spoke not as one priest or bishop here, one school there, one committee in New York, one Order in New Orleans, but in one great voice of prayers and impassioned exhortation. It came down from the liturgy to the Christianity of suffering and of exaltation in righteous combat for the sufferers—both those who endured and those who stood idly and sinfully by.

He doesn't want monuments, but if he did, George Hunton could have none better than this one, not of stone or metal, but of the spirit, one moving the hearts and heads of men toward the most elusive prize of all—love.

Roy Wilkins,
Executive Director,
National Association for the Advancement of Colored People

ALL OF WHICH I SAW,
PART OF WHICH I WAS

Chapter 1

I am no longer a young man. The realization of this fact has been forced on me more brutally than on most. On March 13, 1965, the doctors pronounced me blind, totally and irrevocably blind.

The news was not entirely unexpected. My eyes had troubled me for years. I had endured several operations in my losing battle. But I had never given up hope, never until now.

It is not easy to lose one's sight at the age of seventy-eight. Dedicated researchers and teachers have invented wonderful aids for those to whom God denied or from whom he withdrew the gift of sight. They do much to ease my situation. But their biggest advances are not for me. My age, the state of my health, and the circumstances in which I live, combine to exclude the use of Braille, a seeing-eye dog, or even a metal-tipped cane.

Dear friends do much for me. They read to me and help me handle my affairs. They talk to me and keep me informed of what goes on around me. They have taught me the simple routines which now make up the essence of my life, from my chair along the edge of the rug to the kitchen for a drink of water and a cookie, back to the living room, counting the steps until my outstretched hand connects with the armchair, along the hall to the bathroom, round to the right to my bedroom.

They are very good, these relatives and friends. I thank them many times daily, in their presence and in their absence. But they have their own lives, and they must be off—as I went yesterday—to the bus and the office and the park and the theater. And so I sit here long, lone hours, night hours all, even when the transistor radio that is my constant companion tells me that it is morning or noontime.

Long hours indeed they are, especially those often sleepless ones from two to four in the morning, when the vitality of the blind and of the sighted is equally at its lowest. But they are neither bitter nor empty. If I can no longer look out at the present, I can still look inward at a past which survives in memory, now standing out for me all the more vividly because of the surrounding obscurity.

I have lived a good life. As I look back on it, it presents a certain unity. I can see now, as I could not see when I was living the concrete events, that all of it was designed to fit me for what was to be my principal contribution, the major justification for my living, my work for interracial justice. My revered and devoted parents played their part, as did my schools, my work as a lawyer in New York, the people I met along the way. I have known good people, distinguished people, honorable people. The reader will see as he goes along that it is their story I am recording rather than my own. For what I have to tell is less the story of a life than the story of a movement. The drama is the drama of history, history in which it has been my good fortune to have been a participant or at least a witness.

I think few realize just how historic has been the movement in which I have been involved since 1931. That was the year in which I first met Father John LaFarge, S.J., and became a full-time—if not always fully paid—worker in the Catholic interracial movement. This is something about which I have no false modesty. Let me put it another way. Where would the Catholic Church stand today in the United States, if a few visionaries had not gone out on a limb, risking and often experiencing the displeasure and even the censure of their ecclesiastical superiors, as happened to two Jesuits, the Markoe brothers, out in St. Louis during the 1930s?

The logic of our Catholic principles, as we all know, should keep us well ahead of the sentiment of the general community on any issue of human rights. This is a proposition so obvious that it hardly seems worth stating. Yet the cruel fact is that in the 1930s, the Catholic community was not ahead of the general American sentiment but well behind it in its attitudes toward Negro Americans, even in its concept of them. What is worse, the gap was widening. The big jump forward achieved by the Negro as a citizen in the 1940s and 1950s was already being prepared, while within the Catholic community a vacuum of unconcern still existed.

Up in Harlem, New York, in the 1930s, there was a Catholic grade school in All Saints parish, just north of 125th Street, near Park Avenue. The parish was changing, the white population declining as the Negroes moved north and east from their original nucleus. Some of the Negroes were staunch Catholics, pewholders and dues-payers in All Saints. But not one of their children would be accepted in All Saints parochial school. In a desperate move to keep them out when he had empty desks in the school, the pastor registered the children of the white Protestants of the parish.

It was we of the Catholic interracial movement who put an end to that scandal. But we were not able to do it by appealing to Christian charity or Catholic principle. We had to use the Communist club. We visited the chancery of the archdiocese of New York to warn that the Communists had got a hold of this situation and that they were planning to use it to discredit the Catholic Church among the Negroes not only of Harlem but of the whole United States. This was during the Depression. The Communists were then a domestic force to be reckoned with. They were using all their efforts to penetrate the Negro community, and the remarkable thing is that they had so little success. What we told the Chancery was true. The Communists had the story and were preparing to exploit it. But what was shameful was not the Communist plan but the existence of such a state of affairs and the apathy of Catholic authorities who could be driven to act only for the wrong reasons. And what would have happened if there had been no Catholic interracial movement?

This was an extreme case, but by no means an isolated one. The Catholic community was not prepared at any level for the situation that was developing in the United States. I remember a conversation I had back in March 1934 with Father Louis B. Pastorelli, S.S.J., Superior General of the Josephite Fathers. The specific work of the Josephites was the care of the Negroes in the United States. They had been founded in the 1860s in England by Father Herbert Vaughan, later Cardinal Vaughan, who a short time earlier had toured the United States and surveyed the plight of the emancipated colored Americans. When the first four Josephite priests were ready to undertake a mission, he went to Rome and asked Pope Pius IX to assign them work among Negroes. Pius had recently approved the decrees of the Second Plenary Council of Baltimore, which had appealed for missionary priests to evangelize the emancipated blacks. He told the Josephites to place themselves under the direction of Archbishop Martin Spalding of Baltimore. During the following sixty years, the Josephites had grown to number more than a hundred, and they had continued to carry out their assignment among American Negroes with the greatest dedication, according to the lights.

But what were their lights? This is what Father Pastorelli said to me in 1934 (it was in Philadelphia, at the home of Mrs. Edward Morrell, half sister of Mother Katharine Drexel, two great ladies about whom I shall have more to say later). "I want to talk to you," he said. "We are the ones who know about these people. They are childlike. They have to be treated differently. We don't want them mixing up with the general white community. What Father LaFarge is attempting to do, and if you have any influence over him for heaven's sake stop him, because he is developing a dangerous situation—he is making rice Christians out of Negro converts. They think they are going to come into the Catholic Church because it will provide them with good jobs, when they really are not interested in the Church as such."

At that time and for many years to come, the Josephites did not have a single Negro priest among their members. In fact, there had only been three during the entire life of the society, Fathers Charles Randolph Uncles, John Henry Dorsey, and John J. Plantevigne. All three had difficulty in accepting situations which at that time seemed normal to their white colleagues. "The blood of the Negro boils in resentment of a Jim Crow system in the Catholic Church," one of them once told a conference of missionaries. This and other incidents were distorted by rumor and gossip, and the result was the conclusion expressed to me by Father Pastorelli. Negroes are children. Treat them kindly but firmly. When Fathers Plantevigne, Dorsey and Uncles died, in 1913, 1926 and 1933 respectively, there was no movement to replace them with men of their own race.

The future of the Negro missions was in safe white hands. Few shared the concern which prompted Father John Albert to write to the Holy See, just seven months after the death of his colleague, Father Plantevigne: "During the past six months, out of twenty-four applications for admission to Epiphany Apostolic College, fourteen or fifteen were from colored youths. I believe every one of these was refused admittance. Can this be the will of God?"

It will, I hope, be clear that I do not ascribe any particular malice to the Josephite Fathers in this downgrading of Negro priests in the first third of the twentieth century. The stigma must be shared by the Catholic Church in general. The Josephites were more involved than others simply because they were wholly dedicated to the Negro missions, as they still are. And not all the Josephites shared the official line of the Catholic Church at that time, as expressed to me by Father Pastorelli. I remember a conversation nearly two years earlier, in June 1932, with a Dr. Vincent Warren, also a Josephite. We met at the graduation exercises at St. Emma's Institute, Rock Castle, Virginia, a general and vocational high school for Negro boys, and Father Warren invited me to the graduation exercises to be held the following day at his parochial grade school in Norfolk, Virginia.

Urging me to continue in the interracial work in which I had recently become involved, he said he saw it as a renewal of the program started by the bishops of the United States when they initiated missions for Indians and Negroes. It was a mistake, he insisted, to abandon the original concept of developing internal leadership, just because of isolated negative experiences. "What you are doing is going to produce educated Catholic Negro laymen, and after that, the logic of the situation will give us Negro priests as well."

The process was in fact already beginning. Just about the time I was talking to Father Pastorelli, the Josephites enrolled a Negro seminarian. He was Charles Chester Ball, born in Washington, D.C., in 1913, and his application to study for the priesthood had been rejected by the archdiocese of Baltimore and by six neighboring dioceses before the Josephites took him. He started as a novice at Newburgh, New York, in July 1934, was professed a year later, studied at St. Joseph's Seminary in Washington, D.C., and at Catholic University, was ordained at the National Shrine of the Immaculate Conception in June 1941. He was assigned to a mission church of his own at Glen Arden, Maryland, in 1943, doing graduate work at Catholic University in his spare time, and nine years later he was made pastor of the Josephite Church of the Epiphany in the Georgetown suburb of Washington.

By the time of Father Ball's ordination, the Josephites had charge of a hundred missions in which 135 of their priests looked after 80,000 Negro Catholics and brought adult Negroes into the Catholic Church at the rate of several thousand a year. These missions had 70 schools in which 15,000 Negro children were taught by 300 Sisters and 50 lay teachers. "It is difficult for us today to conceive what a calvary of mis-understanding, of total indifference and neglect the first Joseph-ite missionaries had to ascend in order to inaugurate their work," I wrote at the commemoration of the fiftieth anniversary of their founding, in 1943. And, I added, though their apostolate had vastly increased in diversity and scope, "the missionary to the Negro must still bear a heavy burden laid upon him by the apathy or prejudice of the white majority, Catholic and non-Catholic alike." A quarter of a century later, they continue their dedicated work, still the most important group of Catholic missionary priests working among United States Negroes.

I cannot insist too strongly that all I have to record about individuals and organizations must be kept in the perspective of the times. We were living in an emotional situation which had certain very deep resemblances to that in South Africa today. A dynamism had entered Negro life, causing Negroes to move in many directions into the main stream of American life, and to impinge on the consciousness and sometimes the material interests of American whites, as they had never done before. And the American reaction was as irrational as that of South Africa in the 1960s. They did not try to retain the *status quo*. They tried to push the Negroes back down to a lower level than that to which they had been accustomed. As they probably put it in their own thinking, they slapped them down for getting too big for their boots.

This was not only the general community. It was specifically the institutional Catholic Church expressing the attitudes of its members, high and low. The Catholic University in Washington, D.C., founded in 1888, admitted Negroes from the opening of its school of social science in 1895. When President McKinley visited there in June 1900, the rector could boast that the aims of the university were fixed by those of the Catholic Church, which "knows no race line and no color line." But faculty members, whose leader is believed to have been a Monsignor in charge of—of all places—the philosophy faculty, had the well-established policy changed in the early 1920s. From 1922 to 1936, there were no colored students, in spite of repeated public protests by the Federated Colored Catholics, except a few colored nuns admitted in 1933 at the insistence of Archbishop Michael Curley of Baltimore. Not until 1949 were Negroes admitted to undergraduate dormitories.

I wish that those who say and presumably believe that we shouldn't have pushed so hard, that things would have righted themselves given time, would study the direction of progress during the first third of this century, as well as the direction of progress in South Africa and Rhodesia today. I believe it would convince them of something I wrote in 1953. "Prejudice is an epidemic," I said. "When its virus attacks one group, such as Negroes, it will invariably spread to other minorities— Jews, Catholics and foreign-born. It cannot be cured by fighting any single type of the disease. All the germs must be exterminated before the epidemic can be halted. The most effective way of combating prejudice against any one group is to fight prejudice against all groups." But, I want to repeat, it must be fought. A virus does not die out if you do nothing about it. It spreads until it has consumed the host body.

Much as it grieves me, I must also humbly confess that in this great moral crisis of our nation, the leadership given by the Catholic Church fell far short of that given by many Protestant churches. Their testimony, too, was spotty, nothing to make a Christian triumphalist. But it was relatively good. In the area of higher education, for example, Methodist, Baptist, Congregational, and Episcopal churches, not only the Negro segregated ones but also a fair number of the white, had a long and continuing record of achievement. The white Methodist Church in America was responsible for founding, developing and maintaining nine universities and colleges for Negroes; white Baptist churches were responsible for seven; white Congregationalists and Episcopalians had three or four. In addition, the great universities of the North and Northeast, established in large part under Protestant auspices and still often connected at least emotionally with American Protestantism, were open to Negro students. I think of such institutions as Yale, Harvard, Cornell, Dartmouth, Pennsylvania, Brown, Williams, Columbia. The story was the same with the women's colleges. Vassar, Bryn Mawr, Radcliffe, Wellesley, and Smith all accepted Negro students. Catholic institutions of higher education under their shadow did not. What had Catholics to show? Just one small college, Xavier University in New Orleans founded by Mother Katharine Drexel in 1927, and a handful of Negroes in a few Catholic colleges in the Midwest.

I often ask myself, as others have often asked me, why I stayed all those years in an activity which was unrewarding not only financially but emotionally. By this I mean that you saw so little for your efforts, had to accept the fact that everyone thought of you as a crank, and so forth. I suppose the easiest answer was that I had no choice. You can't leave a spot where you are needed and there is nobody around willing to replace you. But in addition, there were extraordinary compensations, things that sang in your soul and made you know that it was worth the effort, that it had to come right because the people were right.

Just to pick an example, there was the story George Williams had to tell. It was back in the 1930s, and George was a self-confessed hobo in his early twenties. But he was a Catholic. He had ridden the freight cars over most of the country and he had reached a big city in the industrial Northeast when he decided it was time for him to make his Easter duty. It was Saturday, and he decided to go to confession. When he went into the church from the wet and cold of the street, he was told he had no business there.

Next Saturday he tried again in a neighboring city, and this time he was more lucky. They let him go to confession. But that was as far as his luck carried him.

"Sunday morning I went to an early Mass, intending to go to Holy Communion," to continue the story in his own words. "The church was nearly filled and I had to go pretty well up towards the altar. I found a pew where there were only three people, two men and a woman. They turned their heads when I entered, then got up and left the pew.

"Foolishly, I continued to sit there and go on with the service. The church continued to fill more and more, but still I had the entire pew to myself. I looked around and saw people standing, so I said to myself: 'No use of my upsetting the whole church.' So I got up and went to the back, of course feeling keenly the attention I seemed to attract from everybody. Strange as it may seem to some white folks, we have feelings of embarrassment and resentment, the same as they have.

"Off to one side at the rear I saw room in a pew reserved for some religious brothers or clerics, and thinking they at least would understand, I went over and sat there. Rather than let me share their pew, they got up and stood in the aisle. This final humiliation was too much for me, and I got up and left in the middle of Mass.

"On the other hand I have also received kind treatment from both priests and people, and I wouldn't want to give the impression that prejudice is met everywhere, but there is enough of it to do plenty of damage yet."

An incident like that had an extraordinary effect on me, no matter how often I came across it. I knew they were not bad people, these white Catholics. They were my people, people just like myself. Yet what damage they suffered to themselves and caused to others through their insensitivity! The Catholic interracial movement simply had to keep on until wrongs were corrected.

Another incident which affected me profoundly occurred in November 1939. Bishop Joseph M. Corrigan presided, as he did each year while he was rector of Catholic University in Washington, D.C., at the annual meeting of the Clergy Conference on Negro Welfare. There had been considerable discussion earlier that year of the relative lack of success of Catholic missions to the Negro in the United States, and some had been suggesting that there was something in the nature or make-up or culture of the American Negro which made Protestantism more attractive to him than Catholicism. Bishop Corrigan electrified the meeting by reading a long and thoughtful letter he had received on the subject. The writer was a complete stranger, a patient in a tuberculosis hospital in a Southern border state, who identified himself as a Negro, thirty-eight years old, and a Catholic of four years' standing. I published this letter in the *Interracial Review* at the time, and a few extracts will explain why it impressed me as it did.

"The Negro has little sympathy for and much prejudice against the Church," it said. "Sympathy is an emotion that is largely spontaneous and is engendered by things or causes within the province of our understanding. The Negro cannot be in sympathy with Catholicism, when Catholicism smugly refuses to recognize his spiritual needs and complacently closes the door of understanding to him. To be sought and not to seek was not the Savior's teachings. . . . Bewailing the fact that such prejudice does exist and making no concerted effort to remove the cause is not worthy of the Church and contrary to Catholic ideals. The Negro is not largely Protestant because he has a predilection for the Protestant Church nor does his race predispose him to any particular faith, but the very indifference of the Church itself has left him no choice. Is it any wonder he is so cold to the stranger about whom he knows so little? . . . We cannot deny the fact that the Church has acquiesced in the general custom of denying the Negro equality of opportunity in many fields over which it has control. . . . If he is anti-Catholic, it is because the Mother Church has allowed him to become so."

The papal teachings on the social order also played a significant part in keeping me in the interracial movement. As I shall mention later, my Uncle Charles read and taught me to read *Rerum Novarum* when few laymen had ever heard of this encyclical and long before it dawned on anyone that the real meaning of those two words in classical Latin is "revolution." I was further exposed to the papal encyclicals in Fordham, and they marked me indelibly. Although, at first, I did not apply their principles directly to race situations, they preconditioned me for the application when the challenge was offered me. Leo XIII in 1891 had shown the extent to which contemporary poverty and wretchedness resulted from a denial of social justice, and Pius XI elaborated his exposition in *Quadragesimo Anno* in 1931. It was easy for me to see that their analysis was directly applicable to the circumstances of American Negroes, North and South.

These great pronouncements similarly furnished the basis for a Catholic condemnation of the evils of caste and class, and of the heresy of racism involved in common American attitudes to Negroes. They cut the ground from under those Catholics "who were content to abandon to charity alone the full care of relieving the unfortunate, as though it were the task of charity to make amends for the open violation of justice." They proclaimed that "each and every able-bodied man should receive an equal opportunity for work." They insisted that Catholics must not be so preoccupied with the spiritual welfare of others as not to make "a strong endeavor" to help the poor to rise above their poverty.

My study of the history of the period following the emancipation of the Negro also helped to keep me in the Catholic interracial movement. I recall particularly some comments made by Carey McWilliams in his book, *Brothers under the Skin*, published in 1943. They concerned the spiritual collapse of the abolitionist movement, an event assigned by Mr. McWilliams to the year 1876, following the historian Charles A. Beard who had earlier observed that from that time "agitation of the Negro question became bad form in the North." One by one, the great pro-Negro stalwarts of the North, E. L. Godkin, Carl Schurz, T. W. Higginson, and R. W. Gilder, had expressed their doubts that any solution could be found to what was becoming known more and more as the race problem. The high professions of interracial justice of the earlier abolitionist years slipped shamefacedly into oblivion. Historian Albert Bushnell Hart of Harvard, author of *Slavery and Abolition*, of *National Ideals Historically Traced*, and of about a hundred other volumes, set the tone for the new attitude, namely, that the Negro would always remain inferior "in race stamina and race achievement."

There were, no doubt, numerous political and economic causes for this change in Northern sentiment, which had so profound and so disastrous an effect upon the subsequent status of the Negro in this country. But the deepest cause of all was the lack, in the leaders of the Northern emancipation movement, of a genuine, religiously motivated, philosophy of human equality. The Transcendentalists and religious liberals, the Channings and the Martineaus and the Emersons and the Oliver Wendell Holmeses, were personally on fire for human liberty and all good causes. But while their right hand raised the torch of human freedom aloft, their left undermined the sure doctrinal foundations which alone could guarantee that liberty, alone could stand up permanently against the passion and selfishness of man.

It seemed clear to me, as it did to my colleagues of the Catholic interracial movement, that there was a real danger of history repeating itself. In the 1940s and the 1950s, it was clear that a tide was running again with the Negro, that increasing numbers of intelligent and fair-minded Americans were anxious to remedy some of his wrongs. But it was also clear that many of them had no more solid foundation for their friendly emotions than had the earlier Abolitionists, and that consequently a change in the political and economic climate might bring a new wave of defections. I was convinced that it was an error to see the Negro or any other minority group as a problem, for which the general society should seek a solution for its own well-being and comfort. It had rather to be recognized that the problem was the prejudice of the general society, and that the latter could most easily recognize its problem and most effectively act to solve it with the aid of religious principles and motivations. In that light, the modest work of the Catholic interracial movement assumed transcendental value.

It is in this context I look back over my life. Behind the daily routine of pushing bits of paper, of working up small news items, of getting a dozen or twenty people to come to a weekly discussion forum, of scrounging a few dollars to pay the rent, behind all the litter of my extravagantly disordered desk was the human reality. There was a deep disease, a great rottenness in the body politic of the United States and in the Catholic Church as institutionalized in America. It was not something that would cure itself simply by being patient for fifty or a hundred years. On the contrary, it was getting steadily worse both in the nation and in the Church during the first third of the twentieth century. One American in ten was being ground more mercilessly as a human being. He was being progressively denied the opportunity to share in the spiritual riches which Christ had entrusted to the Catholic Church to give abundantly to all.

It has been my good fortune, through circumstances which I shall describe, to be involved in an effort which helped significantly toward correcting that situation. Thanks to my early training and experience, I was imbued with the teachings of the great papal social encyclicals, the concept of universal peace, the urgent need to improve intergroup relations, the importance of the principles enshrined in American democracy. Such ideals have dominated my life as a citizen and as a Catholic. They caused me to throw in my lot with and become part of an aggressive minority, but to do so neither for the sake of aggression nor for the perverted satisfaction of belonging to a minority. I did it, because I saw that in this way it was possible to progress toward the goals that had to be reached, and that otherwise these goals would never be achieved. For the same reason I write this book. It is a story of unfinished business. It is my legacy to those I know will finish it.

Chapter 2

I was born in the little town of Claremont, New Hampshire, on the Connecticut River. The date was March 24, two weeks after the famous blizzard of 1888. My parents were members of St. Mary's Catholic Church, and that is where I was baptized. My father, George P. Hunton, was a native of Vermont; my mother, Elizabeth Dugan Hunton, was born in Charlestown, New Hampshire, about twelve miles south of Claremont.

One of my four grandparents, David Hunton, was a Unitarian minister and a lawyer. The other three derived from the great wave of Irish immigration that reached the United States during the late 1840s and early 1850s as a result of the potato famine. My father's mother was a Kelly and my mother's father a Dugan. My mother's mother was Brigid O'Connor.

Hugh Kelly, my great-grandfather, was probably the first Irishman to settle in Claremont. When he came striding into town along the country roads on his day off, one gossipy neighbor would call to another: "Come on out, there's a real Irishman on view." The Irish often had to stand up for themselves in those days, but that didn't bother Hugh Kelly. In his first job, which was with a family named Jarvis, the other workmen tried to push him around. One day, however, when two of them were loading kegs of cider on a wagon, Hugh taught them a lesson. "Stand aside," he commanded them. Then, single-handed, he picked up the heavy keg and tossed it in the wagon. After that, they respected him.

This Hugh Kelly was a leader. The other Irish families who

subsequently settled in Claremont and were still there when
I was a boy all spoke of the good influence he had been on
them. It was his daughter, Eliza, who married the Unitarian
minister, David Hunton. The marriage did not sit very well
with either of them; perhaps the strain of belonging to different
religious faiths played a part. In any case, they parted before
many years, and my father grew up without knowing his father.
The influences that affected him were exclusively Irish and
Catholic.

My father spent his boyhood in Barnard, Vermont. The area
was suffering from economic depression, and he finally decided
to try his luck in Claremont, from which his mother had come
and where he had relatives. When he was twelve years old,
he teamed up with another lad to drive a herd of eighteen
cattle to a neighboring town, and the money he earned helped
to pay his fare. In Claremont he worked as a grocery clerk
until he finally developed the ambition to own his own clothing
store. One of his uncles, Patrick Kelly, gave him the money
to start his business, advising him at the same time to build
rather than rent. This he did, and the block of stores he constructed is still called Hunton Block. Meanwhile, he lived in a
rooming house along with a man named John Dugan, coachman
for the Baileys, an old New England family. John introduced
him to his sister Elizabeth, and in due course they were married.
My mother had many fine qualities, but there was one in
particular that made for a tranquil home life. She and my
father were always in complete agreement with regard to the
discipline of the children.

Claremont was almost entirely Protestant. There was only a
handful of Catholic families and we then had no school of our
own. But the public school was quite good, and that was
where my brother and sister and myself got our early education.
Our Protestant neighbors were not bigoted. As children, we
were teased a little on St. Patrick's Day, when we wore green
neckties to school, but we were never made to feel uncomfortable

because we were Irish and Catholic. The New Hampshire country around Claremont is lovely, as we learned when we went on long walks with our schoolmates, or on family picnics and trout-fishing trips.

At an early age my parents told me a story about the westerly section of Claremont, or as we always called it, the west part, which was a source of great pride to local Catholics. I recall the occasion very well. We were out for a buggy ride in this part of our little village, when my father reined the horse to a dramatic stop in the roadway between two churches. On the right was the old original Episcopal church, erected in the 1700s; on the left, a small brick chapel that had at one time served as a combination church and school for the Catholics.

More than a century earlier, as my parents told the story, the pastor of the Episcopal church was a Reverend Dr. Daniel Barber. He was married and had a son named Virgil. The pastor, a studious man, spent much time in his study going over the history of the Christian Church. His research finally persuaded him that the Catholic Church was in fact the Church of Christ, and that accordingly he could not in good conscience continue as an Episcopalian rector in Claremont. In 1789, he resigned and moved to Maryland. Subsequently, he became a Catholic and was later ordained to the priesthood. His wife, who had also become a Catholic, entered a convent and took the vows as a nun.

Virgil, who was studying for the Episcopal ministry, followed his parents into the Catholic Church. He studied at Georgetown University, became a Jesuit, and was later sent as a missionary to the village of his birth, Claremont, New Hampshire. Between 1821 and 1823, he built the little brick chapel, the first Catholic church in the entire state of New Hampshire. He soon attracted six Irish-American families to settle nearby, and they were the nucleus of the Catholic population of Claremont.

My parents were proud of their Catholic faith, but there was no exclusivity in their attitude. They were also proud of the fact that a Protestant ancestor, Moses Fletcher, was the ninth person to sign the Mayflower Compact, the agreement for the temporary government of the proposed colony by the will of the majority which was made aboard the *Mayflower* during its historic voyage in 1620.

My parents early taught me to respect the beliefs of others. I remember that one day I happened to mention to a school-mate, the son of an Episcopal clergyman, that I was a descendant of one of the Pilgrim Fathers. To my surprise, he told our teacher, and to my still greater surprise, she asked me to stand up. "An ancestor of Georgie Hunton," she told the class, "was one of the Pilgrim Fathers who landed at Plymouth Rock, Massachusetts, in 1620." Then she turned to me. "George," she said, "what would you like to say about your historic heritage." With more honesty than discretion I blurted out what was on my mind. "I have only heard of this in recent months," I said, "and frankly I am not very proud of my ancestor. I have learned that the Pilgrim Fathers were outspoken in their condemnation of the Catholic Church."

At home that evening I reported the incident to my father. He was not pleased. "My boy," he said, "it is true that in the early days of the Massachusetts Bay Colony, the Puritan Fathers were harsh critics of 'Popery.' They even forbade Catholics to observe Christmas, insisting that Thanksgiving should be the annual festival in America. Subsequently, however, a better understanding developed between the Protestant majority and the Catholic minority in our country. You can see that right here in our own town. Our neighbors and your school-mates are friendly to us, and we to them. Let's keep it that way. Even if we have different backgrounds, we are all Americans. We should be proud to be loyal citizens of our native village."

I think I can fairly claim that my father's respect for the rights of others went all the way. Though there were only two

Negro families in the town, the Norringtons and the Morgans, he treated them just the same as he treated those who had influence. I remember one day Sam Norrington came along with his whitewashing equipment on his way to a job. I must have been about ten years old, and I was standing with my father at the door of his store on Hunton Block.

"Good morning, Sam," my father said.

"Good morning, Mr. Hunton," Sam replied. "I'm coming in soon to pay that bill I owe you."

"That's all right, Sam, no rush," my father said genially.

Anxious to participate in this grown-up conversation, I put in my two cents. "How are things, Sam," I said.

Sam made some appropriate answer and continued on his way. The moment he was out of earshot, my father turned on me with unaccustomed annoyance. "Do you know that man, George," he demanded.

"No, Poppa," I answered, still wondering what had upset him.

"Then don't ever get fresh and call him Sam. Call him Mr. Norrington."

It was my first lesson in interracial manners, and as I found out in due course, my father was fully entitled to give it. The acceptance of Negroes on their merits was a tradition both in his family and in my mother's. When my mother's parents, the Dugans, lived in Charlestown, New Hampshire, a frequent visitor to their home was Bishop James Healy, a Negro who was Bishop of the Diocese of Portland. The diocese then included New Hampshire as well as Maine. A story I often heard repeated was that, if Bishop Healy had not had pneumonia at the time my father and mother were married, he would have performed the wedding ceremony and said the nuptial Mass for them. Bishop Healy was actually very light-colored, and sometimes a neighbor would ask my mother: "When your family had him to dinner, did they really know that he was colored?" My mother always replied: "Of course, everyone knew he was a Negro."

Bishop Healy was born in Georgia in 1830, the son of an Irish immigrant and a Negro slave. He studied for the priesthood at Holy Cross College, where he achieved the highest scholastic honors as valedictorian of the first class to be graduated from the college. I myself went to Holy Cross later, and in course of time I learned much more about this distinguished churchman, the outstanding Catholic orator of New England of his time. He was, until 1965, the only United States born Negro ever consecrated a Catholic bishop.

While our classmates at the Claremont public school treated us well as fellow townsmen, they were not entirely free of prejudice. We were experiencing an influx from Canada of a new minority group lured by the opportunities for employment in our cotton mills. At school we looked down on them, calling them "Frenchies" or more often, "Canucks." They formed their own little ghetto of small, low-rent, wooden frame tenements on the other side of the river. They were Catholics and regular churchgoers. Every Sunday we had two sermons at each Mass in our little church, one in English and one in French.

Like my classmates, I regarded the "Canucks" as a lower form of humanity. But my parents didn't let me get away with it. I remember being sternly reprimanded when I began to make fun of them in our home, mimicking the mispronunciations of the youngsters who came to school with us. My father would always remind us that our own Irish parents and grandparents had gone through a similar experience, and that it would be a poor return on our part if we trampled so quickly on the rights they had won for us.

In due course I also discovered that, though the Irish were more respected than the "Canucks," they also were expected to stay in their place. My father was a public-spirited man. He had a lively interest in community welfare, an interest not too common among the well-to-do of Claremont at the beginning of the twentieth century. But when he decided to run for the state legislature, his best friends counseled him to withdraw.

"You know we all like you," they explained, "but we couldn't vote for you. You're an Irish Catholic." He ran and lost, but he always insisted that his friends had voted for him and that the ballot boxes had been tampered with. He did everything in his power to get a recount, though without success.

He couldn't be kept out of the town meeting, however, and he always participated actively in local affairs. Of course, the matters involved were seldom earthshaking. Even such an issue as the location of four hitching posts near the general cemetery would call for serious deliberation. 1389534

I would often go with my father to these meetings, and one of them was the occasion of a decision which was to influence my entire future. We were on our way home in the company of a man named Perry, the town tailor. "I think you steered that appropriation through very well, George," Perry said to my father. "It's too bad you can't become a selectman, but unfortunately that's out of the question because of what you are."

My father made a gesture of acquiescence, but I could see that deep down he felt the injustice. Suddenly, I realized that the problem was mine as well as my father's. When the tailor had left, I turned to my father. "There must be something we can do about this," I said. "How do you think I should go about it?"

Instead of concentrating on the wrongs that were being done to Catholics by outsiders, my father directed my attention to the part Catholics themselves were playing in maintaining prejudice. "Government in this country is paralyzed by prejudice and corruption," he said. "But don't forget that the organizations run by Irish Catholics are as corrupt as the rest. Take a look at Tammany Hall and at the political machines in Boston and Waterbury. You would be playing a man's part if you helped to clean up some of these. And the way to start is by becoming a lawyer yourself. How about it, young man?"

And so it was decided that I would study law. My Uncle Charles approved wholeheartedly. He was my father's brother, and next to him, he was the big creative influence of my child-hood. Education had not been so easy to come by in his youth, and he had never been able to finish college. But learning was his love, and he was an etymologist and a bookworm. I remember him as the caretaker of Hunton Block, which included my father's store. He educated me painlessly, by answering my endless questions. He had a copy of Webster's big international dictionary, and he would pore over it for hours. "Ask me about a word," he would say. You could mention a word, any word, and he would happily quote from memory, without opening the book, its roots, its derivations and its meaning. Often he would display other feats of memory, such as reciting Daniel Webster's reply to Hayne. He not only admired but studied the papal encyclicals, something not usual among lay Catholics at that time, nor indeed among priests. He knew long extracts by heart, and he would make us learn and recite them. "Stand up over there and do your best," he would encourage us. "Sooner or later, you'll have to learn how to express yourself in public, so you might as well start."

In September 1904 my family moved to New York, where my father went into the real estate business. I was then sixteen and I had already spent two years in Stevens High School in Claremont. I finished high school at Holy Cross preparatory, then entered Holy Cross College. At that time, it was possible to start law school after one year of college. In 1907, accordingly, I registered at Fordham Law. Remembering my father's earlier advice, I quickly became known as an anti-Tammany man. It was not a popular position at Fordham. As most of my colleagues saw it, the Irish Catholics had to stand together to save Tammany, because the Jews were determined to wrest control of City Hall from our good, if corrupt, Irish Catholic district leaders.

My father was always careful not to get involved in attacks on any group. "Two wrongs don't make a right," he would say. "You have to deal with each situation on its merits." Once I started a letter to the New York *Sun* denouncing a Jewish leader who had criticized the quality of the Catholic parochial schools. "Tear it up," my father advised me. "There's considerable truth in his criticisms. In addition, never take a crack at somebody else's faith, if you can help it. Try instead to see why people are the way they are. As a boy, you saw the viciousness of anti-Catholic discrimination in New Hampshire. The Protestant boys have office jobs waiting for them when they leave high school, the Catholics are lucky if they are allowed to tend a loom in the cotton mills or a lathe in the machine shops. What you saw work there against Catholics works in the same way here against Jews. Unless they're twice as good as the others, they can't hope to get ahead."

One of the great influences at Fordham was the radiant personality of Father Terence J. Shealy, S.J. He was a man of immense magnetism, a great orator, the most moving public speaker I ever have heard. Like my Uncle Charles, he was a student of the social encyclicals and a social thinker far ahead of his time. I kept in touch with Father Shealy after I left Fordham. Years later, I became a founding member of a social action study group which he formed, a group that ultimately developed into the Fordham School of Social Work.

I graduated from law school in 1910 and in due course was admitted to the New York bar. My first job was in Harlem, as an employee of the Legal Aid Society. There I quickly learned the basic facts of Negro life as they are revealed to the counsel who defends those too poor to engage their own lawyer.

This knowledge would prove precious to me over the years, yet in many ways it was less decisive than what followed when, six months later, the Society moved me to its office on Manhattan's Lower East Side. This was for me a catalytic experience. Here was a slum, the size of a city, peopled by depressed groups of immigrants, a self-perpetuating jungle in which yesterday's oppressed were too often today's oppressors! But one profound fact stood out. Though the area had troubles aplenty, they were not ethnic in origin. Group and language rivalries indeed existed, yet they never degenerated into religious or national wars.

The phenomenon never ceased to intrigue me, until finally I satisfied myself that it was based on the political district club. A venal and corrupt organization, as I knew all too well, this club nevertheless kept social peace by providing such emotional outlets as picnics, dances and Christmas parties, by meeting financial emergencies, and by giving to all equal opportunity to advance in the organization. Each got the same break irrespective of race, religion or national origin, even of political affiliation or voting record. "One for all and all for one" was not a mere slogan but a philosophy of life.

The lesson stayed with me. When many years later tentative suggestions for an *interracial* organization for Catholics were put forward, many were shocked. I, on the contrary, was elated. I knew it was right. I had seen it work. And I knew that nothing else could work. It was this knowledge that enabled me to help guide the Catholic Interracial Council year after year in the direction in which it moved. It may be, as some of my friends tell me, that I learned the lesson too well. But if I do overrate friendship as a motivation, if I rely on people more than on organizations, surely it is a human fault. Surely the world would be a better place if we had more of it.

On Manhattan's Lower East Side, and afterwards in Brooklyn to which I was transferred in 1915, I got to know a lot of Jews, good, bad and indifferent. Some of the Jewish community leaders I came to admire greatly; others proved almost as ignorant and prejudiced as my Irish Catholic schoolmates.

I still remember a clash I had on my first day in the East Side office. I was tired out from a long day's bootless bickering. Just as I was leaving, one more Jewish client came in looking for help. "All right, I'll stay," I said resignedly. "Go ahead, it's my job." What I got for my enthusiasm was an earful of complaints about dumb, thick and prejudiced Irish Catholics. I stood it as long as I could, but finally I cut him short. "Get out, you damn bigot, yourself," I yelled. "I'm going home." And I did.

Gradually, however, I learned to take the rough with the smooth, and to do what was in my power for all who came to the Legal Aid Society for help. And for this I have been well rewarded. The cause of the Negro would not have advanced as quickly as it has, were it not for the immense help received from Jewish sympathizers. The Catholic Interracial Council itself has constantly been supported by Jewish friends, especially at times when few Catholics were willing to acknowledge it. Here is one group in America which has not forgotten its origins and experience.

Among my own friends there were many who couldn't understand why I'd waste my time, as they said, in such activities. Already I was becoming known by a title that would stick with me all my life, a supporter of unpopular causes. I had no particular desire to be unpopular, still I didn't feel too concerned one way or the other. If I had to be unpopular, I was prepared to be unpopular. What mattered was that I was doing something I felt worth the effort.

At the same time, I realized that I wasn't getting any younger, and that there was not much of a professional future in working for the Legal Aid Society. So after an appendectomy, I decided to hang out my own shingle in Brooklyn. By now, however, the First World War had involved the United States, and Uncle Sam's long arm grabbed me. My martial career was neither more nor less glorious than that of many others. I attained the rank of sergeant and in due course found myself in charge of the Flight Record Office at Scott Field, Illinois. From there I was honorably discharged in January 1919, just two months after the armistice had been signed.

Returning to Brooklyn, I set out once more to build a law practice, engaging in the kind of activities common to young lawyers. I taught moot court practice for a time at Fordham Law School. To the consternation of some of my friends, yet in the spirit of the advice earlier given me by my father, I made common cause with the Brooklyn Independent Democratic Committee against the leadership of the Democratic "boss," the late John H. McCooey. Homer Cummings, also since deceased, was then national chairman of the Democratic party, and Herbert Pell (similarly deceased) was Democratic state chairman. I had contacts with both Mr. Cummings and Mr. Pell, and for a time I thought it might be possible to woo them away from their support of Boss McCooey. One day, however, at a luncheon with Mr. Pell I was made to realize how naïve I had been. I presented him with a concrete plan to ensure a greater participation of the rank and file of the Democratic party in the state primary campaign, thus weakening the power of the "machine" to handpick candidates. All that would be necessary, I said, would be to enact legislation to provide that registration for the elections (done in late September) should coincide with the primaries. This would mean that everyone who registered as a Democrat would at the same time cast his vote in the primaries. To my chagrin, Mr. Pell thought it a very bad idea. "It is highly important," he insisted, "that county and district chairmen retain their authority to designate the party candidates in their respective counties and districts." He had no use for primaries, if they meant a choice of candidate.

After that, I realized that the only way was open opposition. In the primary campaign held the following September, I joined the Independent Democratic Committee headed by the late James E. Finnegan, our choice as Democratic candidate for surrogate of Kings County. I was designated to run for the office of county judge. We waged a vigorous campaign by word of mouth and street-corner rallies, urging our fellow Democrats to join in a movement to reform the courts and the administration of welfare. But tradition was too strong for us.

When the day came, few turned out. The "machine" swamped the primaries as usual. Jim Finnegan succeeded in carrying four assembly districts, but not one of the candidates on our local slate survived.

My interest in local politics, however, was not nearly as great as in the national scene. Already in January 1918, while the war was still in progress, President Wilson had formulated his Fourteen Points for a new postwar order. They were intensely idealistic yet completely practical, and I became totally sold on them. Wilson was convinced that a spirit of revenge would surely breed a new war, a belief in which history was not long in vindicating him. He also knew that the day of unrestricted national sovereignty was over, that world peace required "a general association of nations . . . under specific covenants."

Many in the United States, however, shared the desire of the victors in Europe for a vindictive peace. An even greater number were not ready for the surrender of sovereignty implied by the League of Nations. Those to whom the League was anathema included most Irish Catholics, and they in fact played no small part in the movement that culminated in the rejection by the United States of Wilson's great dream. One of the few who backed it wholeheartedly was Father John A. Ryan, the great apostle of Catholic social action. Years later, I was destined to work closely with him, but already I was totally committed to the ideas he championed.

Just as the war ended in November 1918, Father Ryan was expounding his viewpoint in a five-article series in *America* magazine. Wilson's efforts to secure an armistice before Germany fell into the disorders of Bolshevism, he told his readers, represented a service to the cause of peace and of Christian charity, as contrasted with the "diluted Prussianism" of those Americans who wanted to trample on the vanquished. The League of Nations, he argued, was possible because the war had created a mood of sincerity and of willingness to avert war. It was desirable because it could settle future disputes peacefully.

The following year, when Wilson returned from Paris, Father Ryan renewed his appeal. Those who misrepresented and disparaged the President, he said, were "hirelings of plutocracy, backward-looking Bourbons and players of peanut politics." The enemies of the League, led by the late Senator Henry Cabot Lodge of Massachusetts, were—he charged—substituting slogans for reason when they claimed that the League would mean a lessening of sovereignty. "Those who fear that the League will fail because the selfish interests and purposes of the nations will impel them to disregard its obligations forget that peoples will henceforth be the makers of national policies and the interpreters of national interests, and they will conceive national interests in terms of popular welfare, not in terms of national power, conquest, and economic advantage for a few special groups in the nation. In other words, national interests will hereafter be interpreted as bound up with peace and international justice. The rulers of states will not in the future bring the nations to the verge of war over a dispute in Morocco."

Wilson himself sought popular support by making a wide speaking tour across the United States. It was during this tour, while making his way back east from the Pacific coast, that the strain and fatigue brought on a sudden breakdown in September 1919. Although not all recognized it immediately, he was a dying man from that time. He detached himself from politics and without his dynamic leadership, the cause he had sponsored was hopeless.

Those of us who believed in it, however, continued to fight on. During the 1920 campaign, in which the Republicans pitted Warren Harding against Democrat James Cox, I joined an organization called Woodrow Wilson Democracy. It was a movement which sought to cross party lines in an attempt to mobilize all possible support for the League of Nations. My fellow workers in this unpopular cause included my friend Schuyler Warren, John W. A. Kelley, Judge Westcott of New Jersey, and Hamilton Holt, editor of the *Independent*. I had developed an immense admiration for Woodrow Wilson as a man, and it was for me a matter of the most intense pleasure and pride when I was chosen as one of a delegation from the organization to talk to the President, the first group of citizens to do so as he began to recover from his paralytic stroke. The delegation included Mrs. Schuyler N. Warren, Sr., and Schuyler N. Warren, Jr., Edwin F. Gay, Mrs. Malcolm Forbes of Boston, Mr. and Mrs. John F. Moors of Boston, Professor John Bates Clark of Smith College, the Honorable Theodore Marburg of Baltimore, Joseph N. Price of New York, and other leaders from Massachusetts, Connecticut, Pennsylvania, and Maryland. It was October 1920, shortly before the presidential elections which would bring victory to Senator Cabot Lodge's candidate, Warren Harding, ring the deathknell of Wilson's hope of American participation in the League, and inaugurate an administration that would be stigmatized as one of the most corrupt in American history.

We were received in midmorning in the Blue Room of the White House by the President seated in a wheel chair. He was accompanied by two nurses and by his secretary, Joseph P. Tumulty. After all of us were introduced, two spokesmen told the President that we wanted to work in our various communities for the League, and that we wanted a statement from him insisting that this was one of the most important issues of the election campaign. He was quite happy to accommodate us, and he had in fact prepared a statement in advance. As he spoke, he had frequently to refer to the written text, and his hands trembled distressingly as he did so. His speech also was difficult, and the expression on his face revealed his discomfort. It was unhappily clear that he no longer had the vitality to infuse the needed life into the movement.

The one man who still sought to arouse the country was Father Ryan. Radio had not yet become the direct road to the masses which it would shortly be for Father Coughlin and others. The newspapers were not concerned. So all Father Ryan could do was to needle the bishops and the Catholic press, hoping through them to arouse the Catholic public. With the Catholic editors he could speak his mind openly. Despite the call of Pope Benedict XV, he told them bluntly, they had never been more than "spasmodic and half-hearted" in their application of the principles of Catholic political ethics to international questions. In speaking to the bishops, he had to be more politic. Still his meaning was clear. Not only has the Catholic press been silent, he said, but "no sympathetic voice has been raised in any more authoritative circle." This challenge did in fact produce an endorsement of Benedict XV's approval of the idea of an international organization to place world peace on a solid foundation, in a joint pastoral of the American bishops. But the pastoral had no echo in Catholic opinion. Nor was Woodrow Wilson Democracy any more successful. We kept the organization alive until 1924, although it was already obvious that the situation that had brought it into being no longer existed. The quarrel within the Democratic party over the relative advantages of William McAdoo and Alfred E. Smith as Democratic presidential candidate in 1924 furnished the *coup de grâce*. Hopelessly divided among ourselves on this issue, we decided to wind up our affairs.

It was not many years before I found myself involved in yet another unpopular cause, the one which would be central to my activities for the rest of my life. I had little idea when I started that it was going to become so important for me. At the same time, my interest in race relations was a natural development of my total experience. I have already described the basic preparation made by my parents when I was a child. My apprenticeship in Harlem with the Legal Aid Society had given me a firsthand knowledge of the Negro and his concrete problems in our society. And a further dimension had been added, thanks to Father Shealy, the Jesuit social scientist under whose influence I had fallen at Fordham.

Some time after I had graduated from law school, Father Shealy conducted a course on Catholic social teaching at Xavier

High School, on West Sixteenth Street in Manhattan. The core of the instruction was Pope Leo XIII's encyclical *Rerum Novarum*, on the condition of labor and the reconstruction of the social order. We were also made to study the various statements of the American bishops, in which they applied the papal principles to conditions in the United States. In this way, we got a deeper sense of the values enshrined in American democracy, and we also began to see how serious was this country's unfinished business because one citizen in ten, our entire Negro population, was denied the most basic rights guaranteed him by the Constitution.

At these courses I met a number of men who shared my interest in the problems of our society. I recall in particular John W. A. Kelley and Thomas W. A. Crowe. Kelley was, like me, a native of New Hampshire and a lawyer, a man some years my senior. He was then working for the city, would later develop a big private practice and become a judge. Crowe was for many years one of the attorneys of the Office of the Corporation Counsel of New York City. We were encouraged to form groups and give lectures to existing groups, such as Catholic sodalities and Holy Name societies. This we did. But while we referred in our talks to the principles of Catholic social teaching with which our American treatment of the Negro was at variance, I do not think that any of us took our own words too seriously in this regard. It remained for Father John LaFarge, S.J., to bring the lesson for me down from the realm of theory to the practical level.

My long-time friend Schuyler Warren, whom I have already mentioned as a member of the delegation to meet President Wilson in 1920, was a cousin of Father LaFarge. It was he who told me of Father LaFarge's interest in an industrial school for Negroes near Baltimore, the Cardinal Gibbons Institute. Father LaFarge had organized a fund-raising committee in New York headed by his brother Oliver, who was both a talented artist and an executive of General Motors. Arthur C. Monahan of the education department of the National Catholic Welfare Conference

(NCWC) had been its secretary, but he found in 1931 that he could not continue. It sounded like a job that was worth doing and that at the same time would not complicate unduly my life as a practicing lawyer. I told Schuyler I was interested. Little did it occur to me that I had made the most important decision of my life.

Chapter 3

One's first impression of Father LaFarge gave scarcely an inkling of the profound depths of the man. I remember very clearly the solidly built man of middle height, about fifty years old, who came noiselessly into the small parlor of the Jesuit house on West 108th Street, near Riverside Drive, in Manhattan. It was one of his characteristics. He never seemed to make any noise, just as he never tried to make an impression. But there was a quiet vigor and purposefulness about him. His hair was still dark. The eyes that looked steadily at you through the big rimless glasses were infinitely kindly. Here was a man, I told myself, to whom one could say what he thought.

I already, of course, knew something about him. His family had deep roots in New England. Through his mother he was related to Commodore Oliver Hazard Perry of Lake Erie fame, and to Benjamin Franklin. His father was America's most distinguished mural painter. His great-uncle, Louis F. Binnse, was United States Consul General for the Pope back in the days of the Papal States. His architect brother, Christopher Grant, was co-designer of the Episcopal Cathedral of St. John the Divine in New York. Another brother, Bancel, was an outstanding artist. He himself was acquiring a national reputation as a member of the staff of *America*, which he had joined, at the invitation of the editor in chief, Reverend Wilfrid Parsons, S.J., in 1926.

He had little difficulty in getting me to tell him about myself. Mindful of the purpose of the interview, I stressed my previous associations with Negroes, starting with the experiences in my early youth in Claremont, New Hampshire. I described my work with the Legal Aid Society in Harlem, and my study of the social encyclicals under Father Shealy. But I made no attempt to present myself as a man dedicated to the cause of the Negro. On the contrary, I said, my experiences had left me indifferent and apathetic. It seemed to me that American Negroes themselves had provided little support for the leaders who were trying to win equal opportunities and equal justice for them. While that situation continued, I suggested, there was little outsiders could do for them.

Father LaFarge did not challenge my position directly. Instead, he began to tell me about the Cardinal Gibbons Institute. He had been assigned to mission work in St. Mary's County, in southern Maryland, in 1911, and he had worked there for the following eleven years, except for a break of a year for his tertianship in 1917–18. The project began in 1916, when an $8000 check from Cardinal Gibbons enabled him to buy land at a location called Ridge. It took him several years to arouse any significant additional support. In 1921, however, he was put in touch with Arthur Monahan of the National Catholic Welfare Conference education department in Washington, a man with considerable experience of Negro education in the South.

With Mr. Monahan's support, he organized a committee which met in early 1922 under the chairmanship of Archbishop Curley, who had succeeded Cardinal Gibbons as Archbishop of Baltimore. The committee, as Father LaFarge described it, was mixed in every sense. It included whites and Negroes, Catholics and Protestants, men and women, local southern Marylanders, Baltimoreans and Washingtonians, and people from other parts of the country.

The following year, he got a check for $35,000 from the Knights of Columbus, and he was able to start building. Victor H. Daniel, who had taught at Tuskegee Institute and at the Bordenstown Manual Training School for Negroes in New Jersey, was secured as principal, and his wife was made assistant principal. Negroes all through the county were asked to help a project which would be to the benefit of their children, and they formed a series of auxiliaries, some of which got white support as well. The Federated Colored Catholics, an interstate Negro organization, took an active part. Soon affairs for the Cardinal Gibbons Institute became a recognized part of Negro life. It gave Catholic Negroes an immediate object to work for. They responded with enthusiasm to what in fact was the first national project undertaken by Catholics on their behalf.

Meanwhile, Mr. Daniel, the principal, was talking to neighboring farmers, suggesting that a program of better farming could be developed under the guidance of the Institute and in collaboration with it. As a first step, he showed them how they could improve their homes by putting glass in the windows, by repairing fences, by building simple outdoor toilets. Enough of them listened to him to make a start, and gradually others followed the example.

One thing became very clear to me, as I listened to the low-keyed recital of the trials and modest successes of a project into which Father LaFarge had channeled an enormous part of his apparently endless energies for fifteen years. Here was a man for whom obstacles were simply to be surmounted. It would be an experience to work in such company. I undertook to explore the matter more fully.

The first step, in September 1931, was to meet the committee in New York which raised money for the Institute. In addition to Oliver LaFarge and Schuyler Warren, I then talked to James J. Hoey, Dr. E. P. Roberts, Maceo Thomas and Frank Sadlier, all people with whom I would long continue to be associated. One of the things that impressed me was that the committee had Negro members as well as white. I liked that, because it fitted in with my observations when I had worked much earlier for the Legal Aid Society on Manhattan's Lower East Side. The secret of the success of the political clubs was the principle of social equality. It was a principle that few were willing to apply to work with Negroes in those days. We had to fight hard for it in the following years.

Operating at a distance from the school, as it was, the committee had difficulty in keeping itself fully informed. It was accordingly agreed that I should become committee secretary and fund raiser, and that I should pay a visit immediately to Ridge, Maryland, to see the school for myself, talk to the staff and students, and draw up a realistic plan for financing the operation. I found the physical plant in good shape. In addition to the main school building constructed with the funds provided by the Knights of Columbus in 1923, two fine brick wings had been added through the generosity of James Byrne of New York. A one-story brick and stucco dormitory had been erected with a donation from the Catholics of Pittsburgh. Mr. Daniel and his wife were also well housed. The Institute, in addition to providing both boys and girls with general and technical education of a kind not elsewhere available to them, had a valuable extension program and served as a center for community exhibits, contests and other activities.

The one big problem was financing. We needed $40,000 a year for operating expenses. We received help from the General Education Board of Maryland and some other organizations, but we were in great part dependent on contributions from individuals. These had not been so hard to get while the economy of the country was riding high during the 1920s, but since the onset of the Great Depression, now in its deepest depths, it was going to be a very tough job indeed.

Such was the problem as I presented it at a meeting of the New York committee at the Catholic Club on Fifty-ninth Street on my return. We decided that we would fight to stay afloat as long as possible. Various members of the committee pledged additional contributions. I was given the specific job of trying to reach a wider public for support.

I ran immediately straight into a very hard and unpalatable

fact. Nobody was in the least interested in doing anything for the Negro, or at least practically nobody. This was something Father LaFarge already knew very well. He had struggled on for years against it, getting support for his project through his own personal contacts and persuasive powers. But now circumstances had made it necessary to get beyond this point, and I was the one who was called upon to find a way to pass from the personal to the institutional, to get some significant segment of the Catholic public concerned about their Negro brothers.

This task quickly brought me into contact with the few other activities for Negroes which then existed under Catholic auspices. One of the first and most important was that of Reverend Mother Katharine Drexel, the founder and then Superior of the Sisters of the Blessed Sacrament for Indians and Colored People. For forty years, these Sisters had been devoting their main efforts to the welfare of the Negro. They had established at least thirty-five schools in fifteen states. More recently, they had opened a university for Negroes in New Orleans, Xavier University, the first Catholic college for Negroes in the United States.

I met Mother Katharine Drexel for the first time in early 1932, when she was already seventy-four years old. One would never have suspected her age. She was young in body and soul and continued so right up to her death at the age of ninety-seven in March 1955. She was an extremely vivacious person, always good-humored, a twinkle in her bright blue eyes. When she talked, her head seemed to dance, as she turned rapidly from one to another of the group she was addressing. Her father was Francis A. Drexel, a member of the Philadelphia banking firm which endowed the famous Drexel Institute of Technology. At an early age, she became interested in the problems of the American Indians; and when President Grant decided, after the Custer massacres, to open the reservations to all religious denominations, she began to help Catholic missionaries in New Mexico, California, Tacoma, Washington, and other parts of the West. Her interest in the Indians soon expanded to include the

Negroes too, and she finally decided that she should not only contribute money but give herself to the work. After a training with the Sisters of Mercy, she founded her own congregation, starting with sixteen companions at Cornwells Heights, Pennsylvania, in 1891.

In the fall of 1932, she invited me to attend the dedication ceremonies of the new college buildings of Xavier University at New Orleans. She had already shown keen interest in the work I was doing, and she had said that lack of publicity was one of the unsolved problems of her own projects. Anxious to show her what was possible in this area, I called on the various New Orleans newspapers, and I succeeded in arousing the interest of the editor of the *Times-Picayune* sufficiently to have him send a reporter to interview Mother Katharine. The reporter did her job well. She wrote an excellent account of the work of the Sisters and particularly of the benefits Xavier University was conferring on the city and people of New Orleans.

Not everyone, however, was pleased by the publicity. No sooner had I got back to New York than I got a very distressed telephone call from Mrs. Edward D. Morrell. Mrs. Morrell, who lived in Philadelphia, was a half sister of Mother Katharine, five years younger, and a generous supporter not only of her work but of all efforts on behalf of the Negro. She called my attention to a very caustic report in the religion section of the current issue of *Time* magazine. (*Time* was then in its iconoclastic youth and loved nothing better than making people look ridiculous.) This particular article was particularly offensive. It was from the New Orleans correspondent and was presumably inspired by the totally different story which I had been instrumental in having published in the New Orleans newspaper.

The story, which can be found in the issue dated October 24, 1932, opened with a long account of the Drexel family, its wealth and its connections, then zeroed in on the career of the idiosyncratic daughter who had allowed a casual exposure to some Indian curiosities to channel her life from the impliedly normal frivolities of the idle rich into personal effort and poverty, concurrently diverting her wealth from the high society that could reasonably expect to enjoy it to the support of starving Indians and Negroes.

As if that were not bad enough, she had now reached the further extreme of lunacy of imagining that Negroes could become members of civilized society. At a cost of $500,000, so the article ran on, she had erected a magnificent college building of Indiana limestone, in Tudor Gothic style, enrolled 500 Negro boys and girls for whom she proposed to provide courses leading to B.A. and B.S. degrees, offering in addition to the arts, four-year programs in pharmacy, pre-medical, teaching, and home economics. She had provided this building with such modern conveniences as proper kitchens, and—horror of horrors—a library to which she had donated half of the Drexel collection of books valued at $3,000,000. Her sister, Mrs. Morrell, and herself had guaranteed an eventual $5,000,000 endowment. The faculty included eight Sisters, four laywomen, two priests, six laymen, and a football coach. Only Catholic Negroes would be admitted.

So far *Time*'s recitation of the alleged facts. But *Time*, while calling itself a newsmagazine, always found devices to editorialize. And so the editorial comment followed, in these words: "Resentful of such lavishness, while so many of Louisiana's whites are hungry and jobless, Xavier's neighbors have suggested that the College motto be: 'Is Yo' Did Yo' Greek Yit?'"

I went to see the religion editor of *Time*—its offices were then in the Chrysler Building—and I protested not only the nastiness but the outrageous misrepresentation of important facts easily verifiable by any responsible newsman. It was totally untrue to say that the College was only for Catholics. It had not had before, did not have then, or would not have in the future any religious test. It was undenominational, and students were accepted without direct or indirect reference to their religious affiliation, practice or interest. There was no guarantee or promise of any money from Mother Katharine or other Drexels. The only endowment was that of the gratuitous service of those teachers who were members of Mother Katharine's congregation. The allegation of endowment would increase the difficulty of getting money to run the college. The physical plant was intended for an eventual enrollment of 500, but actually there were only 280 students, and to accept more would require outside aid, because very few Negroes could pay even nominal tuition fees.

The religion editor of *Time* was personally polite but professionally outrageous. Rejecting all notion of an obligation in justice to make restitution to an injured party, or even an obligation to readers to correct misinformation, he insisted that he had full confidence in his New Orleans correspondent and would retract no word he had written. "If you have a grievance," he summed up, "write us a letter or have the principal of the college do so. I won't undertake to print it, but it will be printed if the editors decide it has merit."

I was furious, but there was little I could do. As I rose to leave, I had an idea. "Tell me," I said, "what has been your personal reaction when you talked to a graduate of a Negro university? Did you find that he fitted the description your New Orleans correspondent gives?" He was taken aback. "I don't believe," he admitted honestly enough, "that I ever had such an experience." That was all I wanted. "One day," I retorted, "I hope you will be liberal enough to realize how illiberal is your present stand on a kind of education about which you know nothing."

I did not get the religion editor to alter his stand, but they did print in their Letters section two weeks later a letter, signed by Mrs. Morrell, in which she corrected the more extravagant misstatements of fact. *Time* itself made no apology nor even admission of error, still less offer of restitution. It printed, similarly without comment, two other letters dealing with the subject. One was sort of funny. It was from a reader who felt that the description of the attractive and architecturally imposing buildings of Xavier implied that the South lacked gracious colleges for its white youth, and he listed a number of its stately and spacious campuses, colleges not ashamed of comparison with the best in the North. The other was a fine letter. Its author was Horace M. Bond, who identified himself as a Protestant Negro from Nashville, Tennessee, and his comment was the more significant because he had accepted as correct *Time's* misstatement that Xavier was restricted to Catholics. He lashed out at the authorities of the state of Louisiana who in 1930 had contributed $40.60 to the education of each white child in its public schools, but only $7.84 per Negro. He reminded them that the great tax-supported State University at Baton Rouge was for whites only, and that the magnificent new Medical School in New Orleans had been built and was supported by state tax funds, but it also was for whites only. "No Negro need feel ashamed of liberal arts colleges for the race," he continued. "The writer, a Protestant Negro, ineligible to attend or teach at New Orleans' Xavier (*Time*, Oct. 24) invokes Protestant blessings on the enterprise, thanks God for Mother Katharine Drexel whose Catholic philanthropy promises to give Louisiana Negroes what their State refuses to give them."

So from a publicity viewpoint, the matter didn't end up as badly as it might have. And Mother Katharine was delighted with the retort I had given to the *Time* religion editor about his illiberality. She used to tell the story for years to give her associates a lift, whenever an attempt to get publicity for their work turned out less favorably than they had hoped. The incident, in addition, confirmed her belief that I would finally succeed in breaking through the curtain of prejudice and in getting a better image of the Negro across to the American public, or at least to the American Catholic public, which was our more immediate goal. Her sister, Mrs. Morrell, and herself had already undertaken to pay me an annual salary of $4000 to enable me to dedicate myself full-time to this work in New York.

They said that all previous efforts at getting publicity for the work of the Sisters of the Blessed Sacrament had failed, and that I had for the first time shown that it was actually possible to reach the press. So it was agreed that I should continue my activities in New York, promoting both the work of the Sisters and the Cardinal Gibbons Institute, as well as creating a general climate of interest in the Negro among Catholics.

Small as the salary was, it was not to be despised at the depth of the Depression. And the affairs of the Cardinal Gibbons Institute had reached a condition in which it could offer me nothing. In fact, it had become obvious that we were fighting a losing battle. We stayed with it as long as we could, but in the end we had to admit defeat. On the last day of 1933, we turned over the property to Archbishop Curley of Baltimore. The Provincial of the New York-Maryland province of the Jesuits assigned Father Richard M. McKeon, S.J., a former professor in Georgetown University and in St. Peter's College, Jersey City, New Jersey, to take charge of a holding operation. He was forced to suspend the classes, but he maintained the Institute as a center for various activities of the Negro community, and when things got a little better, it was reopened as a day high school in 1936.

Meanwhile, our work in New York was continuing toward its logical and destined goal. Father LaFarge had always seen the Cardinal Gibbons Institute within a much broader framework. He realized that it was necessary to begin in one particular place and with a concrete activity, but that not even a small problem could be properly solved except in a total context. And the total context was the position of the Negro in the Catholic Church in the United States and the attitude of the average American Catholic toward Negroes, including Catholic Negroes. It was a subject we used to discuss frequently. There were at that time about thirteen million Negroes in the United States, of whom five million were members of various Protestant churches and a quarter of a million were Catholics, leaving nearly eight million with no religious affiliation. "We send missionaries to China and Africa to preach the Gospel," he used to say, "and of course we should continue to do that. But how can we justify our neglect of the eight million right here at home?" However, he would not agree that the attitude of the American whites was usually based on a hatred of the Negroes, as some of the more frustrated Negro leaders were beginning to proclaim. He would insist that the dominant attitude was one of apathy and inertia resulting from ignorance. Thus his solution was an educational program among whites, a program to teach them what Negroes were really like, and what their rights as citizens and as children of God were. Such was his conviction when I first met him, and such it always remained.

To promote his ideas among his fellow priests, Father LaFarge started an organization called the Clergy Conference on Negro Welfare. His early associates included Father James M. Gillis, the dynamic Paulist speaker and writer, long-time editor of the *Catholic World,* and the Markoe brothers from St. Louis, to whom I shall return later. They were both Jesuits, and they have to be counted among the true pioneers of the interracial movement.

Father William M. Markoe had long been active with the Federated Colored Catholics, a fraternal organization of Negroes which was particularly strong in St. Louis and in Baltimore. It was something like the Lions or the Elks, but it inevitably had racial overtones. Each year it held a convention in a different city, and New York was the venue in 1932. It was a big success. St. Patrick's Cathedral was filled for the special Mass. It was an all-Negro congregation, though with a white priest. At that time, there was only one Negro priest engaged in pastoral work in the whole United States. The first ordination of four Negro members of the Society of the Divine Word did not take place until the following year.

I was present at some of the activities of the convention, and I was in full sympathy with the effort to present Negro Catholics as regular and respectable members of the Catholic community, as indeed they were. But I had a deep reservation, and it was one that I entertained about the whole of the work in which we were engaged. It seemed to me that in spite of ourselves, we were caught in a trap. We were involved in trying to improve relations between the races. But the gulf between them was already so deep that we seemed in practice to be building up separate groups on each side of that gulf, on the one side whites, and Negroes on the other. The Federated Colored Catholics were a group identified by race. The stronger they became, the more likely were they to increase race tensions and promote race hatreds.

Father William Markoe had come to New York to the convention as national editor of the magazine of the Federated Colored Catholics, then called *The Chronicle* and later *Interracial Review*. While in the East, he was working with Father LaFarge trying to stir up some interest in other priests in the work of the Clergy Conference on Negro Welfare. The three of us would go from parish to parish, often getting very unfriendly receptions. But it was on one of those drives that I made my decision to cast in my lot permanently with the movement with which I had now been associated about two years.

We had been up to see Father Michael J. Mulvoy, C.S.Sp. Here was a man who was doing a fine job at a time when few Catholic priests had any sense of pastoral obligation toward the Negroes in their parish. He had been pastor for about six years of St. Mark the Evangelist in Harlem, and he had integrated himself thoroughly into the neighborhood. His assistants and himself were attended by a Negro doctor and went to a Negro dentist. He was a member of the major social agencies, the West Harlem Council of Social Agencies, the Housing Committee, committees which dealt with WPA regarding relief and relief work. He was also a friend of the Federated Colored Catholics and encouraged them in his parish.

It may have been what we had seen at Father Mulvoy's that

brought the conversation in the direction it took later. In any case, as we were leaving to take Father LaFarge back to his home on West 108th Street, Father Markoe remarked that they were trying to get away from the concept of an all-Negro organization and planned to change the name from Federated Colored Catholics to the National Catholic Interracial Federation. It was the best news I had heard in a long time, and I told them so. "I always had deep reservations about the direction we were taking," I said. "Long ago, when I worked for the Legal Aid Society in lower Manhattan, I became convinced that the only way to achieve social harmony is by treating all the groups as equal and making them work together. And that means interracial action. Now, you can count me in all the way."

Not all the members were happy about the change. Some of them had become convinced that there was no possibility of ever reaching a mutually satisfactory understanding with whites. A few even objected to white chaplains, although they had no alternative because there were no Negro priests then available. But the majority agreed with Father Markoe and changed the name and finally the attitude also. "We were wholly wrong for years," Elmo Anderson said to me later. Elmo, a New Yorker who was at that time first vice-president, subsequently became a bulwark of the Catholic interracial movement in New York. "We were wrong," he said, "when we went off to a strange city each year for a three-day convention to talk about the people we should have been talking to."

From that time I was indeed wholly committed to interracial work. Father Markoe was pastor of St. Elizabeth's parish in St. Louis, and he had lent the name of the parish to the bulletin which was the official organ of the Federated Colored Catholics. When the organization became the National Catholic Interracial Federation, the name of the bulletin was changed to the *Interracial Review*. But his parish work was proving too much for Father Markoe, and there was absolutely no hope of his getting any help from the Archbishop, who wanted no Catholic participation in any work for Negroes. So we arranged that I should take over the work of editing the *Interracial Review*. Starting with the January 1934 issue, I wrote the editorials and prepared the materials for the printer. Everything was sent out to St. Louis, where Father Markoe continued to read proof and help with the make-up. This procedure continued until the end of 1934, when the entire operation was shifted to my office in New York.

Meanwhile, in New York, it had become steadily more obvious that we could make some dent on Catholic indifference toward the Negro only if we developed an organization committed to this specific objective and prepared to spend the requisite time and effort on the task. Thanks to Father Gillis, we had an audience to which we could present our ideas through the Catholic Hour on the Paulist radio station, WLWL. He would give us a fifteen-minute slot for four weeks, then a couple of months later, offer us another four weeks, and so on. It was our first opportunity, and we formed a temporary committee to take advantage of it. The impact was phenomenal. Franklin Delano Roosevelt had just taken over the office of President of the United States, in the depth of the worst depression the country had ever known. Feeling was intense regarding the program to which he was committed, the repeal of Prohibition and the inauguration of the peaceful social revolution, of which NRA was then the most prominent feature, and of which we think today mainly in respect of the Social Security system that is its permanent monument.

Some of the things we said on these programs sounded pretty shocking to our Catholic listeners. One of our great speakers was the Honorable James J. Hoey, who was then U. S. Collector of Internal Revenue in New York City. Jim Hoey was a dedicated member of our group. He became first president of the Catholic Interracial Council of New York, and his memory is enshrined in the Hoey Award given annually for an outstanding contribution to interracial justice. Hoey lashed out on the Catholic Hour at the injustice of making the Negro bear more than his share of the Depression. He said, and it was a fact, that a Negro, even if he was a college graduate, was lucky to get a job as a porter, a cleaner or an elevator operator.

Not everyone liked this kind of talk. On the contrary, Father Gillis was the subject of abuse and condemnation for stirring up hatred and inciting violence. But some whites and many Negroes listened with understanding. Our committee expanded. We finally decided that we should hold a mass meeting at the Town Hall in midtown New York and invite both white and Negro sympathizers.

From my very first meeting with Father LaFarge in 1931, I was always impressed by his insistence that we would have to count principally on lay people to promote an interracial spirit among Catholics. He worked very hard himself to influence priests, as in the Clergy Conference on Negro Welfare. But what he hoped mostly from them was freedom to allow their lay members to take off on their own initiative. In this he was far ahead of his time, for Catholic Action was then scarcely known, and those who promoted it thought of it mostly as a mobilization of the laity to carry out the directives of the clergy. But that was not Father LaFarge's idea. He wanted a true lay organization, its officers and directors responsible for determining policy and supervising its execution, the role of its chaplain merely one of consultation in matters bearing on Catholic teaching and practice.

Just about the time I met him, Father LaFarge was forming such an organization in New York, the Laymen's Union. It was a modest group with limited objectives, but I think it deserves to be recorded for two reasons. It demonstrates a basic LaFarge technique. He got a few people together to work on a precise and non-contentious task, then gradually pointed them toward further horizons at which they would not even have looked if they had been included in the original package. And it played a major part in establishing the Catholic Interracial Council.

The Laymen's Union started out as a retreat movement for Negro business and professional men. The enclosed retreat movement was then becoming popular among educated Catholics who felt the need for a deeper analysis and discussion of their moral and religious problems than was available through Sunday sermons or public missions. It had not occurred to anybody that there might be Negro Catholics with the same need, but Father LaFarge knew personally the principal business and professional men who were members of the Negro Catholic community in and around New York, and he decided that they were fully ready to take advantage of such an opportunity.

It was a very small group. He arbitrarily limited membership to twenty-five. He knew that there was a better chance of developing an intense spirit and sticking to a precise line of action if there were not too many. Besides, the total potential was small, and he did not want the first few to start out on grandiose recruitment schemes that would be doomed to failure. Actually, not more than twenty usually made the enclosed retreats held each year from 1928 onwards at St. Anthony's Mission House, Tenafly, New Jersey.

All members of the group were in fact Negroes, and it would have been in practice impossible at that time to get suitable white Catholics to participate as regular members of such a group. Father LaFarge, nevertheless, left the door open. When the rules were drawn up, they described the membership as consisting of Negro Catholic business and professional men, with "such other persons as, in exceptional circumstances, the members shall consider particularly qualified to take active part in the Union's program." Father LaFarge, in addition, sought opportunities to create contacts with white Catholics. He was proud, and with good reason, of the level of Catholic practice to which the group attained in a few years. In addition to the retreat from Thursday evening to Monday morning once a year, the members met one Sunday morning every second month for a dialogue Mass (then a rarity) and Holy Communion, a renewal meditation and an exchange of ideas at breakfast. Between meetings, they practiced mental prayer and spiritual reading, and they went frequently to the Sacraments. As the members of the Catholic Evidence Guild and other all-white groups of Catholics discovered when Father LaFarge brought them together, they had more to teach their fellow Catholics than to learn from them.

Father LaFarge had hoped and anticipated that the personal formation would soon seek to express itself in a concrete form. To prepare them for a lay apostolate, he organized a series of monthly meetings at which they were taken through a course in the life of Christ and the social and ethical principles of Christianity as presented in Leo XIII's *Rerum Novarum* and Pius XI's *Quadragesimo Anno*. Armed with this knowledge they began in January 1933 a regular monthly public discussion forum. The location was the parish auditorium of St. Mark the Evangelist Church on West 138th Street, in Harlem, the parish of which Father Michael Mulvoy was pastor. They found keen and spirited audiences. Victims of the Depression, the Negroes of Harlem were ready to listen to anyone who offered them a way out of their misery. Daily, they were being exposed to many kinds of programs, usually panaceas that involved hatred and violence as their basic ingredients. If they were not easy to convince, they were at least willing to listen.

In addition to conducting the monthly forum, the Laymen's Union provided speakers for what we had begun to call the Catholic Interracial Hour over WLWL, and also to send some of their members to talk to church groups, including such groups of white Catholics as Knights of Columbus and Holy Name societies, groups who through them were hearing for the first time something of the Negro's actual problems and situation. They included some outstanding men. Elmo Anderson was president in 1934, the same Anderson who was a vice-president of the National Catholic Interracial Federation and who would become the first chairman of the board of directors of the Catholic Interracial Council of New York and long remain a member of its board. Dr. Hudson J. Oliver was vice-president, Maceo A. Thomas, secretary, and Myles A. Paige, treasurer. They would all become members of the first board of directors of the Catholic Interracial Council, as would Captain Mathieu V. Boutte and Dr. Edward E. Best. And one of the youngest of the group, Emanuel Romero, would also later rise to office and prominence in the Catholic Interracial Council.

The Laymen's Union had started out as Father LaFarge's brainchild and it continued to listen respectfully to his suggestions. But it was by 1934 no paper organization. It had an understanding, a will and a mind of its own. It had its own dynamism and ambitions. It was ready to launch out into bigger things. It, accordingly, was more than happy to become the sponsoring organization for a mass meeting to be held at the Town Hall, New York, on Pentecost Sunday, May 20, and to undertake to bring a representative group of Negro citizens for the occasion.

But we also needed a representative group of white Catholics, and that was not so easy to assemble. The cruel fact was that white American Catholics, with most honorable exceptions, did not know and did not want to know anything about their Negro fellow citizens. Or, what perhaps was even more discouraging was the gradualist or reverse Uncle Tom, the Catholic who had been compelled to listen and to recognize that a problem and a need existed, but who felt that at present nothing could be done about it. "We are in a depression," some would say. "The vast majority of Americans, white as well as Negro, are unemployed or faced with unemployment. This is no time to start a Catholic social action movement. Wait until times are better."

I always think of the late Thomas F. Woodlock as the perfect epitome of this attitude. A well-known Catholic writer, a former editor of the *Wall Street Journal* and the author of *The Catholic*

Pattern, The Age of Thought, and other books, he was widely
and properly regarded as the most learned Catholic lay theologian in America. In response to the appeal of some of his
friends, he came to several of our meetings. He was in total
agreement with our objectives. "Any American who believes in
the principles established by our Founding Fathers, the notions
of liberty, justice and equality as inalienable rights," he used
to say, "must approve of your work. For the American Catholic,
the commitment is still more obvious. He must additionally
hold that all men share equally in the fruits of Christ's Redemption, that they are all brothers under the fatherhood of
God."

But when it came to action, Tom Woodlock and many others
made a distinction. "There's no use beating your head against
a stone wall," was how he put it. "I know how Americans—
Catholics and non-Catholics alike—think about this issue. The
centuries of slavery are too deeply rooted in our traditions to
be disregarded. Maybe in another fifty years something can be
done. But today, nothing. You just must be patient." And so,
no doubt with a heavy heart, they left us. But leave us they did.

But some stayed, such people as Jim Hoey, and Dorothy Day,
and Schuyler Warren, and the first great editor of the *Commonweal,* Michael Williams. And I am proud to be able to
record that I also stayed. And when Pentecost Sunday, May 20,
1934, finally arrived, we had succeeded in rounding up enough
white citizens to make a respectable showing. The Town Hall
was decently filled, an audience of about 800 persons, and the
races were about equally represented.

We had got together an impressive group. Father Gillis, Elmo
Anderson, Michael Williams, and Mr. E. P. Roberts (of the New
York Urban League) were our principal speakers, and Dr. Hud-
son Oliver presided. Others on the platform included Father
Wilfrid Parsons, S.J., editor of *America,* Reverend Dr. George C.
Haynes, of the Interracial Committee of the Federal Council
of Churches in America, Father Christopher Plunkett, a former

pastor of St. Mark the Evangelist and then Provincial of the Holy Ghost Fathers, and Father Timothy J. Shanley, pastor of St. Benedict the Moor. Cardinal Hayes had sent Monsignor Michael J. Lavelle, Vicar General of the archdiocese of New York, to represent him.

Not everyone liked what they heard. In particular, as we learned to our cost later, some of Monsignor Lavelle's colleagues at the chancery of the archdiocese of New York were displeased by the straight talk. And that was what they got. "The crimes of the white men against the black men and the discriminations against colored workers were denounced in no uncertain tones by prominent speakers at the interracial mass meeting held at the Town Hall on Sunday afternoon." Such was the opening sentence in the long report of the event printed in New York's *Catholic News*.

Michael Williams set the tone when he asserted that the problem of the Negro in the United States was the most important of all the nation's grave current problems, and that for Catholics the Negro question was a test or standard of Catholic Action in all its many fields. "White American Catholics have terribly and most lamentably neglected, and in some ways plainly violated, their duties as Catholics towards American Negroes. We have been indifferent and cold and callous, to say the least, even when we cannot be charged with openly and flagrantly denying love and justice to the Negro. . . . We cannot degrade our own charity with mere almsgiving—it must be the fraternal sharing of common responsibilities and common burdens. The same thing applies even more strictly, if that be possible, to the dispensation of our justice. We cannot satisfy the claims of justice in a spirit of condescension, by mere doles and make-shift expedients. By the way we apply our principles in this particular matter, so, I believe, shall we succeed or fail in our efforts to solve the whole social crisis now inescapably upon us."

Father Gillis spoke in the same vein. "It behooves any and

every white man who presumes to speak at an interracial meeting," he proclaimed with his inimitable oratory, "to commence with a public confession of the sins and crimes he and his race have committed against the black man. Like the priest at the beginning of Holy Mass, he must bow the head, bend the body in token of contrition; he must strike the breast and cry *Mea culpa, mea culpa, mea maxima culpa*. When thus purified in spirit he mounts the steps of the altar, he must still cry again *Kyrie eleison*, Lord, have mercy on us. For in all the long history of man's inhumanity to man, perhaps the cruelest pages are those whereon is written the record of the treatment accorded the Negro by the *dominant* race that achieved and maintained its dominance with injustice and brutality and falsehood and hypocrisy."

The two Negro speakers were more reserved but not less impressive. Mrs. Roberts presented a reasoned and documented exposition of the economic, social and educational disabilities under which Negroes suffered at that time in New York. "Somehow, white workers must be made to realize," she said, "that there can be no security for American labor as long as the Negro is excluded—and thus remains a constant threat. Industrialists must be shown that markets for their wares will remain more limited as long as so large a part of our population—potential consumers—is excluded because of sub-subsistence wages. Self-protection and selfish interests prompt this even where no sense of social justice exists."

"Many people, both white and black, in the South and in the North," Mr. Anderson added, "assume that the Negro in his relationship to whites, is essentially inferior, and they base upon this, as upon a proven proposition, the whole relationship, complex as it may be, between the races. I have been taught—and I believe I have been taught correctly—that the Catholic Church recognizes no such distinction. She knows only one race—the human race, though broken into many groups from diverse causes—just as she teaches one Creator and Redeemer of this human race. To the individual soul the Church bears her message, irrespective of the group to which it has been assigned by climate, by language or by human conventions."

Jim Hoey summed up the situation and presented a program of action in a series of resolutions which were adopted unanimously. Promotion of relations between the races based on Christian principles is a matter of supreme concern to New York and to the whole country, he said. In addition, the needs of the Negro constitute a challenge to Catholics to aid in establishing such harmonious relations. In consequence, a Catholic Interracial Council should be set up in New York, and other cities across the country should be urged to follow this example.

An organizing committee to work out a constitution and develop a program for such a council was approved. Jim Hoey was to be its chairman. The members were Elmo Anderson, Miss Mary Byles, Mathieu Boutte, Miss Dorothy Day, Thomas J. Diviney, Nicholas A. Donnelly, Hugh J. Grant, James V. Hayes, George K. Hunton, Francis S. Moseley, Dr. Hudson J. Oliver, Eugene Savage, and Schuyler Warren. I am glad to say that both races were solidly represented and also both sexes. And I think it is noteworthy that it was an entirely lay group. This would also be true subsequently of the composition of the board of directors of the Catholic Interracial Council. We have always had a chaplain, and we always have listened respectfully to his advice. But we anticipated by more than thirty years the spirit of the Second Vatican Council when we staked out the social order as being specifically the realm and the obligation of the layman. We looked to the Church for principles, but we were never afraid to accept our own duty to apply them. Another thing I am proud to be able to say is that from the very start, the Council was not only in name but in reality interracial. There was never a majority and a minority. There was always a single mind, the mind of all the members. In its entire history, the board never once divided on racial lines. And with our tradition, I am sure it never will.

We left the Town Hall with Father Gillis's majestic and prophetic words ringing in our ears. "Now there can be no good purpose in the public confession of our sins and the sins of our forebears unless it is to prevent obstinate continuance in sin," he had thundered. "In the Catholic system, confession without sincere repentance is sacrilegious and the only sure evidence of genuine sorrow is a purpose of amendment. Any Christian who creates or perpetuates or tolerates race hatred or race prejudice contradicts and crucifies Christ; any human being who discriminates against his fellowman because of the color of that man's skin or because of the fanciful opinion that any other man's blood differs essentially from his own, is guilty of a crime against not one race, but against the human race. 'One Lord, one faith, one baptism,' and one Father in heaven of all men upon the earth. We are, in consequence, not many races but one race."

I walked out of that meeting into the balmy May afternoon with my head touching the clouds. A miracle had happened. A representative group of New Yorkers had demonstrated that progress was possible, that the time was indeed ripe for action. It was for me a justification of the three years since I had committed myself to the interracial movement by going to work for the Cardinal Gibbons Institute. All the drudgery and penny-pinching, all the snubs and insults, all the rejections and disappointments were unimportant beside these results. My original intention had been to spend two years, more or less, with the Institute. But now all that was changed. I had already become the managing editor of the *Interracial Review,* now the organ of the National Catholic Interracial Federation but likely to become (as it shortly did become) a part of the operation of the Catholic Interracial Council of New York. The plans to organize that Council were posited on my availability as secretary and executive officer. There was no going back, nor indeed did I have any desire to go back.

But even when my head is in the clouds, my feet have a habit of staying solidly on the ground. Father LaFarge once described me as combining Irish enthusiasm with Yankee caution and canniness. And later, in the solitude of my sparsely furnished one-room office at 11 West Forty-second Street, the cautious Yankee had his hour. It was all very well to fool oneself with the momentary enthusiasm of a few hundred people, whipped up by the magic of Father Gillis and Michael Williams, but that did not change the reality of American life as stated so objectively by Tom Woodlock. "Today, you can do nothing," he had said. And, in fact, we lacked the money to do anything, to meet the rent, to publish our magazine, to pay my salary.

This is part of the reality of the 1930s that is almost impossible to appreciate after a whole generation of unparalleled prosperity. There was literally no money in those days. The Negroes were really desperate. With sixty per cent unemployment in Harlem, even professional men could hardly keep their families alive. Much of their work was free, and much more was billed but never paid. Some among our white supporters had formerly been comfortable or even wealthy. But the collapse of the market had wiped out their assets and in some cases shaken their self-confidence too.

I did not like it, but I knew that there I was. The Chinese proverb says that the longest journey starts with a single step. And that was what I proceeded to do. I began to walk, cautiously, one step at a time.

Chapter 4

Those first steps of the Catholic Interracial Council were very modest ones. But they were the only ones we could take. I had around me from the start a dedicated group of people. Most of them I had met only during the previous three years, since I had become involved in the interracial movement. But many had already become personal friends, and the others would also prove year after year that they were good friends, honorable people, and serious in their undertakings.

The summer months after the Town Hall meeting were devoted largely to organizing the Council and deciding precisely what it should do. We also talked long and learnedly about the way its work should be underwritten, but that was largely academic. Neither then nor later did we ever succeed in creating any solid financial base for our activities. We just moved ahead from crisis to crisis, and something always turned up. Usually the one who saved us was Father LaFarge. He had the most extraordinary range of acquaintances of all races, faiths and walks of life. All who knew him revered him for his integrity and disinterestedness. He could always find someone willing and able to give the sum needed to save us from bankruptcy. And thus through his ingenuity and that of the board of directors, we struggled along.

The control of the Council, as I mentioned earlier, was entirely in the hands of lay people. Membership, however, was limited to Catholics. That was one of the policy decisions which the organizing committee had to make. It was not that we lacked an ecumenical outlook. In that respect, Father LaFarge was way ahead of his times, even causing raised eyebrows by his close friendships with Jewish and Protestant theologians. And I, for my part, would give top priority to establishing close working relations with individuals and groups representing other religious beliefs who might help our work.

Our decision to organize ourselves as a denominational group was based on the fact that what was needed was specifically a denominational group. Negroes already had in the National Association for the Advancement of Colored People (NAACP) a strong and growing community interracial organization with which we would later establish excellent understandings. But it had no way to do what we wanted to have done, to persuade American Catholics that they were failing to live up to their own principles in their treatment of Negro Americans. For one thing, the NAACP lacked the specific knowledge of the facts. And for another, American Catholics would not listen to it, were it to attempt to tell them their duties. If that was to be done, only a Catholic organization could do it.

The Catholic Interracial Council thus started from the principle that the various movements established for the education, the civil rights, the social welfare, and the opportunity of the Negro could not attain their ends in a satisfactory manner unless they were supplemented by a movement specifically aimed at removing the barrier of race prejudice, a movement specializing in that particular field and serving as a clearinghouse for everything that could possibly help to cure that disease. We did not look on our work as primarily a service to the Negro, but a service to the nation as a nation, and to the Catholic Church as the Church of Christ. We saw it as a work of as much interest to the white man as to the black.

We needed the authorization of the authorities of the archdiocese of New York to include the word "Catholic" in our description. There was little sympathy for our ideas among most of the Catholic clergy of the archdiocese, but we had taken the precaution of picking a strong board of directors, and the Chancery had little choice but to let us go ahead. James J. Hoey was the first president, with Elmo Anderson and Dorothy Day as vice-presidents, and Nicholas A. Donnelly as treasurer. The other members were Dr. Edward E. Best, Harry L. Binsse, Mathieu V. Boutte, Gerard L. Carroll, Thomas J. Diviney, Hugh J. Grant, James V. Hayes, Maurice Lavanoux, Francis S. Moseley, Dr. Hudson J. Oliver, Myles A. Paige, and Schuyler N. Warren. Father LaFarge was our chaplain, as he would continue to be until the late 1950s. I was a member of the board as well as executive secretary.

I had been editing the *Interracial Review* since the beginning of 1934, although Father Markoe continued to figure as editor on the masthead until the September 1934 issue, and the publication office remained in St. Louis. But Father Markoe was getting deeper into hot water out in St. Louis because of his open championship of Negro rights, a championship that would ultimately result in his transfer. He, accordingly, was more than relieved when the Catholic Interracial Council took over the full responsibility for the *Review* and made it the official organ of the Council. The change was announced in the October issue, the first published in New York. An editorial board, consisting of Dr. Best and Messrs. Boutte, Hayes, Moseley and Warren, was created, and I was confirmed as managing editor.

I had already been writing editorials and other unsigned pieces in the *Review,* as I would continue to do until the early 1960s but it was in this same issue of October 1934 that my first and one of my few signed contributions appeared. The title of the article was "Mr. Mencken Muddles." Thanks, presumably, to my high percentage of Irish blood and environment, my boiling point has always been low, and on this occasion my ire and my inspiration were aroused by an article contributed by H. L. Mencken to *The Crisis.* It was a strange, cynical piece, in which the distinguished essayist and literary critic turned his talents to condemning Negroes for not recognizing that their white fellow Americans had been very generous to them already. "The general feeling in the country, unless I misjudge it sadly," he wrote, "is that the Negro has gone far enough, that he already has as much as he deserves, and should be content for a while."

The trouble, I told the Sage of Baltimore, was that the vast majority of white Americans were not sufficiently concerned over the Negro to have any "general feeling" either for or against his progress. This was, of course, our basic attitude as far as Catholics were concerned, and I used Mencken to deliver a lecture to the readers of the *Review*. The great stumbling block was the lack of interest of the white majority, the complete indifference and almost abysmal ignorance regarding existing wrongs and the aims and objectives of the Negro's strivings.

To the extent permitted by our limited resources, the Catholic Interracial Council began right away to do something about the abysmal ignorance. We already had the basic tools that we would gradually perfect through the years. They were the *Review*, the radio talks by courtesy of Father Gillis on the Catholic Hour, the lectures to Catholic organizations already begun by the Laymen's Union. I had during the previous few years established a series of press contacts, mainly with editors in the Catholic field but also with editors of publications for Negro readers. I now set out to expand this chain of contacts in order to multiply the impact of our efforts by the widest possible use of the media of mass communications. That was a slow and heartbreaking task, often likely to lead to a rebuff, as had already happened when *Time* picked up the story about the dedication of the new buildings of Xavier University in New Orleans. But it grew and grew, so that ultimately the office of the Catholic Interracial Council became a major distribution center for news about Negroes in the United States, especially whatever dealt with religion or with human rights. In the beginning, most of our output reached only to the editorial wastebasket, but that changed in due course. Most of the editors I have known were honorable men, if sometimes squeezed between conflicting obligations. Most of them, too, were real professionals. Once they knew they could rely on the news source, they read the copy carefully, and they used it if it was news. And that was the reputation we acquired, a reputation for being reliable and for delivering copy that was news.

Back in 1934, however, the more immediate task was to establish the facts. The ignorance about the Negro went all the way from the top to the bottom. He was the forgotten man in society, and he was the forgotten man in the Catholic Church. So we started to publish some basic information in the *Review*. There were then about 12,000,000 Negroes in the United States. The biggest concentration in the North was in New York City, which had 328,000. In Chicago there were 233,000; in Philadelphia, 219,000; in Washington, 132,000.

Figures for church affiliation were vague, but we figured that 7,000,000 were Protestants and 250,000 Catholics, which left nearly 5,000,000 with no church affiliation. About 200 priests and 1000 Sisters were working in what were known as the Colored Missions, that is to say, in parishes in which the congregation was entirely Negro. There were 210 churches in these parishes and 205 schools with an enrollment of 35,092 pupils.

We were particularly interested in the educational situation, because we were all totally convinced that the way to penetrate the barriers of segregation in the Church was through the schools, a belief which time was to vindicate. In 1934, however, the view was dim. Although the Negro community was still miserably served as regards higher education, the situation was changing rapidly in the Negro's favor. Fewer than 2500 Negroes were in college in 1915, but the number had passed 23,000 by 1933. A survey made by a magazine during the 1931–32 year came up with a total of 20,277 Negroes in higher education, 19,256 in college courses and 1021 in professional schools. Of this number, 16,981 were in Negro colleges and the other 3296 in Northern non-racial institutions. All these students were in Protestant schools or purely secular institutions, with the exception of 237 in Xavier University, New Orleans, and 36 in Loyola University, Chicago.

Xavier was then the only Negro Catholic college in the United States, and Loyola University in Chicago was the only other Catholic college with any significant Negro enrollment. The magazine survey had missed a few places off the beaten track. Creighton University, Omaha, did have a handful of Negroes who were not included, and so did some other Catholic colleges. But the number was probably not more than a dozen. And that was the total Catholic contribution to the higher education of the Negro. A second Catholic college for Negroes was not opened until 1936, a very small institution at Guthrie, Oklahoma, conducted by the Benedictine Sisters.

Even Xavier was still very young, but thanks to Mother Katharine Drexel, it was good and it was becoming known. It had started as a high school in 1915, and its first college class was graduated in 1927. When the new buildings were dedicated in 1932, it was not expected that the planned capacity of 500 would be reached for many years. In actual fact, the enrollment passed 800 within four years, and if the facilities had existed, it would have gone even higher. All of which added up to one very simple fact: Negroes were begging from the Catholic Church the services she was supplying to other Americans but not to them; when she offered even a token service, it was taken with gratitude and used enthusiastically.

Everywhere, it was the same story. Dorothy Day, who had become a Catholic six years earlier, began the *Catholic Worker* in May 1933. She insisted specifically from the beginning that her paper was for the Negro and the white worker alike. She had a white worker on one side of the masthead and a Negro on the other, and she encouraged Negroes to write for her not only on problems of the Negro race but on social justice in general and all the problems of the worker. She was very impressed by a sketch drawn by a child, which she published in an early issue. It showed a group of Negroes in stripes and chains, with their guard in back, and the barred auto truck which carried them to and from work. "Look closely," Dorothy would say, pointing to that simple drawing. "The little girl didn't color the Negroes black. She didn't think in terms of color. She was thinking of them as human beings, as prisoners. That is the general attitude of children before race prejudice is instilled in them by others."

Dorothy was deeply concerned by the efforts the Communists were making to infiltrate Negro youth. Her purpose in founding the *Catholic Worker*, she said, was to combat Communism and atheism by showing the social program of the Church, and she insisted that the only way to counter the Communist propaganda to the Negro community was to give young Negroes the same opportunity as other young Americans. Dorothy was a founding member and a director of the Catholic Interracial Council. "The criticism of the Communists is just," she used to say. "It is the remedies they propose and the techniques they use to bring about justice that we as Catholics object to."

Paul Daly, a lawyer, got Dorothy a place at 1070 Seventh Avenue in Harlem, and in 1934 she began to organize some activities there. Liturgical artist Ade Bethune, who was staff illustrator for the *Catholic Worker* and who frequently contributed her beautiful work to the *Interracial Review* also, conducted art classes for the children. It was the kind of interracial group in which she delighted—Negroes, Puerto Ricans, Italians, Greeks, and other Americans. She specialized in liturgical subjects, so that the children learned their Christian doctrine while developing their drawing skills and a taste for art. In the evenings, groups came together to discuss the problems of the workers.

The problems at the time were so grave as to seem to defy solution. Jim Hoey about the same time set out some of them in a talk on the Catholic Hour. "I made an investigation of the unemployment problem among our Negro citizens in Harlem," he said, "and I was alarmed to find that the unemployment of the Negroes in our city is more than sixty per cent. Incidentally, I am informed that in some cities it is as high as ninety per cent. I have learned that wherever there is a condition of unemployment, the Negro is the first to be fired, the last to be rehired when things improve."

Negroes as a group, he continued, were the ones who suffered most from the Depression and benefited least from the provisions of the NRA. "In fact, the minimum wage provision of NRA acts to the distinct disadvantage of the Negro. For example, where an employer had a Negro elevator operator at ten dollars a week, finding himself forced by law to pay a minimum wage of fifteen dollars weekly, he fires the Negro and hires a white operator."

The Negro was more likely to have no job, and to be paid less when he had a job, but it cost him more to live. The median rental paid by Negro families was three or four dollars a month higher than that paid by all families in Manhattan, although, of course, the quality of his housing was significantly lower. The population density in Harlem was more than three times that of the city at large, and one square block there had the doubtful distinction of being considered the most densely populated block in the world. Families were housed in what were known as old-law tenements, which contained just about every known hazard to life and health. A carelessly dropped cigarette converted one of them into a funeral pyre.

Father Michael Mulvoy, pastor of St. Mark the Evangelist, was one man who did heroic work to correct this situation. I already have mentioned his participation in the various social agencies that were then beginning to concern themselves for the health and welfare of the poor of Harlem under the WPA and other emergency relief programs spawned during the Depression. One specific organization developed by Father Mulvoy in his parish was the Race Relations Bureau. It was a Catholic Action group, and its function was similar to that of the Urban League on a national level, namely, to expand job opportunity for Negroes. The Bureau both co-operated with other welfare organizations in the section and operated its own youth center and labor school.

This particular labor school began as a project to train Negroes for the lower civil service positions that were opening up for them at that time, particularly in the city administration. Gradually it broadened its efforts to prepare young people for private employment also and to agitate for the opening up of job opportunities denied to qualified Negroes simply because they were Negroes.

Even today the Negro is far from having resolved this issue in New York or elsewhere in the United States. But he has come a long way from the early 1930s. In this effort to open up to the Negro every avenue of employment for which he was qualified, the Catholic Interracial Council co-operated from the beginning with other interested agencies, including the National Urban League and the National Association for the Advancement of Colored People. The sentiment was so strong that an office that employed a Negro in any but the conventional menial activities of porter, cleaner or elevator operator had trouble with the landlord. Even for our own office of the Catholic Interracial Council the issue was real. I always had Negroes working with me, when I could afford any help; and even when I couldn't pay, I had volunteer Negro help. No landlord wanted that kind of setup. He would say that it gave his building a bad name and caused him to lose other tenants. It was like the block-busting in private housing at a later date. If one Negro appeared, the whites wanted to get away.

One of the things we tried to do was to persuade individual Catholics to set an example, something which Jim Hoey, our president, was more than willing to do. I remember Jim saying on one occasion that he had made a statement in Harlem, when he was running for public office, that if he ever had the opportunity, he would test his belief that a Negro could measure up to a white person in any responsible position. When he was made Collector of Internal Revenue for the Second District in New York, he delivered on his promise. He appointed eleven Negroes to his staff, something absolutely unheard of previously, and all but one of them proved entirely satisfactory. They not only worked well at their jobs but they took night classes to improve their efficiency. Several of them went to law school, and one graduated from St. John's Law School with higher honors than any student, white or Negro, had won up to that time.

Jim had one particularly impressive story about his experience with a Negro who came to him for a job. "This man had been working as an elevator operator," he used to say, "and he was recommended to me by one of my family who was impressed with his education and personality. I sent for him and learned that he had taught in a Maryland high school. I gave him an application to fill out, and he entered his age as fifty-seven. 'Check on your age again,' I told him, handing him back the form. 'The upper age limit for appointment is fifty-five.' He took the application and went away. Two hours later, he was back. 'Mr. Hoey,' he said, 'what's the use? I'm fifty-seven, and a job isn't worth a lie. Thanks very much just the same.' I was so impressed that, after he had left, I wrote a special letter to the Commissioner of Internal Revenue. It turned out that the age limit was a departmental regulation, not a law. And for the first time in many years, it was waived."

Hardly any one else around was as willing as Jim Hoey to go out on a limb, but there were some who recognized the need for change. The politicians were beginning to understand that Negroes in the North were becoming a force to be respected, a reality that was brought home forcibly by a Harlem riot in March 1935. It was not much of a riot as compared with some of our subsequent experiences. It lasted only one night, and the damage caused was moderate. But it was a danger sign. An investigation conducted by a committee named by the Mayor of New York established that it was not a race riot in any true sense of the word. It was a spontaneous explosion on the part of people who happened to be Negroes, people whose specific grievance was that their living conditions were intolerable.

An editorial on the Committee's report in the New York *World-Telegram* summed up what was wrong and how it could be remedied. The Negroes, it said, were "virtually imprisoned" in a narrow area of decrepit houses, high rents and unsanitary surroundings. Population density had reached such an extreme that even new low-cost housing could not suffice. New areas would have to be found to take care of a considerable proportion of the inhabitants.

To make recommendations was easy, but it was less easy to implement them. The state of New York got into the act in 1937, naming a commission of twelve members to undertake a more thorough investigation. Harold P. Herman, assemblyman from Nassau County, a lawyer, a Catholic and a believer in justice for the Negro, was the chairman. Other Catholic members included State Senator Walter Mahoney from Buffalo and Father Michael Mulvoy, the pastor of St. Mark's, who was secretary.

A week of hearings in December 1937 brought out a shoddy story of abuses in schools, hospitals, industries, and housing. One of the most sensational bits of evidence was the revelation of a continuing policy on the part of the skilled-labor trades unions to keep out Negroes. The first person to put it in the record was a white man, Mr. Sidney Lake, principal of New York Industrial High School. His school was located in Harlem, but when he became principal, only 68 of the 1200 students were Negroes, the others coming from a distance. He had instituted a policy of giving equal opportunity to the neighborhood boys, with the result that the Negro enrollment had grown to 648, about half the total. The Negro boys learned their trades like everyone else, Mr. Lake testified, but when they were finished, they had practically no chance of finding jobs as skilled craftsmen. "There are no colored boys in any of the skilled labor unions," he insisted.

Other witnesses were called to challenge or confirm his claim. Most of them were reluctant, but in the end the validity of his evidence was established beyond doubt. In most instances, the regulations and bylaws of the unions and corporations did not actually bar Negroes, but their practice did.

This was an issue which had come up many times before, and because of the predominantly Catholic composition both of the leadership and membership of organized labor, it was one on which the Catholic Interracial Council had expressed itself strongly. We, however, were not the prime movers in this area. The honor and the credit go to A. Philip Randolph, a devout Protestant and a great Negro leader. From the time I first met him in the early 1930s, he has been my good and honorable friend. I shall say more about him later, but at this point I want to mention just two things. In 1935, he won a fight that had been going on for ten years. Through the National Mediation Board and an impartially conducted election, he ended the efforts of the railroads to control their labor in a company union and won recognition for his Brotherhood of Sleeping Car Porters. He also got the American Federation of Labor (AFL) to give a guarantee that it would end discrimination against Negroes in its ranks. It was a fight that he had been conducting for a long time. Each year, he would have himself elected as a delegate from the Brotherhood to the AFL convention, and each year he would repeat the same plea. At first, they hurled insults at him or walked out of the meetings. But he stuck at it, and finally AFL president William Green began to take notice, with the result that in 1935 a resolution was passed affirming that the AFL would discipline unions which discriminated against Negroes.

This was a decisive advance, and ultimately the entire labor movement came to recognize that it could protect its own interests only if it defended the rights of all workers. But the change did not come automatically with the passage of a resolution. At the Harlem hearings two years later, several witnesses testified to the continuing union discrimination against Negroes. Some unions, it was asserted, had constitutional provisions under which Negroes could only form auxiliary unions, these auxiliaries to be under the control of the white locals. Extracts from the bylaws of the Sheet Metal Workers Union and the International Brotherhood of Blacksmiths were put in the record as direct evidence of discrimination. And just at that same time, Mr. William Green (AFL) was on the wrong side of one of the most outrageous jurisdictional disputes ever waged. About four thousand longshoremen, mostly Negroes, employed as freight handlers on railway piers in the port of New York, asked to be admitted to the Railway Union. They were refused on the ground that the Railway Union did not admit Negroes. Thereupon, Joseph P. Ryan, president of the Longshoremen's Union, began to organize them. Green, however, would have none of it. "You cannot organize these men as longshoremen," he told Ryan, "because they are railway employees." And Green was so powerful that he was able to force Ryan to desist.

As can be imagined, A. Philip Randolph had to have himself elected to several more AFL conventions and to throw in their teeth at each of them their refusal to stand by their own resolutions. At least as late as 1941, he was still at it. At the AFL convention in Seattle in the early fall of that year, he presented a strong bill of particulars, listing the names of AFL unions which continued to exclude Negroes on grounds of color. Again the delegates wrung their hands, and again they refused to challenge the offenders. They "reaffirmed the stand taken last year at New Orleans," but blocked the Randolph proposal that a committee be authorized to make a survey "in order to determine the extent of the discrimination within the Internationals and Locals of the AFL." Pearl Harbor was then only a few months away, and as we shall see, the Second World War changed many things.

To come back to the 1937 Harlem hearings, however, union and corporation officials alike assured the Commission of Enquiry that they did not practice discrimination. The facts, however, were against them. It was brought out, for example, that only six per cent of the employees of the BMT subway system were Negroes, all in low-salaried jobs, that the New York Telephone Company did not employ a single Negro, that savings banks employed a few Negroes, but that generally one did not find them in banks. Less than three per cent of the members of Local No. 3 of the Electrical Workers Union were Negroes. The Astor Hotel never employed any, except as strike-breakers when they had a conflict with their regular staff. Neither did major restaurant chains, such as Childs, Longchamps, Bickfords, and the Waldorf cafeterias.

The NAACP and the National Urban League used all their resources to publicize the results of these hearings, just as we did at the Catholic Interracial Council. One concrete result came within a few months. The IRT subway system was in economic trouble, and Thomas E. Murray, Jr., a New York businessman who subsequently became a member of the Atomic Energy Commission, had been named receiver. In a letter to Charles H. Houston, special counsel of the NAACP, Mr. Murray promised that Negroes would be given jobs in grades higher than elevator operator and porter, which up to that time were the only ones open to them. The subways had become a sort of test issue. When the municipally-owned Eighth Avenue system was opened in September 1932, some Negroes were immediately employed by it as station agents. After several years of effort, Negroes were also admitted to the civil service examinations for guard or conductor, and still later to those for motormen. The result was that by 1938 the Eighth Avenue system had a broad spectrum of jobs open to Negroes, whereas the two privately-owned systems, the IRT and BMT, still kept Negroes only in the most menial positions. Mr. Murray's undertaking to open up the IRT consequently was a major breakthrough, and it was not long until the BMT followed suit.

Another controversy that was starting to hit the headlines about the same time, and would continue to do so for many years, was the admission of Negro baseball players to the major leagues. Negro track and field men under the leadership of Jesse Owens and Ralph Metcalfe saved the honor of the United States in 1936 at the Olympic Games in Berlin. The newspaper comment at home had been extremely favorable because of the attempts made by Hitler and his cohorts to snub the Negroes as members of an inferior race. And it was not long until correspondents were pointing out that Berlin had no monopoly on racism. I recall one fan who wrote to the local paper insisting that the Brooklyn Dodgers would not be languishing at the foot of the league if they would hire a few players like Satchel Paige and Walter Ball.

Jimmy Powers, then and for many years subsequently sports editor of the New York *Daily News,* gave a classic answer to the basic question asked by all segregationists. One day he dropped the suggestion that perhaps the time was coming for Negro players in the major leagues. The response from his readers was substantial and impassioned. It added up to an overwhelming no. They would fight, they would have cliques, they would lack cohesion. Then came the clincher: "How would you like your sister to marry one." And back shot Jimmy: "Are we discussing ballplayers or brothers-in-law?"

Such was the general climate into which the Catholic Interracial Council was thrust when it was established in 1934. The nature and extent of the discrimination suffered by Negroes in New York at the hands of the general public, at the hands of employers, at the hands of labor unions, at the hands of the city authorities, even at the hands of most representatives of the Catholic Church, seem scarcely believable when viewed from a distance of only a single short generation. At the same time, it was clear that important movement had begun. As bad as things were, they were no longer static. People could do something about them, were in fact doing something about them. And it was supremely important that Catholics should play their part in the correction of ancient wrongs.

That was how the picture looked to us when we reviewed the situation at the end of our first year. What was to become an annual get-together took the form of a Catholic interracial conference, and it met on September 8, 1935, at St. Anthony's Mission House in Tenafly, New Jersey. The conference had been well planned in advance. I had been at Candlewood Lake, Connecticut, for a two-week vacation in August, and I invited Father LaFarge to come up one day to lunch and spend the afternoon working out the details. The first issue was where to hold it. The chancery office of the archdiocese of New York was suspicious of everything we did. Some statements at the Pentecost Sunday meeting in the Town Hall the previous year had caused grave offense (as I shall explain later), and we lived in constant dread that our precarious approval would be withdrawn, if we became too prominent. We decided, in consequence, to cross the Hudson to a retreat house of the Society of African Missions at Tenafly. Father LaFarge had friends there, and he had already secured it for several years for the annual enclosed retreat of the Catholic Laymen's Union.

The next step was to prepare the agenda. We decided to start with a dialogue Mass, following the practice of the Laymen's Union at its meetings. The conference itself would have two main items. One would be a talk by Monsignor Francis J. Gilligan of St. Thomas Seminary, St. Paul, Minnesota. He had just won a doctorate at Catholic University for a thesis on race relations in the Church, "The Morality of the Color Line," the first such study ever made under Catholic auspices in the United States. We decided to ask him to talk on this subject. The other major business was the presentation to the members of a statement of policy and program of action which I had drawn up over the previous months with the co-operation of the board of directors.

September 8 is a day that stands out in my memory. I had been through a tough year, with many rebuffs and disappointments, an excess of apathy and inertia and ignorance on the part of many who should have cared. I needed some kindness and friendship and concern, and here I found them in abundance.

The Hudson River was obscure in the early-morning mists as I drove out over the George Washington Bridge, marveling at the majestic structure which had been opened just four years earlier. But by the time I reached St. Anthony's, it was already a day of surpassing loveliness, the gray, barracks-like building softened and beautified by a warm, gentle September sun.

There were about twenty-five of us, almost equally divided by race, and with women forming a substantial minority. Two priests were present, Father LaFarge and Father Gilligan. The Mass was a new experience for many of the white members of the group. It followed the procedures long practiced by the members of the Laymen's Union at their meetings. The whole congregation read the Ordinary aloud, and Elmo Anderson recited the Proper of the day. It was an anticipation of what the Mass would be thirty years later as a result of the reforms of the Second Vatican Council.

Our day-long discussions, held informally outdoors in the shade of great trees and interrupted at noon for a buffet lunch, produced very important conclusions. Father Gilligan had been invited, because it seemed necessary to clarify fully the basic principles on which the movement was to operate, and he became the storm center of an animated discussion as to whether prejudice is a transgression or a disease. We may never have reached theoretic agreement on that issue, but we did reach the practical conclusion that most progress could be achieved by regarding it as a disease and applying a primarily educational therapy.

As an outcome of this meeting, a statement of policy was prepared and a program of action was drawn up, and that meant that the Catholic Interracial Council was in business for keeps. It started out by proclaiming that it had two objectives, the combating of race prejudice and the establishment of social justice. It then developed strictly religious and theological motives for its stand, as befitted a Church-related organization. All men, it said, are children of one heavenly father, all are brothers through the Redemption, and all are members of the Mystical Body of Christ through the Holy Spirit. There are, it added, important secondary motives for the work of the Council, such as attracting Negroes toward the Catholic Church, securing civic peace and promoting the common good of all men.

The Conference went on record as proclaiming that the goal of the organization was to recognize the right of the Negro to full equality of opportunity, something that represented a significant departure from the then common view that Negroes were childlike and had always to be kept in a condition of tutelage. "It is necessary," the statement declared, "that the Negro secure all the essential opportunities of life and the full measure of social justice. All educational and cultural opportunities should be made available to Negro youth, both as a matter of right and in order to develop Catholic leaders."

Turning to means to achieve our ends, the statement gave first place to purely spiritual means, intercessory prayer, expiation and penance, the Mass and Eucharist, and the liturgy. It affirmed "the primacy of the moral issue in appealing to Catholic consciences, to each individual's moral responsibility for his racial attitude," urged a change of heart as a prelude to right action, and emphasized "the positive merit of justice and charity as the Catholic way of life in dealing with our neighbor and the humanization of all our relations with our fellow-men."

What was to be my concrete work as executive secretary of the Council and editor of the magazine was then spelled out. I should commit the Council to "a broad program of education, informing the public as to the facts, the motives and the moral issues, and the most practicable and effective means of establishing social justice." An essential part of this program would be to get the co-operation of organized Catholic forces. In particular, all social justice activities should be urged to expand their self-definition and their concrete programs so as to include the interracial sphere. The Catholic press and social service groups should be encouraged to emphasize the importance of interracial problems and the need for interracial justice.

Finally, we should reach out beyond the purely confessional sphere to co-operate with and invite the co-operation of all groups with shared interests. This would mean the creation of contacts with those engaged in special religious, charitable and educational works for the Negro, whether under Catholic, Protestant, Jewish or civic auspices. Even more widely, we decided that we should seek the support of charitable and human welfare institutions, even if they were not specifically concerned with Negro welfare, and that in particular we should seek the help of every educational institution and every cultural movement.

It was indeed an all-embracing program, and year by year we were to implement a great portion of it. It had already become clear, however, that some areas offered more prospect of progress than others, and that consequently we should concentrate a major part of our limited resources on them. It was indeed a very old fact of human experience that we were verifying once again. Those who are old are hardened in their views. To change them takes much time and effort. But the young are more likely to have open minds and to be willing to listen.

At our meeting at St. Anthony's I had told our colleagues about an extraordinary experience some time earlier at a Catholic girls' college in New York, an experience which I planned to follow up and which I was hopeful would make history in the Catholic interracial movement. At that time, there was scarcely a Catholic university or college in the New York area, or indeed in the whole northeast of the United States, which admitted Negro students. Resistance to the idea of integration of women's colleges was probably even more intense than for men's. Yet I had had a reaction that showed that it might not be as remote a dream as it seemed. The story, as it developed over several years, is so important as to merit a separate chapter.

Chapter 5

Manhattanville College of the Sacred Heart, situated at 130th Street in New York City, on a cliff overlooking Harlem, was about as unlikely a place as one could imagine to start a movement for the racial integration of Catholic education in the United States. It was a residential college whose students were drawn from the prosperous professional and merchant groups of upper-middle-class Catholics, dedicated to enhancing their own social standing. Their virtues were conservatism and conformity.

Manhattanville College, however, had the good fortune of getting an unusual president in the early 1930s, in the person of Mother Grace M. Dammann, R.S.S.C. She was one of the most remarkable persons it has ever been my privilege to know. When I first met her in 1933, she was in her middle thirties, but she already had the poise and personality of a much older person. I do not mean that she was set in her ways. On the contrary, she retained the curiosity and enthusiasm of the young people around her. She was fully informed about current events and she had a sense of commitment to society that she communicated to her students, together with an awareness that the way to get things done was to get up and do them.

She told me a story at one of our early meetings which I think projects many of her qualities. She had just had a visit from a former student, now graduated and married in New Jersey. This young lady had decided to implement some of the ideas she had imbibed from Mother Grace, and she got together a few of her acquaintances and formed a group to discuss current social issues. Within a few weeks, she had been summoned by the pastor, who told her that he had been running the parish before he baptized her and was still fully able to run it without her unsolicited assistance. She was understandably flabbergasted, and she came to Mother Grace to ask where she went from here. With her magnificent incisiveness, she summed up the situation. "You can only be patient, child," she said. "We have so many of these old priests of European extraction who long ago earned their way into heaven, and I think what we can do is to pray the Lord with greater fervor that he will not delay unduly their eternal reward."

Mother Grace had organized a group from the senior class under the name of the Banner Students. They were girls who took a special interest in Catholic social action and in the civic responsibilities of educated Catholics. In the spring of 1933 she invited me to give a series of five lectures at weekly intervals to this group. It was the kind of opportunity of which I dreamed, and I pulled out all the stops. Our first meeting was on a Monday afternoon at three o'clock, and we had two hours for lecture and discussion. I began by reviewing the doctrinal position of the Church in order to establish the obligations of the Catholic in the United States toward the American Negro. I then contrasted the duties with the normal level of fulfillment, or rather, non-fulfillment.

When I came to the performance of Catholic colleges, the report was almost entirely negative. Apart from the small group in Loyola University, Chicago, and the other scattered individual cases in the Midwest, to which I have referred earlier, the only positive action I could record was Mother Katharine Drexel's work in founding Xavier University, New Orleans, as an all-Negro Catholic college.

One of the following lectures was devoted to the Catholic teaching on race, on prejudice and racism, and on the equal dignity of all men in the sight of God. I impressed on them several points Father LaFarge always insisted were basic. One was that the cause of interracial justice was an expression of the fundamental principles on which the United States system of government was founded, namely, liberty, equal opportunity and freedom. Another was that the Catholic interracial movement had the full support of the teachings of our faith, particularly in the area dealt with in the great social encyclicals.

The response from the students was electrifying. I believe that this was the first time they had been exposed to a formal discussion of the race issue in the concrete context of their own society. But Mother Grace had laid the groundwork well. They knew what social justice was. And they had open minds. They were not afraid to draw the conclusion, once they agreed on the principle.

Each day the discussion became more animated and concrete. Finally, a student voiced the question that proved to be the catalyst. It was during the discussion period at the third or possibly the fourth lecture. "Mr. Hunton," she asked, "can you make a suggestion as to how we here at the college can do something more to get these principles implemented than simply talking about them to each other in this group and to our classmates?" The question drew an immediate echo from the group. All agreed that they felt the need to strike a blow.

I was naturally pleased at having made so deep an impact, but I was also taken aback. I had enough experience of audiences to know that a speaker is very quickly downgraded if he builds up a great climax at the level of theory, but pulls away when challenged to spell out the practical implications. Fortunately, I had an idea. "What would you as a group think," I asked, "about formulating and adopting a series of resolutions that would set out the responsibilities in the sphere of race relations of those Catholics who enjoy the privilege of a Catholic higher education?" It was the right question. The response was unanimous: "When do we begin?"

Of course, we began right away. And within a short time the

students, with the help of a number of expert consultants, drew up a series of twelve specific propositions for Catholic action, under the heading of "The Manhattanville Resolutions." They were no more than a broad statement of the principle that the Negro was by right an equal co-sharer in the fruits of the Redemption, and that his God-given rights had long been ignored in a country which professed to be freedom-loving. Specifically, the Resolutions enjoined those who had the privilege of a Catholic higher education "to maintain that the Negro as a human being and as a citizen is entitled to the rights of life, liberty and the pursuit of happiness, and to the essential opportunities of life and the full measure of social justice."

Five weeks passed after the conclusion of my course of lectures, and I began to resign myself to the realization that nothing more was going to be heard about the famous Manhattanville Resolutions. To my gratification, however, Mother Grace telephoned my office one day. For several weeks, she said, copies of the proposed Resolutions had been displayed on bulletin boards, and the entire student body had been engaged in warm discussion of Catholic teaching on race relations. "We have decided to hold an Assembly next Wednesday morning at eleven o'clock. Two students have been selected to make an exposition of the subject. Then there will be a question-and-answer period. And at the end, the Resolutions will be read and a vote taken."

Mother Grace invited me to be present, and I was more than delighted to accept. The discussion reflected the same high quality as those I had led during my course of lectures. When the issue was finally put to the vote, the approval was unanimous. As the only man present, I was accorded the privilege of having the last word. "Students of Manhattanville College," I said, "what you have done here today is a matter of interest not only to yourselves, or even to students and faculties of other Catholic colleges. It is a matter of national interest and concern."

I thought the words perhaps a trifle grandiloquent as I spoke them, but they turned out to be far short of what the moment demanded. It was in fact a historic moment. Outside the country, the significance of the event was quickly appreciated. The semi-official Vatican newspaper, the *Osservatore Romano*, printed the Resolutions in full. They were translated into the major European languages. They were carried by Catholic newspapers throughout Asia and Africa.

There was also a gratifying murmur of approval both in the Catholic and in the Negro press within the United States. But that was only the beginning. The Resolutions were reprinted in pamphlet form and distributed to Catholic editors and educators. They were taken up, endorsed, elaborated, and commented on by all manner of bodies. The following year, for example, an interracial committee of graduates and undergraduates of Catholic colleges sent out a student-to-student appeal. Under the title, "All Men Are Equal: A Brief for the Black Man," it circularized the 162 Catholic colleges in the country, challenging faculties and student bodies to become articulate in the cause of justice for the Negro.

Let me note in passing that I believe this was the first pamphlet on interracial issues ever published under Catholic auspices in the United States. The man responsible for its preparation was Francis S. Moseley, then a teacher at John Adams High School in Brooklyn, and later principal of the same school. In the fall of 1932, he heard me talk on the Paulist radio station, and he invited me to speak to the Brooklyn Catholic Action Council, of which he was then president. My address to the Council consisted in large part of extracts from papal documents and from the writings of Negro educators and of others interested in race relations. When I had finished, he asked if I had any objection to the preparation of a booklet incorporating the material. I assured him I had none, and in due course he produced the text of "All Men Are Equal." In addition to what I had said to the Council, it included the Manhattanville Resolutions.

The impact of this presentation on the Catholic students to whom the pamphlet was distributed took a very concrete form the following year. The Catholic Students' Mission Crusade, representing half a million college and high school students, went on record at its annual convention as supporting the identical interracial program which we had set out. Soon I was being asked to speak at one Catholic college after another, at St. Joseph's in Brooklyn, at St. Francis College for Men and St. John's University, also in Brooklyn, and Manhattan College.

The reader will undoubtedly have noticed that all this discussion has never got down to the concrete question of admitting Negroes to the Catholic colleges that were putting themselves on the record as defending the rights of the Negro to equality of opportunity. I knew very well, as did my colleagues of the Catholic Interracial Council, that my opportunity to state my case would end if I was so undiplomatic as to present that issue squarely. But we also confidently felt that if we kept the discussion alive, others would sooner or later get down to cases. And so it happened.

When the National Federation of Catholic College Students was formed in 1937, it named a committee on interracial justice, and this committee organized a drive among the student bodies of the constituent colleges to get the students to bring pressure to bear on the faculties. This was a major step towards getting out of the vicious circle which came up in every discussion, namely, that the students blamed the prejudice of the faculty members, while the faculty members blamed the prejudice of the students and their parents. For seven years in succession I went each year to talk at Mount St. Vincent College. They were very friendly and full of righteous indignation about the wickedness of discrimination. A group from the class of 1936 formed a committee, immediately on graduation, "for the study of, and participation in interracial problems." But there was no question of admitting a single Negro student to this New York Catholic college. The Reverend Mother and her associates would get me in a corner to tell me how much they'd like to admit Negroes, but the students wouldn't stand for it. The students in turn would tell me the same story in reverse.

At least in some cases, the problem of the administration was that it had thought the issue through to its logical conclusions, but was not prepared to face those conclusions. I remember being invited, in the early 1940s, to address the students of a girls' academy in New Jersey. The usual procedure on such occasions was for the Reverend Mother to introduce the speaker and tell him something about the backgrounds and social attitudes of the students. This time, however, I was received a little differently. Reverend Mother was waiting for me in her office, with the Dean, the head of the mathematics department, and one or two other weighty Sisters.

"We like the girls to know what the various Catholic social agencies in our neighborhood are doing," the Reverend Mother told me. "In the case of the Catholic Interracial Council, however, my associates and I have some misgivings which I think we should express before you speak to the student body. We understand, for example, that you people are advocating that Catholic high schools and colleges should admit qualified Negroes."

I was quite taken aback by the reception, and I framed my reply so as to indicate on the one hand that we did indeed advocate the opening of Catholic educational facilities to qualified Negroes, and on the other to find out what was the real problem in the minds of the Sisters. The Reverend Mother was quite frank. "Suppose," she said, "that we admitted a few good Negro girls to this academy. There might at first be a little unpleasantness or misunderstanding here or there. But that wouldn't worry me. I'm sure we could handle it. In due course, however, those Negro girls would become sophomores, juniors, seniors. Then they would graduate. And that is when we would really be in trouble. Because I can see some of their classmates walking into this office and putting me on the spot. 'It was all right to have Negro companions in class with us,' they would say, 'but apparently it's not all right to have them as members of your community.' That, Mr. Hunton, is our problem in a nutshell. It would be unthinkable to have Negroes in the same novitiate or as members of the same community."

That was in the 1940s, and many communities of Sisters were still thinking in those terms, though a few of them were starting to accept Negro postulants and novices. But the strange thing was that, though this Reverend Mother and her council were quite clear as to where the line had to be drawn, they did not stop me from talking to the students in their academy. And within a few years, the attitude of this academy and of this community of Sisters had changed radically.

It was not only the Sisters who resisted the social equality that would necessarily follow educational opportunity. The association of alumnae, the International Federation of Catholic Students, was very hostile for a long time, and even in the 1960s it was still bringing up the rear. The corresponding federation of alumni, the National Catholic Alumni Federation, was not a great deal better. This group, founded in the mid-twenties, could have exercised a lot of pressure on Catholic colleges through its 12,000 members. I remember making a major effort to get it moving in 1936. I arranged a symposium for its New York chapter on the interracial issue at the Centre Club on Central Park South in Manhattan. It was a strong battery of speakers. In addition to myself, there were Father LaFarge and Reverend Cornelius J. Ahern, pastor of Our Lady Queen of Angels Church, in Newark, New Jersey, Dr. Hudson J. Oliver, a leading Negro physician and current president of the Catholic Interracial Council, and Elmer A. Carter. Elmer was then editor of *Opportunity*, the organ of the National Urban League, and later he was the first man named by Governor Thomas E. Dewey to the New York State Human Rights Commission. He was not a Catholic, but he was then and always a good friend of mine and of the Catholic interracial movement. They listened to us politely enough, as we laid down the principles and urged them to get the national body to take action. But it went no further.

It was at the student level that the big breakthrough occurred. Students of Catholic colleges in the New York area established the National Federation of Catholic College Students in 1937, as a result of an organizing drive sponsored by Pax Romana, the international confederation of societies of Catholic college and university undergraduates. Colleges in Philadelphia and Washington joined the association almost immediately, and before long it spread also to New England and elsewhere. One of the first things they undertook was the formation of undergraduate interracial groups in the colleges and the co-ordination of the work of such groups where they already existed, as in St. John's College in Brooklyn, and in Manhattanville and Mount St. Vincent in New York. It was actually at Manhattanville that the Federation itself had its founding meeting, in October 1937.

I was in constant contact with the Federation from its inception, and I was fortunate in that its first president, Miss Louise Quigley, was an enthusiastic champion of interracial justice. With her help, I was able to organize an interracial symposium at Manhattan College just before Christmas 1938, under the combined auspices of the Federation and the Catholic Interracial Council. Five hundred students from the New York area attended, and the meeting revealed a dynamism and concern which seemed a century away only a few years earlier. Strong resolutions were ratified, including one to organize committees on each campus to collect signatures in favor of federal legislation against lynching, a live issue at the time. Actually, ninety-five per cent of the student body on each of the thirty-five campuses represented at the meeting signed the petitions within a short time. In addition, an interracial unit of the Federation was established on every single one of those campuses.

With this kind of activity on the Catholic campuses, the problem of Negro admission was already beginning to solve itself. I doubt if it will ever be possible to determine with certainty which Catholic college in the New York area deserves the credit for being the first to re-admit Negroes in the 1930s. I stress *re-admit*, because I think my alma mater, Holy Cross, can take credit for being the first to admit a Negro, since Bishop James Healy was an honor student in its first graduating class in 1849. But Holy Cross had subsequently fallen by the way with the others. And when the doors started to reopen slightly in the 1930s, this was done with the utmost circumspection. Everyone feared that publicity would start controversy and embarrass all parties. I do know, however, that the student sodality magazine, *The Queen's Work*, published a small item in 1939. "As far as we know," it wrote, "the first Negro girl to be graduated from a Catholic girls' college in recent years is Genevieve Green, who was graduated from the College of St. Elizabeth in Convent Station, New Jersey, in 1937." And as far as I know, *The Queen's Work* was correct. As regards men students, I think there were a few even earlier than Miss Green, and I think that St. Francis College in Brooklyn has a strong claim to the record. I know that in 1937 a young man named Edwin P. Kane, who was then president of the Interracial Relations Society of St. Francis, said the college was proud to number several Negroes among its graduates. "Contrary to what is ordinarily thought," he said in a statement circulated to every Catholic college editor in the country, "there has never been any difficulty between Negro students who have attended St. Francis and the white students."

It was also in 1937 that Catholic University in Washington broke with its all-white policy by admitting some Negroes to its summer school. This was an action that drew national attention. Congress at that time had separate provision for the education of the races in the District of Columbia, and private institutions have generally followed the cue of the Government. In addition, Negroes in Washington were better served through Howard University than those of any other part of the country, and the availability of Howard was widely used by educators to justify their segregationist policies in other universities.

We in the Catholic interracial movement felt that we had played a part in opening up Catholic University. Monsignor Joseph M. Corrigan, who was named rector of Catholic University in 1936, had long been an enthusiastic member of the Clergy Conference on Negro Welfare. I recall first meeting him at the home of Mrs. Morrell, Mother Katharine Drexel's half sister, in Philadelphia, and I attended several of the meetings of the Clergy Conference on Negro Welfare which he arranged at Catholic University each year while he was rector. He was made a bishop in 1940, but unfortunately died almost immediately afterwards, in June 1942.

In any case, Father LaFarge buttonholed him not long after his nomination as rector of Catholic University was announced. "I hope," he said, "that you will change the policy which excludes Negroes from the university." Monsignor Corrigan had the tact that makes university presidents. "I have no idea what policies Catholic University has followed in the past in the admission of students," he said with just a hint of a twinkle in his Irish eyes, "but I can assure you that if an issue has ever arisen about the rejection of a student on the ground of race, it is not going to arise again." He was as good as his word. Not only was the summer school opened to Negroes in 1937, but the following year the university announced that it was expanding its nurses department, and that Catholic Negro girls would be welcomed. There was great excitement. Mrs. Mabel Stoupers, who was president of the Guild of Negro Nurses, called me. "We have fifteen students down here in Washington," she said, "who would like to get into Catholic University. Can you help us?" "You know I am always ready to help you, when help is needed," I replied. "But this time you don't need my help. Just send them to register." She was a little doubtful, because doors didn't usually open that easily. But she sent them, and they were accepted on their merits.

Also in 1938, the senior class at Manhattan College voted to set up a $1000 four-year scholarship for a Catholic Negro, tenable at the college. One of the points made when the project was under discussion was that a Negro with a high scholastic record had been accepted for matriculation at Manhattan a few years earlier but had been forced to withdraw because of financial difficulties.

In the same year, Manhattanville College of the Sacred Heart reached the logical conclusion of the road on which it had embarked with the Manhattanville Resolutions. There was always a style about Mother Grace Dammann, and it came out strongly in the way she handled this incident. She was, of course, not caught unprepared. She and I had often discussed what decision she should make when a Negro girl with the educational, cultural and moral qualities required by the regulations should apply for admission. When such a girl did apply in May 1938, her strategy was planned. She first presented the facts to the faculty and the board of trustees, and they agreed that the girl was qualified and should be accepted. Then the student body was informed of the decision and asked to comment on it. In a written ballot, eighty-two per cent of the girls approved.

But as Mother Dammann and I had anticipated, the die-hard minority would not yield without a fight. No sooner had the news spread to the families of the girls than a group of seven alumnae addressed anonymous letters to the alumnae throughout the country. A first-class controversy ensued, and the objectors called for a showdown at the Class Day meeting. Although I had supreme confidence in Mother Dammann, I looked forward to the event with no little trepidation. My judgment was on the line as well as hers. But I need not have worried; she was her usual superb self. In a serious and hard-hitting speech she set out the reasons for the decision. "We have been accused of lowering the standards and traditions of Manhattanville College," she said. "On the contrary, we have given the college new prestige by daring to defy prejudice. Our prejudices and our principles may exist side by side until some call is made upon us which reveals the depth of the one and tests the strength of the other." Mother Grace had done her work well. The alumnae were forced to recognize the justice of her stand. The meeting closed the controversy, and the girl was admitted.

The process went on slowly and painfully, and it took a long time to get any significant number of residential schools to accept Negroes. I shall mention just one incident which made headlines in 1939. Father Michael McLaughlin, a young priest working among Negroes in Brooklyn, told the story at a conference of Catholic high school teachers and principals. William O'Dwyer, who later became Mayor of New York and who was then district attorney of Kings County, had been the previous speaker, and he had told the educators that nothing could take the place of moral training as a preventative of crime. Agreeing with Mr. O'Dwyer, Father McLaughlin asked the Catholic educators how they expected young Negroes to get the needed moral training, when they were methodically excluded from Catholic schools. "A very refined and well-educated Negro lady, a teacher in the public school, came to us at St. Peter Claver's," he said, "and asked us to suggest a Catholic boarding school for her son. We took it on ourselves to write to Catholic institutions, vouching for the boy as well trained and a member of a highly respectable family." Producing the five or six replies received, Father McLaughlin stated that all were refusals. One, from Wisconsin, commented that the writer did not know of any Catholic boarding school which admitted Negroes. The reporters, who had come along to cover Bill O'Dwyer, recognized news when it was served up to them. The New York *Times* and the *Herald Tribune* splashed the story the following day, and it was widely reprinted. For some it was bitter medicine, for they felt that the newspapers were glad to needle the Catholic Church. But none could deny the legitimacy of the criticism, and I for my part was glad to give it publicity as the only available way to ensure corrective action.

The resistance to admitting Negroes to Catholic colleges extended also to seminaries. In the nineteenth century, several Negro candidates were ordained to the priesthood and acquired acceptance in the Catholic community in the United States. Of these, the most famous were the three Healy brothers, one of whom became a bishop. Ordained in Paris in 1854, Georgia-born James Augustine Healy was first chancellor of the diocese of Boston in 1855, then pastor of the cathedral and of the biggest church in Boston (St. James) from 1866 to 1875, and Bishop of Portland, Maine, from 1875 until his death in 1900. His brother Sherwood was theologian to Bishop John Joseph Williams of Boston at the Baltimore Council in 1866 and at the First Vatican Council (1870), and he was rumored to be in line to be named Bishop of Hartford, Connecticut, when he died in 1875 at the age of thirty-nine. The third brother, Patrick, was a Jesuit. He became president of Georgetown in 1873 and erected the main building on campus which still bears his name.

The records in Boston and Portland establish that it was generally known that the Healys had Negro ancestry, and as I mentioned earlier, this was known by my parents, who were friends of Bishop Healy. But they were very light-colored, and the legal and social criteria determining race were not so absurd in nineteenth-century America as they subsequently became. Under the law in Virginia, for example, only those were Negroes who had at least one quarter of Negro blood. That was the position until 1910, when the legislators decided that one sixteenth was enough; and it was not until 1930 that they proclaimed that Negro blood is so powerful that a single drop determines the race of the proud possessor.

Following this same kind of reverse evolution, attitudes among

Catholics toward Negro priests became less and less sympathetic
in the early part of the twentieth century. Part of this process
I described in the opening chapter of this book when referring
to the three early Negro members of the Josephite Fathers,
Fathers Charles Uncles, John Dorsey and John Plantevigne.
Father Adrian Esnard, of New Orleans, who was ordained at
Louvain, Belgium, in 1905, never worked in the United States.
Father Joseph Burgess, C.S.Sp., a native of Washington, D.C.,
ordained in France in 1907, taught at a seminary at Cornwells
Heights, Pennsylvania, until 1919, then worked briefly in Haiti
during the United States occupation of that island, and was
assistant pastor of St. Joachim's Church, Detroit, a French-Ca-
nadian parish, from 1920 until his death in 1923. Father Joseph
John, a native of the little island of Carriacou in the West
Indies, ordained in New York in 1923 at the age of forty-three
after overcoming unbelievable obstacles in his determination to
become a priest, could not get a bishop in the United States
to give him an assignment, although it had been publicly announced that his mission work would be among the Negroes of
the South. A member of the Lyons Society of African Missions,
he taught English, literature, Latin and homiletics to the seminarians at St. Anthony's Mission House, Tenafly, New Jersey, until 1927. He was finally assigned to a parish, in Corpus Christi,
Texas, in that year, but gave up two years later and transferred
to Trinidad in the West Indies to a successful pastoral career
that continued until his death in 1944. Another West Indian, Father Augustine Derricks, known in religion as Augustine of the
Ascension, was a Trinitarian monk trained and ordained in Italy.
He did some light pastoral work in the United States between
the completion of his studies in 1928 and his death from appendicitis the following year.

One unchanging positive element in the Catholic life of the
United States is the universal high regard in which the priest
is held. I knew that one of the most effective ways to improve
the image of the Negro in the mind of the average Catholic

would be to familiarize this average Catholic with Negroes who were priests. I realized that quick results could not be expected. The stereotype of the Negro extended even to the Negro priest. But I was confident that over the years the American Catholic, if exposed to Negro priests, would gradually see them less as Negroes and more as priests. And we did have one Negro priest in the United States in the early 1930s who was in a position to expose himself publicly, and who had a reputation which made it desirable from our point of view to give him every possible exposure. He was Father Stephen L. Theobald, known as "the fighting archbishop's protégé."

The fighting archbishop was, of course, Archbishop John Ireland, a native of Ireland and first archbishop of St. Paul from 1888 to 1918. He was a man who never spoke; he always thundered. And on the race issue, he thundered in terms that enshrine him for all time as a great Christian who understood the implications of his faith. At a commemorative service for the anniversary of Lincoln's Emancipation Proclamation on January 1, 1891, he challenged Americans to be loyal to the Constitution and allow Negroes to enjoy all the political rights of the citizen. "If the education of the Negro does not fit him to be a voter and an office holder, let us, for his sake and our own, hurry to enlighten him. I would open to the Negro all industrial and professional avenues—the test for his advance being his ability, and never his color. I would in all public gatherings and in all public resorts, in halls and hotels, treat the black man as I treat the white. I might shun the vulgar man, whatever his color; but the gentleman, whatever his color, I would not dare push away from me."

From the pulpit he spoke in similar terms. "I know no color line," he said once. "I will acknowledge none. I am not unaware that this solemn declaration of mine shall be deemed by many upon whose opinion I set a high value as rash and untimely. Yet I fear not to make it. I am ahead of my day. But the time is not distant when Americans and Christians will wonder that there ever was race prejudice."

In due course, he received the direct challenge. "Would you admit a Negro to your seminary?" "Yes," he thundered back without hesitation. "And if the other students objected, or embarrassed him because of his color?" "I'd expel every single one as unworthy to be a priest." In 1905, Stephen Louis Theobald, thirty-one years old, a native of British Guiana and a law graduate of Cambridge University, England, was admitted to the archdiocesan seminary in Minnesota. Five years later, Archbishop Ireland ordained him. After a short period as canon law expert on the Archbishop's staff, he was made pastor of the racially mixed parish of St. Peter Claver in St. Paul, and there he labored with great success for twenty-two years until his death in 1932. Thanks to Archbishop Ireland's continuing protection, he was able to express himself locally and nationally, and to both white and colored audiences, on race relations in the Catholic Church, a task he performed with tact but in straightforward language. Negro Catholics revered him, and in 1917 he helped Dr. Thomas W. Turner of Baltimore to start an organization which in 1925 assumed national proportions as the Federated Colored Catholics of the United States.

His status was well assured by the time Archbishop Ireland died in 1918, and his new superior, Archbishop John Murray, gave him full freedom to continue the many works with which he was associated. He remained active in particular in the Federated Colored Catholics, and when St. Louis was chosen for a convention of this body in 1931, Father LaFarge and I decided to join in a tribute to him. Father William Markoe, S.J., who was still editor of the publication that would shortly be renamed the *Interracial Review* and a man of influence in St. Louis, was in full agreement. He organized a big procession through the streets to the cathedral for the opening of the convention. It was led by the boys' band from his parish. Archbishop J. J. Glennon spoke at the High Mass celebrated by Father Theobald, referring to the kiss of peace given by the Negro celebrant to the white deacon (Father Edward Kraemer) as a symbol of peace between Catholics of the two races. Much as Father Theobald appreciated the gesture, however, he was too much a disciple of Archbishop Ireland to be satisfied with less than the reality. At a mass meeting in the auditorium of St. Louis University that evening, he called for an ending to discrimination in St. Louis, particularly in Catholic schools, hospitals and other institutions, and specifically in the Jesuit university in which he was speaking. Applause greeted his words, and action was not long in following. But he did not live to see it. Just ten months later, he was stricken with appendicitis, as had happened to Father Derricks earlier, and succumbed to peritonitis. Five bishops and a hundred priests attended his obsequies. A thousand people could not get past the door of the thronged church.

That left a single Negro priest engaged in pastoral work in the United States at the time I became involved in interracial work. He was Father Norman DuKette, the youngest of twenty-six children, born in Washington, D.C., in 1890, ordained in Detroit in 1926. He was assigned to parish work in Detroit the following year, soon transferred to the Christ the King Mission in Flint, Michigan, and remained there for the rest of his life, respected for his hard work and revered for his great charity. I came to know him well, and I can make my own the words written by an admirer in 1947. "He is a plain man, delicately formed, slight in stature, modestly reserved, quiet and dignified. To see him in his long, black cassock, his close-cropped head bent slightly forward as he talks, his gentle eyes beaming behind his shell-rimmed glasses, is to take with you a picture you cherish forever; an impression that you have touched something a little holier than common things."

In one of the first issues of the *Interracial Review* edited by me, I recorded the ordination of the next Negro to be admitted to the priesthood in the United States. He was Father William

Le Roy Lane, a native of New York, ordained in Pittsburgh on December 23, 1933, and he celebrated his first Mass in St. Charles Borromeo, a Negro parish in New York's Harlem. A few months later, on May 23, 1934, four Negro members of the Society of the Divine Word were ordained at the Society's seminary of St. Augustine at Bay St. Louis, Mississippi. Bishop Richard Oliver Gerow of Natchez was the ordaining prelate. The four new priests were Maurice Rousseve of New Orleans, Vincent Smith of Lebanon, Kentucky, Anthony Bourges of Lafayette, Louisiana, and Francis Wade of Washington, D.C.

These ordinations, in the presence of two bishops, a hundred priests and about two thousand lay people, were the culmination of a hard struggle. Exactly twenty years earlier, in 1914, Father Matthew Christman, S.V.D., had presented a paper on the need for Negro priests to a conference of Society of the Divine Word missionaries. The public opposition at the time was so bitter that the project was shelved. Within a couple of years, however, Father Christman had opened a high school at Greenville, Mississippi, the mission which had been entrusted to him. Here there was no question of a junior seminary but simply of a regular high school. Yet even that was such a novel venture in the field of Catholic education for Negroes that it was made the butt of bitter opposition and hostile criticism.

In 1919, a colleague of Father Christman, Father James Wendel, S.V.D., went to Bishop John Gunn of Natchez, pointed out to him the success of the high school at Greenville, and asked his approval for a junior seminary for Negroes. The Bishop agreed, and the Provincial of the Society of the Divine Word put Father Christman in charge of the undertaking as first rector of Sacred Heart College. The Catholic Board for Mission Work among the Colored People gave publicity and financial aid. Mother Katharine Drexel and a Mr. Murphy of New York sent donations large enough to provide scholarships for the first three students. Applications came from many parts of the United States, from the West Indies, and even from Africa. Eight candidates were chosen to begin their secondary studies at Greenville in November 1920.

In 1923, the seminary moved to permanent quarters at Bay St. Louis on the Gulf, and the name was changed to St. Augustine's Seminary. In 1926, the first class completed its six-year course of classical studies and moved on to philosophy and theology, a course that occupied a further seven years before the first ordinations. St. Augustine's in those early days also supplied some vocations for the diocesan clergy. The first two were Father Philip Marin, a native of British Honduras, who returned to work in his homeland after ordination, and Father Max Murphy, a Texan, who completed his studies and was ordained in Prague, Czechoslovakia, and then went to work in the archdiocese of Port-of-Spain, Trinidad. Before going to the West Indies, Father Murphy approached thirty bishops in the United States with offers to serve in their dioceses. Many ignored his letters. The others regretted that the time was not ripe.

Subsequently I came to know Father Max well. He always stopped by the Catholic Interracial Council's office in New York on his frequent visits to his homeland, and he often spoke at one of our weekly meetings. He has spent most of his life as pastor of Chaguanas, a thriving town in the heart of Trinidad's sugar region, to which he has contributed among other things a fine high school. When the United States Occupation authorities in Germany wanted a youth specialist with fluent German in 1952 to plan a program for education, recreation and welfare services for underprivileged and unemployed young Germans, the man they picked was the Texan pastor of Chaguanas, Trinidad.

Even in the 1960s not all white Catholics in the United States are prepared to accept Negro priests to minister to them, and in the 1930s there was no question of assigning the first Negro priests to white parishes. Even some, who spoke from their prejudices more than from their knowledge, disapproved of assigning them to Negro parishes, claiming that Negroes wanted white priests. Pope Pius XI, however, had recently taken the wind out of their sails when he wrote to the Superior General of the Society of the Divine Word to express his approval of St. Augustine's. "If we wish to accomplish some solid and useful work in this field," Pius wrote, referring to the conversion of Negroes to Catholicism, "it is indispensable that priests of the same race make it their life task to lead these people to the Christian faith and to a higher cultural level."

What was decided, accordingly, was to send all four young Negro priests to form a separate community of the Society of the Divine Word and take charge of a newly created parish in a Negro section of Lafayette, Louisiana. The intention was to make it the center for the future activities of Negro priests in Lafayette and other Southern dioceses. And so it continued, very successfully, until a growing awareness of the content of the message of Christ brought more people to appreciate the distinction between the function of the priest and the color of his skin.

That, however, took time. Meanwhile, many of the very small number of Negro priests were either shipped overseas or relegated to some community activity in which they would have minimal contact with the general public. This was a technique with an old history. Back in 1905, the Immaculate Heart Fathers had ordained in Belgium a Negro from New Orleans, Father Adrien Esnard. Soon afterwards, they sent him as head of their mission band in the Philippines, which had come under United States rule a few years earlier. The United States authorities refused to let him function as superior of a group of white priests, and so he was shipped back to Belgium. From there he went to the Congo and worked as a bush missionary for forty years until his death in 1947.

History repeated itself in June 1937 when the first Negro from New York, at least in modern times, was ordained. He was Father Marcus Glover, born in the Yorkville section and baptized in the parish of St. Francis de Sales. He became a member of the Congregation of the White Fathers, studied in Quebec and subsequently in Carthage, Africa, where he was ordained. He returned to New York for his first Mass, then went off to work on the Gold Coast of West Africa, now Ghana.

We at the Catholic Interracial Council felt very strongly that a high priority should be accorded to the effort to have Negro priests accepted everywhere as priests. Accordingly, whenever a Negro priest visited New York, we went out of our way not only to help him but to expose him in ways which would make a favorable impression on white Catholics. Some of our visitors were men of very high caliber indeed. I think the first was Father Gladstone Orlando Wilson, a Jamaican convert who was ordained in Rome in 1931 by Cardinal Van Rossum, head of the Sacred Congregation for the Propagation of the Faith. Father Wilson had a brilliant mind. Here he was competing with picked students from more than fifty different countries, yet he led consistently in all his classes. He wrote a thesis on the living wage for his degree in philosophy and one on the marriage bond for his degree in theology, receiving first-class honors in both subjects and a gold medal for outstanding excellence. He was selected to deliver the baccalaureate address to his classmates in the presence of Pope Pius XI.

On completing his courses, he was awarded a scholarship for graduate work in canon law in Rome. He continued to lead the new class also in scholarship, and during his last two years he gave theology courses to the underclassmen. He again graduated with the highest honors and was again selected to give the baccalaureate address in the presence of the Pope.

After traveling through various European countries and acquiring a speaking knowledge of five languages, he returned to Jamaica. In September 1938, he arrived in the United States to take a course in social service at Fordham University and at the same time to promote the Catholic interracial movement. I had previously corresponded with him, and one of his first stops was our office, which was then at 220 West Forty-second

Street, near Times Square. He charmed me personally and delighted me professionally. Here was a man who would grace
any social or intellectual situation. One who met him even
briefly could never again swallow the old shibboleth about an
inherent inferiority of the Negro race. I determined to use him
as fully as possible, and he was more than ready to be used in
this cause. I arranged for him to talk to many white and Negro
audiences in Harlem and elsewhere in New York City and
vicinity. He was a featured speaker at the annual conference
of the Catholic Interracial Council and at several of its monthly
Communion breakfasts. He contributed several very thoughtful
articles to the *Interracial Review*, and he continued to write
for it frequently after his return to Jamaica. Many of his articles
were reprinted and commented upon in Catholic publications
throughout the country. One point that he liked to make was
that he himself had never been so color-conscious in all his life
as when he was in the United States. It seemed to him extraordinarily naïve of Americans to take a single element in
something so complicated as a human being and determine the
entire civil and social status, and by necessary consequence the
economic status as well, of that human being on the issue of
the presence or absence of one drop of a particular kind of
blood indistinguishable by chemical analysis from other kinds
of blood. Shortly after this first visit to the United States,
Father Wilson was given the title of Monsignor and made
chancellor of the diocese of Kingston, Jamaica, a position he
still occupies.

Another Negro priest who made a big impact was Father
Basil Matthews, O.S.B., a member of the multiracial Benedictine
monastery of Mount St. Benedict, Trinidad, West Indies. Father
Basil had been educated in Trinidad and at the University of
Louvain, and he came to the United States about 1941 to study
for a doctorate in sociology at Fordham University. He also
gave retreats in Benedictine abbeys in various parts of the
United States. Father Basil was a powerfully built and striking

young man, full of charm and persuasiveness. Mother Grace Dammann of Manhattanville College of the Sacred Heart took a great liking to him, and she decided to give him a part-time job as instructor in religious knowledge to help him pay the cost of his studies. She was a little bit doubtful about the reaction and she called me up to ask what I thought. "Mother," I said to her, "I think by now I know the temper of the students. They won't have the slightest objection. I can vouch for them, if you can take care of the staff." "I can take care of the staff," she answered without hesitation. And she did.

But prejudice has many faces. It was much easier to open doors for a Negro from another country, even a distinctively dark-skinned West Indian like Father Gladstone or Father Basil Matthews, than for an American-born Negro, no matter how light-colored. They were different, people would say. They were more educated, more cultured, more this or more that. They clung to any straw to justify their refusal to treat their fellow Americans on their merits, unable even to see that the admission that some Negro, any Negro, could be different upset their entire basic position.

I recall discussing this subject with Bishop Andrew J. Brennan of Richmond, Virginia, and getting from him a very curious excuse. I had been invited to the Commencement exercises of St. Emma's Industrial and Agricultural Institute (now St. Emma Military Institute), a trade and general high school for Negroes founded in 1895 by Colonel and Mrs. Edward Morrell at Rock Castle, Virginia. Bishop Brennan was a Northerner, a native of Scranton, Pennsylvania, and like myself an alumnus of Holy Cross College, Wooster. I felt I could speak freely to him, and I did so during the luncheon.

"I understand," I said, "that you have no Negro priests in your diocese. I hope you are planning to change this, that perhaps you already have some candidates in training."

"I'm sorry, Mr. Hunton," he said, "but that would be quite impossible. You see, it would interfere with the annual visit of the clergy who in this diocese have the practice of spending two days for conferences at the Bishop's residence."

I made a gesture indicating that the explanation was not fully clear to me. The Bishop repeated himself more explicitly. "What I mean is," he said, "that none of the priests, pastors or curates, of my diocese would attend, if Negro priests were included in the annual diocesan conference. But obviously, if I had Negro priests, I'd have to invite them. So, no Negro priests. The others just would not attend."

That was in the South, but things were not greatly different in the North. Even into the 1940s, most American Catholics continued to treat the few Negro priests around as second-class priests. The very religious congregations that had accepted them as candidates and trained them took the easy way out. By the time the United States entered the war in 1941, the Society of the Divine Word had fourteen Negro priests, but several of them were working in Africa, where they would have and create fewer problems. In that year a Negro newspaper, the New York *Age,* summed up the situation very aptly. Commenting on the announcement that four Negroes had been ordained to the priesthood at St. Augustine's Seminary and were about to set off for Africa "to carry the teachings of their Church to their own people," it made the following caustic observations.

"While we consider it a laudable ambition for anyone to become a missionary and pioneer, we think that it would also be a fine thing if the Catholic Church would place some of its Negro priests in parishes in this country where they may become leaders of their own group here. As splendid a field as foreign service offers, there is still much work to be done in this country to civilize and christianize the masses of Negroes and whites of the South, as well as our large industrial centers. A Negro priest in New York would do more to bring members of his race into the Catholic Church than a dozen white priests, for his example would be living proof that the Church practices as well as preaches the principles of democracy."

Twenty-five years later the views expressed by the *Age* sound very moderate and reasonable. When they were written, however, they were regarded by most Catholic priests in the New York area as insulting and provocative. And the *Interracial Review* came in for its share of criticism for daring to reprint them in a context that showed that we agreed completely. It will already be clear to the reader that the interracial movement had from the outset the backing of individual priests. But they formed a mere handful. Most of the clergy were firmly opposed to our basic principle that color was irrelevant in church. They regarded us as mischief-makers, and as I shall describe in the next chapter, they treated us as such.

Chapter 6

"I am here tonight to honor a man of whom the archdiocese is proud," said Auxiliary Bishop John M. A. Fearns of New York. "I am here as representative of the archdiocese and as representative of Cardinal Spellman. But while my presence is official, I am delighted to be here. This is a part of my work that gives me a very deep personal satisfaction and pleasure."

Among the 500 guests at the Statler-Hilton banquet on that Thursday evening in September 1961, there were several on whom the irony of the moment was not lost. Judge Harold A. Stevens was there, and Maurice Lavanoux and Maceo Thomas and Gerard L. Carroll and Daniel J. Sullivan and Theophilus Lewis and Father LaFarge. It imposed no strain on the memory of any of them to recall a time when the archdiocese of New York had been anything but proud of George Hunton.

All through the 1930s, there was scarcely a single representative churchman, priest or lay, in the greater New York area who wanted to have anything to do with Catholic work for Negroes, or even approved of the idea of lending the Catholic name and prestige to any effort to have the Negro recognized as an equal citizen. It was with the greatest reluctance that we got Cardinal Hayes in 1934 to approve of the founding of the Catholic Interracial Council in New York. The sum total of his contribution during the four years until he died was that he didn't stop us. We were always fearful that he would stop us, and indeed he was under constant pressures to do so. We had to move with the greatest caution and circumspection in order not to get our necks chopped off. I used often to feel frustration, but Father LaFarge would say: "Let's count our blessings. With one word, Cardinal Hayes could put us out of business. But he hasn't said that word, and while he doesn't, the mere fact that we are here is something."

I do not know that I could have found the moral and spiritual strength to struggle on in my lonely unpopularity in those days if it were not for the tremendous faith and singleness of purpose of Father LaFarge. I remember working myself into a state in the summer of 1935. We were making our plans for the first annual meeting of the Catholic Interracial Council (which was held at Tenafly, New Jersey, in September, as I mentioned earlier). It had been agreed that I should formulate a policy and program of action for the Council, to be submitted to the meeting. As I went ahead with this work, it seemed to me each day more hallucinatory and chimerical. We were purporting to present as Catholic principles concepts at which I knew Catholics in high places scoffed. We were calling for the cooperation of organized Catholic forces in interracial interests and action when the major ones were on the record as opposed to our position. We were looking for the support of a Catholic press, most of which regarded us as utterly irresponsible.

I finally reached a point where I felt unable to proceed. I telephoned Father LaFarge. "May I have fifteen minutes of your time after supper this evening," I asked him. "Of course," he said, as he always did to whoever asked his help. "You know our situation," I said to him, when we met. "Our every pronouncement and even every news item we print in the *Interracial Review* is studied microscopically in the Chancery. You know that they want no association of the Catholic Church with advanced views on Negro rights. And it is not only here in New York but all across the country. Catholic editors, educators and bishops are almost unanimous in insisting that this is no time to rock the boat. Do you really think we should stick our necks out so far as this proposed statement of policy is going to project them?"

For the first and I think the only time in our long association, Father LaFarge gave full vent to his emotions. "They are not right," he said in a voice of thunder, clenching his right hand and pounding the desk emphatically with his fist. "It is we who are right, and time will prove us to be right. But we must have the courage of our convictions. We have to go forward, alone if necessary. In due course, the entire Catholic Church in this country will follow us."

I shall never forget the elation with which I left the little parlor in the Jesuit house on West 108th Street where we had talked. As I rode back on the subway to my home in Brooklyn, I knew that another milestone had been passed.

A continuing obstacle to the progress of our work at that time was a priest named James L. McIntyre, who by coincidence was appointed chancellor of the New York archdiocese in 1934, the year in which the Catholic Interracial Council was formed. His status and power increased in 1940 when he was consecrated as an auxiliary bishop to Archbishop (later Cardinal) Spellman, who had been named to New York the previous year on the death of Cardinal Hayes. Bishop McIntyre continued to head the Chancery until he was made Archbishop of Los Angeles in 1948. The reputation he subsequently acquired for arbitrariness and obscurantism as Cardinal Archbishop of Los Angeles came as no surprise to my early associates in the interracial movement and myself. In our dealings with him, we had experienced the same treatment.

Shortly after Archbishop Spellman had been named, we asked him and Bishop Molloy of Brooklyn for an annual contribution of $2500 each towards our work. Archbishop Spellman turned over the application to Monsignor McIntyre, who sent for Father LaFarge and myself. We went up to the chancery office to meet Monsignor McIntyre and Monsignor (later Bishop) Joseph P. Donahue. A priest active in the labor movement, Father

John P. Monaghan, was also present; and he was as astonished as we were by our reception. He called me up afterwards and said: "I never realized that I was going to be a witness of such a grilling as you two got."

Monsignor McIntyre opened the interview by turning on Father LaFarge and saying to him: "Father LaFarge, you have for these years been advocating interracial marriage." "I have never advocated interracial marriage," Father LaFarge replied. "When the question was asked of me, I have simply said that the Church does not make of race an impediment to matrimony." Then he turned to me. "As for you, you have something here in this brief you submitted to the Archbishop, you have something about the Negro which I think it is preposterous for you to say. You claim that even today he is the victim of racial despair, that even Harlem stores won't employ him. Why should he suffer from racial despair? I'll tell you how little you know about this thing. You don't even know how many priests are working for the Negroes up in Harlem, or how many of the Negroes up there are Catholics, and how many Negro children are getting an education in Catholic schools."

As it happened, I did have the figures right in my pocket. I took out my notebook and I reeled off for him not only the number of priests working in Harlem, the number of Catholic Negroes and the number of Negro children in the Catholic schools, but a number of additional facts concerning discrimination in employment suffered by qualified Negroes. "Even in stores whose customers are ninety per cent Negro," I said, "no Negro is employed as salesman or saleswoman. Marian Anderson or Dr. Ralph Bunche couldn't get a job selling dustpans in the bargain basement of any of our department stores."

"I must admit that you have your statistics right," Monsignor McIntyre said grudgingly. But he still refused to accept the conclusion I wanted him to draw. His viewpoint was that the economic disabilities suffered by Negroes were no concern of the Catholic Church. It was, in fact, the almost universal viewpoint at that time among Catholics. They were satisfied that they were more than fulfilling their Christian duty toward Negroes and found it hard to understand how the Negroes could be so unappreciative of their generosity. So Father LaFarge and I had to take the chancellor's tongue-lashing mildly. And we got some benefit from it, too. Bishop Molloy of Brooklyn had already agreed to give us the $2500 a year we had asked, a pledge he kept until he died in 1957, and which his successor has continued with minor modifications since that time. This action of Brooklyn rather squeezed New York, so Monsignor McIntyre recommended to the Archbishop that we be given $1000 a year. At this time, I was still not able to get to Archbishop Spellman direct. It was a couple of years later when I had my first audience with him. I took advantage of it to tell him that Brooklyn was giving us $2500 a year, and he immediately agreed to match that figure.

I was naturally glad to get the money, which we always needed desperately just to stay in business. But giving money did not automatically change attitudes. On the contrary, it could tend to harden them, because the donor could delude himself into substituting his charity for his concern. He could continue to keep the Negro at arm's length, and that is precisely what most Catholics in and around New York were doing.

I remember, for example, when the national council for a permanent Fair Employment Practices Committee (FEPC) was set up in the office of A. Philip Randolph. Among the charter members, there were two Catholics, Monsignor John A. Ryan of the Social Action Department of the National Catholic Welfare Conference in Washington, and myself. After some smaller meetings, we decided to hold a meeting in Madison Square Garden in June 1942, and I was asked to get the chancery office to send an Auxiliary Bishop of the archdiocese of New York, or failing that, at least a Monsignor or a priest. When I sent in the request, it was turned over to an assistant in the chancery office. In due course, this minor official phoned me. "We have decided not to send an archbishop, not to send a bishop, not to send a monsignor, not to send a labor priest. We are going to send a Catholic layman." I interrupted him. "Pardon me," I said. "I shall relay to the organizers of the rally your refusal to designate a priest to take part along with the Rabbi and the Protestant clergyman who have already been named. It will be for them to request a layman as representative of the archdiocese, if they want one." They decided to forget about it. Instead, they put me on the program as a speaker, along with Mrs. Eleanor Roosevelt, Senator Wayne Morse, Helen Hayes, and Senator Dennis Chavez of New Mexico.

Monsignor Ryan was a most unusual man for those times, and I suppose I should say for any times. I have already referred to the lone battle he waged to make his fellow Catholics understand the importance of the League of Nations. His long years as a champion of social justice had by now won him a national reputation, and he had no hesitation in identifying himself publicly with even so unpopular a cause as that of the Negro. But he had no illusions about the price he was paying. I first met him in 1931, shortly after I became secretary of the New York committee for the Cardinal Gibbons Institute. "I'll never make bishop," he used to say jokingly. "I speak too plainly." He came from St. Paul, and some of the integrity and fearlessness of Archbishop Ireland had rubbed off on him. He was reluctant at first to get deeply involved in Negro problems. His great commitment was to the cause of labor and to the promotion of the human rights principles of the social encyclicals. But he gradually came to recognize that the Negro issue was part of the wider issue to which he was dedicated, and from then on he was always with us. He became a very close friend of the Hoeys and always stopped at their home when he visited New York. Jane Hoey, Jim's sister, had been his student at Catholic University, where he was professor of Social Action at the same time as he headed the Social Action Department of NCWC.

Few were able or willing to speak out as Monsignor Ryan did.

Most of our friends felt the need to be circumspect. But actually there were few who were even privately well disposed. In the whole of New York, there were only two priests at what I might call the policy level of the archdiocese in the 1930s that I could call friendly to our work. They were Monsignor John Voight, superintendent of schools and later secretary of education of the archdiocese, and Father Philip J. Furlong, then secretary of education and later (1955) named auxiliary bishop. They were both open-minded men, with an ecumenical outlook and advanced ideas in social action. I knew Bishop Furlong first, but I became closer to Monsignor Voight, whom I met through him. He was a man in whom I had implicit confidence. I could go to him, lay my case before him and ask his candid advice and counsel. He had no previous exposure to interracial affairs, but he quickly developed understanding and sympathy.

I could say the same of Father Furlong. It was he who always advised me to go ahead and speak at the round tables sponsored by the National Conference of Christians and Jews. The idea of these meetings was that a priest, a minister and a rabbi would express the viewpoints of their respective faiths; but the opposition to any ecumenical encounter was so strong in New York— even under Archbishop Spellman—that for five years I was the unofficial Catholic spokesman, with the approval and behind-the-scenes guidance of Father Furlong.

Things became easier for us when Archbishop McIntyre left the Chancery and crossed the continent to Los Angeles in 1948. Monsignor George Higgins, who had joined the staff of the Social Action Department of NCWC under Monsignor Raymond A. McGowan four years earlier and who subsequently succeeded him as director, was in my office the day the news came over the radio. "Does the Catholic Interracial Council have a statement for the press on the appointment to Los Angeles," Monsignor Higgins asked me teasingly. "In principle, we are very happy that the west coast of the United States is so far removed from the east coast," I answered in the same vein.

Another of our bitter opponents was Monsignor William J. McCann. He was a famous and successful preacher. He and his brother belonged to the New York mission band, of which Monsignor Cornelius J. Drew was also at one time a member. It was a bad day for the Catholic interracial movement when he was named pastor of St. Charles Borromeo Church in Harlem and unofficial representative of the archdiocese to the Negro community. He enjoyed a supervisory authority over neighboring parishes with Negro memberships, including St. Mark's, St. Joseph's on 125th Street, and the Resurrection. He was the kingpin, the one whose voice carried weight with the Chancery. I met him in the days of Cardinal Hayes, when I was invited to speak at a luncheon of the alumni of Catholic University at the Hotel Pennsylvania, New York. I overheard a conversation between him and the wife of one of the professors, after I had explained what the Catholic Interracial Council was. "You, Monsignor, must feel very happy," she said, "that you have here in New York a Catholic interracial council which can be helpful to you in interpreting to the Negro community the work of the Church and its attitudes on race problems." "Catholic Interracial Council," he said. "I have heard of it. I don't know where it is. I don't know what it does. And I don't care."

This was typical of the man. He was overbearing and intolerant. Dr. Edward E. Best, a Negro physician, one of the founders of the Catholic Interracial Council, was his parishioner at St. Charles Borromeo. Dr. Best once invited Father LaFarge and myself to a fair which had been organized to raise money for the parish. The pastor made a brief appearance. "I'm very glad you all have come here," he said. "I hope you will succeed in selling a great many books of chances. I'll just say 'God bless you' in the work you are doing for the parish. Good night." According to his lights he was a fine priest and did much good. But his lights had a tinge that did not belong in our times.

He was the eyes and ears of the archdiocese as to what was going on in the Harlem community, and the lead he gave was followed by the other pastors. That situation improved only when he was replaced after his death in 1949 by Monsignor Drew. "I sent to Harlem my very best priest," Cardinal Spellman once said to me, referring to Monsignor Drew, and that was indeed so.

Father Drew was an active supporter of the Catholic interracial movement even before he was assigned to succeed Monsignor McCann. He told me, many years later, of a humiliating experience in which he had been involved, an occurrence curiously enough in the very parish in which he was later to be pastor. When Father LaFarge was promoting the Clergy Conference on Negro Welfare in the early 1930s, he brought Father Gillis of the *Catholic World*, Father Cornelius Ahern of Newark, Father Joseph Corrigan, who was later rector of the Catholic University, and Father Drew, to talk to Father McCann at St. Charles Borromeo and ask his help. "I never felt so embarrassed in my life," Father Drew told me. "Father McCann deliberately ignored Father LaFarge throughout the interview, showing him nothing but open contempt."

Monsignor Drew's first assignment after the Mission Band was as pastor of St. Paul's Church in New York City from 1940 to 1943, and he was then transferred to St. Augustine in the Bronx. It had been a white parish, but the Negro population was growing rapidly, and the scaremongers were having a wonderful time going around and stirring up hatred. Monsignor Drew called a meeting of his parishioners. "This is your church," he said to them, "and your rectory and convent and school. You paid for them and you own them. Should you turn around and run away from your brothers in Christ, because of the color of their skin? Should you not welcome them and ask them to share these things you own, your church and your school?" His attitude really made a difference, and the integration of the neighborhood was effected peacefully and with a minimum of economic loss. It was an example to which I often referred subsequently in lectures and in the *Interracial Review*. It is an extraordinary fact, but one not sufficiently stressed, that our history of race riots in this country shows that riots never occur in areas where white and Negroes have been living together. They always start in segregated areas.

Father Drew never changed. When he later lived at St. Charles Borromeo, from 1949 until his death in 1964, he was the most beloved man in all Harlem. He was a man of immense energy. He never wore a hat, and even in the depth of winter, one seldom saw him with an overcoat. When he arrived as pastor, the parochial grade school was still the old church which had been converted into a school about the turn of the century when a new church was built. His first concern was for the quality of the education, and soon the children were averaging over ninety per cent in the New York State Regents examination. Then he started on a monumental project, a community center to include a new school, adult education facilities, and cultural and recreational units. All Harlem joined him in making this program a reality, including such non-Catholic leaders as Dr. Channing H. Tobias of the Phelps-Stokes Fund, Roy Wilkins of the NAACP, and Jackie Robinson of the Dodgers. "Don't try to make Negroes white or whites Negro," was one of his sayings. "Give both the opportunity to meet as equals, and you'll find that friendship, respect and understanding are inevitable."

Father Drew's gentle concern was always for others. When he was dying of cancer at the Memorial Hospital in New York, the doctors allowed him to go home for a week-end. As a friend, Bernard O'Shea, was driving him up to his rectory in Harlem from the hospital, he suddenly interrupted their conversation. "Can you turn into Ninety-first Street for a minute, please," he said to him. "My friend George Hunton is having an operation for a detached retina, and I'd like to stop by to cheer him up." And he did, chatting with me as though he himself hadn't a care in the world. It was a visit I will never forget.

Father James Gillis was another good friend of the interracial movement. As a Paulist, he was not under the jurisdiction of the archdiocese, and as editor of the *Catholic World* and a radio commentator of national distinction, he could speak his mind freely. This he did. He was superb equally as a writer and a speaker, and he didn't care who he offended. I first met him at the Paulist radio station, WLWL, where (as I already mentioned) we had for a number of years a regular slot on the air for the interracial movement. He had a passion for knowledge. Although he was already extremely well informed on Negro issues, he was constantly accumulating new facts. Each time I met him, he would probe some current problem or perhaps a historical or philosophical point.

We needed such friends, but they were also a danger to us. At the first meeting of the Catholic Interracial Council at the Town Hall in New York, on Pentecost Sunday 1934, Father Gillis had made a remark which long rankled in the archdiocese. "Catholics must recognize the wrongs they have done to the Negro," he had said. "We should join in a humble *Confiteor,* Through our fault, through our fault, through our most grievous fault." That was far from the official line in the triumphalist archdiocese of New York, where such weakness was unseemly. Monsignor McIntyre reminded me of it during his meeting with Father LaFarge and me several years later, which I described above. It is things of that kind that give the Catholic Interracial Council a bad name, he commented bitterly. Of course, Father Gillis made similar charges not only once but many times. He was so outspoken on the Catholic Hour in his defense of Negro rights that the Southern stations finally cut him off.

Among the thorns in our sides back in those days, Monsignor John Louis Belford of Nativity Parish in Brooklyn was one of the sharpest. He was consistently hostile to Negroes, and he was able to turn many of the priests around him against us when we started the Interracial Council. On one occasion Father LaFarge suggested to Bishop Molloy that he should take a subscription to the *Interracial Review* for priests in parishes with Negro members. Pleading that it would be discriminatory to subscribe on that basis, he took out a subscription for every one of the 375 priests in the diocese of Brooklyn. No sooner had we sent out a letter telling the priests that their bishop had paid their subscriptions than I got a phone call from Monsignor Belford. "Keep your magazine away from my door," he said. "I don't want it coming there. I'll be very frank and say that I'm not interested in the parish that has been erected within a thousand feet of my parish." He was referring to the recently established parish of St. Peter Claver which had a heavy Negro population. When I asked if I might drop down to chat with him some time at his convenience, he answered revealingly: "I will not see you. Frankly, I wouldn't want to be convinced."

Monsignor Belford was more outspoken than most, but actually his views were widely shared by his colleagues. I remember one of them telling me so in an expansive moment. He was Monsignor Raymond J. Campion, a cultured man who taught at Cathedral College, Brooklyn, for many years and later followed Monsignor Bernard J. Quinn as pastor of St. Peter Claver Church. He also became a member of the Brooklyn Council of the State Commission Against Discrimination. "There was a time, George," he said to me, "when you folks were marked lousy by every priest in the Brooklyn Diocese and every priest I knew of anywhere. That went for the whole group, including Father LaFarge and the Catholic Interracial Council, but particularly you."

Monsignor Campion's heart was in the right place. He worked hard for the people of St. Peter Claver's as their pastor and treated them as human beings. In an article he contributed to the *Interracial Review,* he wrote that the Catholic priest in a Negro parish is acutely conscious of the disabilities under which his people labor. "He sees their sufferings, their hardships—he knows they are denied educational opportunities. He sees them brutalized by the unfairness, the insults and the degrading housing situations in which they are forced to live. His people, because of racial discrimination and inequality, find it extraordinarily difficult to obtain a job in keeping with their abilities and needs. It is a common axiom that the Negro is 'Last hired and first fired.' Furthermore, he frequently has to accept employment for wages much less than his white brother receives for exactly similar work. Therefore, in addition to regular priestly administrations, the priest in a colored parish has to get out and fight for his people. He has to secure them jobs if at all possible."

Each year that Father Campion stayed at St. Peter Claver, he identified himself more fully with the hopes and aspirations of his Negro parishioners. When the late Mary L. Riley, who was active in the development of the New York Plan to which I shall refer later, set out to form a Brooklyn Catholic Interracial Council in 1944, he gave her his full support. He also played a major part in the establishment of an Institute of Interracial Justice in Brooklyn. And, as I shall describe later, it was he who hit the first home run in the epic struggle to open the major baseball leagues to Negroes. He was a prince among men, even though at times quite unpredictable, especially if you found him in a bad humor. "George Hunton," he challenged me one day, "the next time you come over here with your damn-fool ideas, I'm going to throw you out the window." I found that rather amusing, because he was a little bit of a man who couldn't throw a kitten out the window, to say nothing of a man my size.

Perhaps I found such bias hardest to excuse in Brooklyn, because it was the last place in the world that should harbor such sentiments. This was the essential melting pot of America, where Catholics of every race were welcomed and given a chance to become full Americans while practicing their faith in freedom. But I do not want to convey the impression that Brooklyn had any monopoly. Catholic priests all across the country looked down on Negroes. I remember the way one of them put it on the line at a meeting of the Federated Colored Catholics held in Cleveland in 1936. "We priests in Cleveland know our duties towards Negroes," he said. "We will do everything in our power as pastors, give as many special novenas for Negroes as they want, preach them as many missions, as many spiritual devotions. We'll work untiringly for the salvation and spiritual welfare of their souls. But when they come up to us and say, 'Why don't you do something about getting jobs for Negroes in Cleveland, and why don't you condemn anti-Negro discrimination?' then I say we are not interested."

The clergy who wanted to keep Negroes at arm's length were ably seconded by the Catholic organizations. The New York Council of Catholic Men was very hard to move. It was not only that they did not encourage Negroes to participate in their activities. They didn't want even to hear about them. Occasionally, we would get an invitation from a parish Holy Name Society to send someone to talk to them about racial justice. I was the one usually picked for the job, and I'll never forget some of my experiences. Even when the officers had been interested enough to extend an invitation, it was impossible to present the most modest set of propositions without arousing intense opposition and hostility from our good Catholic audience. "You are a hypocrite," I would be told. And the speaker would invariably have the same question to prove his point. "Would you," he would ask, often speaking in a thick Irish brogue, "would you allow your daughter to marry a Negro?" Usually an Irish audience can be diverted by a frivolous answer, but on this issue it was no good to reply dolefully that unfortunately I had neither wife nor daughter. The jaws remained clenched. This was no subject for jokes.

I found the Knights of Columbus an even tougher nut to crack. I spent a lot of time trying to get them to take an objective look at the race issue, because they potentially have a great role to play in the social life of the country, but I never got anywhere. When Harold A. Stevens, a member of the board of the Catholic Interracial Council, and later a judge, was elected an assemblyman of the state of New York, a friend invited him to join the Knights. He was very happy to accept. A few days later, the friend phoned him. "I'm sorry, Harold," he said, "I can't get you into our chapter, but there's one branch up in the

Bronx known as the St. Patrick's chapter that will take you."
"Forget it," said Harold.

As a result of this incident, I tried to find out how many Negroes were members of the Knights, and all I was able to identify was one man in Pittsburgh and an integrated chapter in Hanson Place, Brooklyn. Still it was impossible to get anyone excited. The only Church leader who took a public stand was Archbishop John Gregory Murray of St. Paul, Minnesota. There was a prominent physician there, whom the Archbishop respected highly and had helped to bring into the Church. The Knights blackballed him on no ground other than the fact that he was a Negro. Archbishop Murray was incensed. "Your policy is unchristian," he said. "As long as I am Archbishop, you will never come as a group into my cathedral, no matter who is being buried, no matter who is being honored." And he kept his word to the day of his death. But his example was not contagious. With well over a million members, the Knights were able to brandish their influence and their money. So those who could have compelled them to change kept silent. And the Knights continued to drag their feet, long after the national consensus had passed them by.

One might argue that up to the Second World War the Knights were simply adjusting themselves to the common pattern of American life at the time, if that is an excuse, that the YMCA—for example—was equally derelict. But the progress of the Knights toward a situation of true integration has been much slower than that of the YMCA and most other social and fraternal organizations, and even in the mid-1960s many of the Councils continue to practice segregation brazenly without any effective disciplining on the part of the regional and national controlling bodies. It is true that the Supreme Council, after long years of vacillation, is today publicly committed to a policy of "absolute racial equality," and I am glad to say that members are resigning in increasing numbers from the Councils that flaunt this policy, but I can show from a few examples that the top leadership has not yet faced up fully to its responsibility.

My first skirmish with the Knights occurred in Brooklyn. I'm pretty sure the year was 1934. I was a member of the Brooklyn Catholic Social Action Conference which held its monthly meetings at the Columbus Council of the Knights of Columbus. We invited the public to talks on social action, the lecturer being Father Ignatius Cox, S.J. In return for this service, the Knights gave us a free meeting place. They had a big building, and they wanted to protect its tax-exempt status by showing that it was being used for educational activities.

Father Edward Swanstrom, who was later head of NCWC's War Relief Services and made a bishop, was our chaplain. He had just graduated from the New York School of Social Work and he was engaged in writing a book he published a few years later, *The Waterfront Labor Problem.* Two months after Father Swanstrom's appointment, I was elected president of the Conference, and thereafter the leadership devolved mainly on the two of us. Father Swanstrom's special interest was the layman's role in social action. He was an assistant at the Holy Name Church, and his pastor didn't look with too much favor on his extracurricular activities. We met at his office the Sunday afternoon I was elected president, and I remember that the pastor stuck his head in and asked petulantly what was going on. When Father Swanstrom explained, he said, "Well, don't take long. This is not intended to be a gathering place." But Father Swanstrom went ahead and soon he had organized a monthly meeting at which the delegates of fifty or more Holy Name societies discussed contemporary problems, the Catholic press, the Church in Mexico, the Brooklyn waterfront, and so on.

I had little difficulty in getting Father Swanstrom to include the issue of Negro rights on our agenda. Accordingly, we had a full-scale discussion at a meeting attended by four or five hundred delegates from different parishes in Brooklyn. A resolution which was in effect a restatement of the Manhattanville

Resolutions was introduced and approved. It called for equal civil rights for the Negro as a citizen and a recognition of his title as a Catholic to equal status and treatment in the Church.

The resolution was distributed to the Catholic, the Negro, and the general press, and it was accorded sufficient publicity to come to the notice of the local executive committee of the Columbus Council, in whose building the meeting had taken place. They took a very dim view of our action. "This is a gross abuse of our hospitality," they told Father Swanstrom and me. "You should have submitted this controversial resolution to us for our study before presenting it at your meeting, and from now on, we want it to be clear that we must be given the opportunity to rule on the orthodoxy of any statement you propose to publish."

Father Swanstrom was as outraged as I was by this insolent demand, and he gladly approved the reply I prepared. "Not all the members of the Social Action Conference are Irish," I told them, "but enough of us are Irish to establish as the Conference's policy what has always been the Irishman's attitude to his landlord. No landlord of ours will ever tell us what we may or may not talk about in the premises we occupy as tenants."

In the following months the Conference grew and expanded, so that we soon had delegates from nearly a hundred diocesan chapters of the Holy Name Society. I recall a particularly big turnout when our featured speaker was Monsignor John A. Ryan. But when our year's tenancy expired we were faced with an ultimatum. The executive committee of the Columbus Council came to a meeting of our board and demanded a veto over our activities as a condition of our continuing occupation of quarters in their building. Needless to say, we shook the dust off our sandals.

I had one other experience with the Knights of Columbus which failed to improve my image of them. A good friend who worked on the *Catholic News* in New York was a member of a

Council in Yonkers, and he arranged to have me invited to speak to the Council. They could not give me an honorarium, they said, but they would take care of my travel expenses. The chairman made a preliminary announcement. "We have two speakers tonight," he said. "The first will talk about the Negro and the Catholic Church." I got polite applause before I spoke and pretty sharp criticisms when I finished. "You obviously haven't been much into the South," I was told, "or you would know that the South knows how to treat the Negro and how to keep him in his place; and we have to be careful of the feelings of these good people in the South." The thought behind the words was clear enough to me and to everyone else. It was that the Knights of Columbus had councils in the South and we should all be realistic enough to know where they stood.

The chairman then presented the second speaker, Chief Wahahow of the Oklahoma Indians, and the audience applauded vigorously. The Chief proceeded to demonstrate the tribal bird and animal calls and to dance a few of the traditional ritual dances, and the members of the Council expressed their appreciation of the finer things of American culture vociferously. Afterwards, they invited me to the downstairs bar for a beer on the house, and several of them availed themselves of the opportunity to assure me that they knew a lot more than I did about Negroes, and that I'd be well advised to slow down. Finally, a little Irishman came over to me. "I'm the treasurer," he said. "Would you mind stepping outside. It would be less embarrassing for both of us." So we walked round the corner. "I understand from Bill," he said, "that we agreed to take care of your expenses. What did they amount to?" I said that the round-trip ticket was sixty-nine cents. Straining himself, he put his hand down in his pocket. "Suppose I give you a dollar," he said. "Suppose you keep it and let it be on me," I said. And that was the last time I spoke to a Knights of Columbus chapter.

Indignant as I was with the Knights for their shabby treatment of me and their refusal to take a stand on principle, I realized that they were too important to ignore. They were by far the biggest Catholic fraternal organization in numbers, and their members were very influential and had a real potential for service. I was accordingly very pleased when a contributor to the *Interracial Review* undertook to prepare an article about them in terms that held promise of getting them off their seats. He was Thomas F. Doyle, a young newsman from Ireland, who had reached the United States by way of Argentina a few years earlier, and who was already making a name for himself in Catholic journalism in this country. I shall have more to say about him, because he played a major part in bringing Irish and Irish-Americans into the Catholic interracial movement.

Tom wrote a magnificent article, moderate and charitable. Under the heading "419,111 Catholics," he pointed out that along with priests, doctors, lawyers and other professional men, the Knights had a solid representation of businessmen and tradesmen, a Catholic elite with extraordinary power and influence. "Its members are already well versed in the fundamental truths inherent in the interracial program and should need but a summons to join in a work that is of great ultimate good to the social order."

He recalled the many charitable works of the Knights at home and abroad, including appeals in their magazine for the Negro Catholic missions and the gift of $40,000 in 1923 toward the cost of the first buildings of the Cardinal Gibbons Institute in Maryland. He insisted, however, that more remained to be done. "Not indefinitely can the members of this great Catholic society continue to walk as blind men while about them millions of ill-paid, ill-educated, ill-housed and economically handicapped Americans plead for recognition of their rights as defined by Catholic teachings and the Constitution of the United States. This should be deemed not a work of mere election for any group linked to Catholic interests; it is rather a compelling obligation. The Negro is the poorest among the poor; he has the highest ratio of unemployment; receives the lowest wages; is denied the opportunity to work in many fields; is excluded from membership in countless labor unions. In no other country in the world will the Knights of Columbus find more destitution, more heart-rending need than that which exists in vast areas of this nation. Here are conditions of hopelessness and despair that outrage the Christian conscience."

I am sure that Tom's eloquent words helped to get some Negroes into Catholic colleges and schools, helped to open labor unions to them, helped them to get jobs with firms previously barred, helped to get fairer allocations to Negro neighborhoods for schools, houses, clinics and playgrounds. I am sure of it, though I cannot prove it. For they had no recorded impact on those to whom they were addressed.

In February 1954, Bishop Floyd L. Begin, then Auxiliary Bishop of Cleveland and since 1962 Bishop of Oakland, California, gave a direct challenge by appealing to the Supreme Officers of the Knights of Columbus to grant a charter to an interracial council. While continuing to insist that race was no element in its laws or practices, the Supreme Officers refused the Bishop's appeal, and the rejected group of Negro and white Catholics formed their own interracial organization as the Cavaliers of St. Michael.

One positive effect was to bring to national attention the history of St. Columba Council, No. 1119, in Brooklyn. This Council, in 1950, had admitted a Negro member, James Pierce, in spite of dire warnings to Grand Knight Michael Corrigan that he was killing his Council. "You will lose your current white members," he was told, "and never again will a white apply for membership." In the following year, the Council added thirty-seven members, twenty-seven of whom were white. By 1954, one hundred two new members had joined, fifty-nine white and forty-three Negro, with whites proposing Negroes, and Negroes whites. The membership had more than doubled, and not one of the original eighty-one white members had left in protest.

I did everything in my power to spread the experience of Council No. 1119 on the public record, both in the *Interracial Review* and through releases to the Catholic, Negro, and general press. The old attitudes, nevertheless, continued. Later in 1954 Bishop Gerald T. Bergan of Omaha, Nebraska, publicly condemned the blackballing of three Negro candidates by the Father Flanagan Council of Omaha as "backward and unchristianlike." The Grand Knight of the Council publicly apologized to the three rejected applicants, saying that he and a great majority of members had favored admission, but "a very small group held fast to the old racial position." Yet even this clear situation could get no statement from the Supreme Board, nor was there any move to discipline councils which publicly admitted that they were violating the admission criteria spelled out in the rules of the organization.

About the same time, James Pierce, the first Negro member of St. Columba Council in Brooklyn, made an attempt to get a friend, John T. Yancey, into another Brooklyn Council, Columbus Council No. 126 on Prospect Park West. In due course, Mr. Pierce was summoned as sponsor before the admittance committee. The committee questioned him at length as to his motives in proposing Mr. Yancey for the Columbus Council rather than his own Council of St. Columba, which was already integrated. Apparently, they were not satisfied with his explanation that Mr. Yancey was a city employee and had several fellow employees of the city (all white) in Columbus Council, whereas he would be a stranger in the other Council. Mr. Pierce withdrew and Mr. Yancey was invited in and informed that he was barred from membership. To his question whether his race was the reason for denial of membership, he received an evasive answer. When Mr. Pierce learned of the decision, he gave the chairman of the committee a tongue-lashing. "You are unfit for the Church and unfit for membership of our

138

Order," he stormed. The chairman was unmoved. "You don't tell me how to run my life" was the extent of his answer.

To pass over scores of later instances recorded in the files of the Catholic Interracial Council, let me note two issues that came to public notice in 1966. A sports reporter for the *Clarion Herald,* New Orleans, charged in April that the Knights had failed to invite to a sports meeting the outstanding Negro Catholic high school of that city, an event in which sixteen teams participated. According to Hal Berrigan, the team of the Negro school fulfilled all the requirements and standards except one. Among the invited teams, he wrote, "color was the common denominator."

In the same month, a drama that had been unfolding for some time in Detroit came to light. Charles K. Jackson, a Negro policeman and member of the homicide squad, had been proposed for membership of the Monsignor Flanagan Council No. 3180 by Chief of Detectives Vincent Piersante. He was rejected the first time, and Piersante put him up a second time. On the second rejection, Piersante himself resigned, charging that the denial "was on the basis of Jackson's color." Monsignor Francis X. Canfield, rector of the Sacred Heart Seminary, was a candidate on the night of Jackson's second rejection. He was accepted, but he resigned immediately, stating that he would not want to be a member of an organization which flouted its own rules.

When the protests got into the newspapers, Supreme Knight John W. McDevitt promised to investigate, and an investigation did take place at the level of the Michigan State Council. The Council, having gone through its own mysterious processes, refused to intervene. "There is no way to determine the mental processes of each man who voted against him," the statement asserted. Mr. McDevitt informed me in September 1966 that the Supreme Office had also investigated, and its inquiry "established that there was no violation of any rules or procedures in the handling of Mr. Jackson's application for admission to the Order." Echoing the statement of the Michigan State Council, he added that there was no way to determine the motivation of the men who voted against Jackson.

The claim that there is no way to determine a man's mental processes may sound plausible to the layman, but it does not hold water. Under our legal system, every time a man goes on trial for his life, a jury is called upon to determine his mental processes, and the courts equally rule on a man's mental processes a thousand times a day in lesser matters. The same principle applies in Church law. Pope Leo XIII expressed it excellently in his encyclical of September 1896 on Anglican Orders. "The Church does not judge about the mind and intention in so far as it is something by its nature internal," he wrote, "but in so far as it is manifested externally she is bound to judge concerning it."

After the Knights of Columbus, the two most important Catholic fraternal societies back in the 1930s were probably the Central Verein and the Kolping Society. These were primarily for people of German descent, and in that sense it was easier for them than for the Knights to take a stand on principle, because the principle would not be used against themselves to compel them to admit Negroes. On the other hand, this was early in the Nazi period in Germany, and the German societies might easily have acquired some of the racist attitudes. In fact they did not. They took a very open and proper stand on Negro rights from away back. As early as 1925, the Central Verein went on record at a convention in Cleveland, Ohio. "The spirit of the Constitution of our country," they said, "makes for that true tolerance among our citizens which Christian justice and charity enjoin on all men . . . It especially behooves us to guard against the temptation of fostering racial strife, while we should do what lies in our power to promote peace and goodwill among men, always ready to actively assist in the solution of our racial problems. Mindful of the fact that one of the first and foremost saints of the New World, Saint Peter Claver, devoted his life to the Negroes, and even ahead of such glorious martyrs as Isaac Jogues, an American Negro was beatified by the Church, the Blessed Martin de Porres, let us in a special manner devote our attention to relieving the condition of the members of the Negro race, subjected to so many injustices, not merely denied the rights guaranteed to them by the Constitution, but made to suffer slights and indignities which deeply offend them. They too are our neighbors, both under the law of Christ and that of our country. We therefore wish to impress on our members the obligation to labor for amicable race relations and to grant their assistance to all efforts to bring them about."

Catholic hospitals were in line with other Catholic institutions. They had no place for Negroes either as physicians, interns, nurses, or patients. I had a telephone call one day in 1939 from a director of St. Vincent's Hospital, New York. He thought I ought to be happy to learn that the hospital had finally accepted a Negro nurse on the staff, a girl who was so light-colored that she would pass as white, and that was how she was being presented by the administration to avoid fuss. The man was astonished at what to him was the irrationality of my reaction.

The first significant breakthrough in the hospitals, I am sorry to say, resulted not from virtue but from economics. With the Depression and the resulting development of social services under President Franklin Roosevelt, the charity patient rose to a determining position in the financial structure of the voluntary hospitals. And to qualify for state and city subventions, they were forced to accept anyone who applied for admission to the wards, regardless of race, creed or color. And thus we reached the absurd situation in which a destitute Negro could get a bed in a ward in a Catholic hospital, but a well-to-do Negro was refused admission as a private or semi-private patient because he was a Negro.

The decision of Catholic University in Washington, under

Monsignor Corrigan, to accept Negro students in its school of nursing, as I described earlier, marked a milestone. Gradually, other hospitals and training schools began to open up, particularly when the Second World War brought personnel shortages. The lifting of quotas on Negro nurses in the Army Nurse Corps in 1944, and the abolition of the regulation restricting Negro nurses to the four Army hospitals serving Negro troops within the continental United States, was a big forward step. But it brought no automatic response from Catholic schools of nursing. When in September 1947, St. Camillus Nursing School, Borgess Hospital, Kalamazoo, Michigan, admitted its first Negro student, it was only the eighth of 368 Catholic nurse training schools in the country with even one Negro student. In this, as in so many other areas, the Catholic institutions lagged behind the national consensus. Miss Alma Vessells, executive secretary of the National Association of Colored Graduate Nurses, was able to report in November 1947, that even the Southern states were ending the discriminatory practice by which Negro nurses had been denied professional status by exclusion from the American Nurses Association. Florida had been first to drop the barrier in 1942, and by 1947 it had been followed by Delaware, Maryland, Tennessee, and part of Missouri (including St. Louis). And three years later, the National Association of Colored Graduate Nurses decided to dissolve on the ground that the function it had been created in 1908 to perform was substantially accomplished. Although only 330 of the nation's 1200 nursing schools were admitting Negro students, the movement was progressing so fast that the Association decided it would continue of its own momentum and might only be retarded by the continuation of an organization which was discriminatory by definition. One of its last official acts was to write me a letter thanking the Catholic Interracial Council for the contribution it had made toward the integration of the nursing profession.

The fight in the Catholic area was nevertheless far from

finished. By 1949, half the Catholic nursing schools asserted that they had no racial barriers to admission, yet the total enrollment of Negro student nurses in interracial Catholic nursing schools was only 109. And in the spring of 1951, the twenty white nurses in St. Francis Hospital, Charleston, West Virginia, walked out in a body when Sister Helen Clare, the hospital superintendent, refused their demand that she fire three Negro nurses she had just hired. Sister Helen Clare stuck to her position and was supported by her superiors. "As a Catholic institution," she said, the hospital "will continue to uphold Christian principles of charity and justice, as well as the spirit of the United States Constitution." The incident just about marked the end of open resistance. I am glad to say that I contributed to the wave of outraged reaction that helped to bring Catholic institutions into line with the general conscience of the country.

Chapter 7

The Second Vatican Council has made it possible for Catholics to discuss in public issues which previously we had been discouraged from entertaining even in our innermost thoughts. Nowadays, we are suddenly asking ourselves to what extent the officials and representatives of the Church shared in the responsibility for the division of Christendom into warring Eastern and Western halves in the Middle Ages, and for the subsequent splitting away of the Protestants in the sixteenth century.

As I go back in memory over some of the incidents I have recalled in the previous chapter, I ask myself to what extent the blame should fall on Catholic leaders, who alone had then the freedom to speak out in the Church, for the deterioration of the attitude toward Negroes among rank-and-file Catholics since the Reconstruction period, and particularly between 1900 and the Second World War.

What are the facts? Archbishop Ireland spoke out fearlessly at the turn of the century, in the words I quoted earlier. After that, I have to move forward to 1936 to find another bishop who lays the facts on the line. "The responsible people of this community must be made to recognize their duty to work for the elimination of the Negro slum districts of Cincinnati," Archbishop John T. McNicholas, O.P., of Cincinnati, said that year. "Let us secure a few competent individuals from white and colored groups who will give them their serious attention and will work harmoniously in a constructive way. . . . I am anxious to see Negro priests in the ranks of the clergy of this diocese.

I would also like to see colored Sisters. We have been praising the little work that we have attempted; but let us recognize very frankly that we have merely scratched the surface. We need at the present time several other Negro churches; and even more necessary than churches are schools. I am consoled to know that many of our young priests, earnest, zealous and capable, are anxious to give themselves to the Negro apostolate. I wish all the religious communities of men in this diocese would be willing to take over a catholic mission for Negroes some place in this diocese."

After that, we have the joint statement of the American bishops in late 1943 on the essentials of a good peace. Recalling that millions of Americans were Negroes, it said: "We owe to these fellow citizens, who have contributed so largely to the development of our country, and for whose welfare history imposes on us a special obligation of justice, to see that they have in fact the rights which are given to them in our Constitution. This means not only political equality but also fair economic and educational opportunities, a just share in public welfare projects, good housing without exploitation, and a full chance for the social advancement of their race."

It was a good statement; but issued in 1943, it was bringing up the rear of American public opinion in its recognition of the humanity of the ten per cent of Americans whom Hitler had described in *Mein Kampf* as "half apes." And by that time, not a few were wondering why it had taken them so long to absorb the spirit of the encyclical Pope Pius XII addressed specifically to them in November 1939, an encyclical in which he expressed his "special paternal affection, which is certainly inspired by heaven, for the Negro people dwelling among you; for in the field of religion and education we know they need special care and comfort and are very deserving of it. We therefore invoke an abundance of heavenly blessing and pray fruitful success for those whose generous zeal is devoted to their welfare."

But to say nothing of the South, where Catholics after all were nearly everywhere a tiny minority, how much of this penetrated to the Northeast of the United States, where we were strong and influential? Part of the answer I have given already. Here I feel I should be more explicit. I have been going to Mass regularly all my life, and I've heard plenty of Sunday sermons on subjects pertinent and impertinent. But I have never heard a sermon on racial justice in a Catholic church, except on those occasions on which a sermon was specially arranged for the meeting of an already interested group, such as a Communion breakfast of the Catholic Interracial Council. Our general Catholic public was never exposed to a discussion of the moral issues.

This was a fact with which I was continually challenged as, through the years, I went back and forward throughout the country, to talk to any group willing to listen to me. "You tell us, Mr. Hunton, that what you say is Catholic teaching," was the rebuttal thrown constantly in my teeth. "But I am a Catholic, and I go to Mass every Sunday, and I listen to what the pastor tells us. Our priests are not afraid to speak out on issues of right and wrong. You know that. Everyone knows it. Then how is it that at no Mass, at no novena, at no mission or retreat, have I ever been told that I have a moral obligation to treat the Negro the way you say? Can you explain that to me, Mr. Hunton?"

Of course I couldn't or I can't give any satisfactory explanation of this silence on the part of the overwhelming majority of the clergy. There is no doubt, however, that it existed, and that the Catholic conscience was long able to live with it. If one is to pick a dividing line, I think the decisive moment was the issuing in 1958 by the American bishops of their statement that racial prejudice and discrimination were moral problems concerning which no Catholic could be indifferent. The statement defined the issue in the very words we had been using for a quarter of a century. "The heart of the race question is moral and religious," it said. "It concerns the rights of man and our attitude towards our fellow man. If our attitude is governed by the great Christian law of love of neighbor and respect for his rights, then we can work out harmoniously the techniques for making legal, educational, economic and social adjustments. But if our hearts are poisoned by hatred, or even by indifference towards the welfare and rights of our fellow men, then our nation faces a grave internal crisis." Since that time it has become the practice of a substantial number of our bishops to instruct their pastors to preach periodically on the Catholic doctrine regarding the equal dignity and eternal destiny of all men.

It so happens that a few months before the 1958 statement of the bishops, the Catholic Interracial Council of New York had prepared a 126-page booklet entitled "Sermons on Interracial Justice" and made it available to Catholic dioceses throughout the country. The timing was just right. Many priests welcomed the material and used it. But if we had distributed the same booklet twenty-five years earlier, it would have gone straight into rectory wastebaskets from coast to coast. We had to begin with the fact of total clerical apathy, and we had to begin with it in an atmosphere in which the clergy would not take kindly to suggestions from the laity. The start had to be made in a different way. Accordingly, while the Laymen's Union and the Catholic Interracial Council plugged away at a general audience of influential Negroes and whites, the Clergy Conference on Negro Welfare concentrated on the narrower but even more vital task.

I have mentioned the Clergy Conference on Negro Welfare many times already, but it deserves more formal notice. It was Father LaFarge's special concern, if one can speak of the special concern of a man who gave the same total dedication to each of his myriad activities. He never measured the boundless energy and enthusiasm with which he infused the Laymen's Union, the Catholic Interracial Council, liturgical renewal, the ecumenical movement, St. Ansgar's League for Scandinavian Catholics, *America* magazine, social progress in Latin America, and the Lord knows how many other interests.

Yet I think I can say that among them all, the CCNW had a unique place in his idea of his own life mission. It took shape at about the same time as the Catholic Interracial Council, its first meeting being held in November 1933 at Newark, New Jersey. Father LaFarge had a very pragmatic approach to all his activities. He had no objection to mass support, but he was happy if he had two or three or half a dozen who really shared his stand and were willing to work. His two principal helpers in forming the CCNW were Father Cornelius Ahern, pastor of Queen of Angels, Newark, where they met, and Father Harold Purcell, C.P., editor of *Sign* magazine. They established contact with priests from several dioceses and various religious orders, and a small handful undertook the task of educating their fellow clergy in the United States on their duty toward their Negro fellow citizens.

Most of the work was by word of mouth, at clergy meetings, at informal discussions in presbyteries, in articles in obscure publications. But there were also dramatic confrontations. In the fall of 1934, ten thousand Catholic priests in the northeastern United States got a letter whose seven-word opening paragraph must have surprised many and encouraged not a few to read further. "This is *not* an appeal for contributions," it read. It then recounted some facts: twelve million Negroes, millions of them with no church affiliation, a scant quarter million Catholics served by some two hundred priests and a thousand Sisters.

"Mission works for the Negro in this country will be effective in proportion to the Negro's conviction that the Catholic Church really wants him," it continued. "The American Negro wants the Catholic Church. Among this naturally religious people, there is an immense yearning for something more satisfying to heart and mind than the brands of Christianity with which they have been acquainted. But there stands in the way a dread question mark: Does the Catholic Church *want me?*

"Plenty of people are on hand to inform the Negro that the Catholic Church does not *want* him. Anti-Catholics and interested persons among their own group; Communists ready to exploit every instance of unfairness or lack of consideration on the part of Catholics towards Negroes, proclaim that Catholics despise him. . . . Obviously we can make the colored people feel that the Catholic Church *does* want them. There are several ways in which this may be done.

"Nothing will more readily create a conviction in the mind of the colored people that the Church is genuinely interested in their salvation, than to see the Catholic priest give them a helping hand in removing the obstacles that they daily encounter in trying to do their duty—obstacles that their more fortunate white brethren little suspect. They are told that it is their duty to lead industrious lives and support their families. Yet of all people in this country the Negroes have the greatest difficulty to obtain employment.

"They are told to bring up their children in the fear of God. Yet they find that their attempts to provide decent homes or suitable education for their families meet with resentment. The Catholic Negro, in particular, is often prevented by insuperable obstacles from giving his children a Catholic education."

The eight signatures on the letter show the kind of priests Father LaFarge had gathered around him in the CCNW. They were Father Wilfrid Parsons, editor of *America*, Father James Gillis, editor of the *Catholic World*, Father John Ryan of NCWC's Social Action Department, Father Hugh Lamb, chancellor of the archdiocese of Philadelphia, Father Joseph Corrigan, rector of Overbrook Seminary, Philadelphia, Father John Delaney, secretary to the Bishop of Newark, and two professors of Catholic University, Father Francis A. Walsh, O.S.B., and Father John M. Cooper.

Although the meetings were intended for priests only, Father

LaFarge was able to smuggle me in to a few of them. They were held on an average three times a year from 1933 until the war conditions forced their suspension in 1942. From the time that Father Corrigan became rector of Catholic University in Washington, D.C., in 1937, until his untimely death in 1942 shortly after he had been made a bishop, the principal yearly meeting of CCNW was held at Catholic University. The meetings were always off the record, and every effort was made to encourage priests to speak their doubts frankly.

Father LaFarge, who was secretary during the entire period, has summed up in his autobiography, *The Manner Is Ordinary,* what these meetings achieved. The participants, he wrote, became convinced of two things, "first, that public opinion is a capital factor in the Negro's spiritual welfare and in the material circumstances that affect that welfare; and, second, that the combating of false opinion and the building up of a sound one cannot be left to mere chance. It cannot be left, as has been so often falsely said, to the good works merely to speak for themselves. There must be set on foot a systematically and intelligently organized propaganda for the spiritual welfare of the Negro and its material implications, and the clergy themselves should be leaders in such an undertaking."

In 1935, at a meeting at Cornwells Heights, Pennsylvania, the CCNW drew up a very simple program of race relations. It asked a full Catholic life for the Negro, and a full equality of opportunity for him to fulfill his duties toward God and his fellowman. It was further elaborated by Father Corrigan at a meeting of a Philadelphia committee of the CCNW in February 1936. He urged organized use of the media of communications, promotion of devotion to Blessed Martin de Porres, training of young Negroes in the spirit and techniques of Catholic Action, letters from priests to their priest friends, and talks to seminarians and college students. The first meeting at Catholic University was in November 1937, and the growing influence of

CCNW was indicated by the presence of a bishop, the co-adjutor of Richmond, Virginia, Bishop Peter L. Ireton.

On his return to Richmond, Bishop Ireton set to work so effectively that the following May, a hundred priests of the diocese were given two talks on the CCNW at their semi-annual conference. With the approval of Bishop Eugene McGuinness of Raleigh, who was also present, a Richmond-Raleigh unit was created. A little later, another unit was formed in Mobile, Alabama, under Bishop Thomas J. Toolen, and yet another in the Midwest under Bishop Edwin V. O'Hara of Kansas City.

The Clergy Conference on Negro Welfare did more than create an awareness among priests of the existence of a moral issue. It gave them a sense of solidarity with the other priests who felt as they did, and it encouraged them to speak up and to take action on social issues about which they had previously been silent. A very good example is the part they played in the opening up of competitive sports to all qualified athletes.

We got off to a false and embarrassing start on this tough issue in December 1939. The Jesuit-directed Boston College had received an invitation to play Clemson at the Texas Cotton Bowl. It accepted subject to an express stipulation that all team members would be permitted to participate. "Racial barriers should be banned in the field of sport," the athletics manager of Boston College spelled out in his telegram of conditional acceptance. A news dispatch from Dallas announced that the Cotton Bowl committee had withdrawn its objection to Boston College's star halfback, Lou Montgomery, a Negro. The Negro press went wild with delight. "The character, courage and sportmanship shown by Boston College has advanced the progress of interracial justice in America to an encouraging degree," went a typical editorial. "Here we see Catholic principles being put into practice." The Catholic press agreed, and so did the general press. "Historic," was the editorial comment of a New York daily.

Then the denouement. The game was played, but Lou Montgomery was left at home in Boston. No official explanation was given for his absence, but it was quite obvious to everyone that Boston College had made a secret deal with the Cotton Bowl committee. The one small consolation was that Boston College lost. But the victory was a Pyrrhic one for the segregationists. The reaction to Boston College's fence straddling was so vigorous, and we made it our business to keep the issue alive, that college after college faced up to the reality, with the Catholic colleges making more yardage than most.

Even before this time, there was widespread discussion of the absurdity of exluding qualified Negroes from major baseball, but it was not until another priest who had been exposed to our movement got into the act, that things really livened up. He was Monsignor Raymond J. Campion, whom I have earlier mentioned as pastor of St. Peter Claver's Church in Brooklyn and who subsequently helped to found and became chaplain to the Brooklyn Catholic Interracial Council. Looking round his parish and seeing what hardship discrimination worked on its Negroes, and specifically on the Negro boys and girls emerging from his orphanage, well qualified to work but unable to get jobs, he had an idea. There had been talk for years about opening the major leagues to Negroes. Jimmy Powers of the New York *Daily News* and Dan Parker of the New York *Mirror* were not the only sports writers who openly urged it in their columns. As a matter of fact, it was common knowledge that the major leagues were using Negroes, bringing them in through the back door disguised as Mexicans, Indians, Cubans, and Portuguese. But Negroes as such were barred, and Monsignor Campion decided that it would not only give Negroes a psychological lift but quickly open other doors to them, if they were officially acknowledged and made the grade in America's most universal sport. And where better than in the melting pot of Brooklyn? So he sat down on a hot July day in 1942 and wrote to Colonel Larry MacPhail, president of the

Brooklyn Baseball Club. MacPhail was a sloppy fielder. He wrote a reply, blaming the rules of the two major leagues for the situation, then compounded his error by publishing the reply, along with a copy of Monsignor Campion's letter, without observing the courtesy of first delivering the reply to the Monsignor.

It was no way to endear oneself to Monsignor Campion. So he called up some reserves, forming an interracial committee to open the major leagues. It included Dan Burley, sports editor of the *Amsterdam News,* Joe Bostic of the same paper, Ferdinand Q. Morton of the Civil Service Commission, and myself. I should clarify that I was not simply there as executive secretary of the Catholic Interracial Council of New York. Brooklyn has been my home since the time of the First World War, and I have always rooted for the Dodgers. We Brooklynites are not like the natives of Manhattan. We do not think that everything on the far side of the Hudson is still Indian territory. We recognize that the rest of the world has its values. But they are not the values of Brooklyn. They do not—or at least they did not—own the Dodgers. Simply as a Brooklynite, I felt I had rights in this matter. I called with the other members of the committee on Colonel MacPhail and told him so. "Let's have sportsmanship in sport," we said. The Colonel expressed agreement with our viewpoint and promised that he would issue a statement declaring that he opposed discrimination in baseball. But he never did. He was at that time preparing to return to active service in the Army, and he left Brooklyn without having delivered on his promise.

Monsignor Campion kept on going. His next stop was Judge Kenesaw Mountain Landis, baseball commissioner, and he had strengthened his committee by the addition of Paul Robeson, when we called on the judge and the presidents of the two major leagues at Roosevelt Hotel, New York, in December 1943. Judge Landis was completely on the level. There is no rule or agreement, written or verbal, to prevent a major or minor league team from employing a Negro. "Each club is entirely free to employ Negro players to any extent it pleases," he told us.

And that was that. The rest is history. Branch Rickey, who had succeeded MacPhail as president of the Dodgers took Commissioner Landis at his word. He signed Jackie Robinson. And in due course, the falsity of every one of MacPhail's arguments was demonstrated. There were Negro players of major-league quality. Their colleagues accepted them on their merits. The other teams raised no objection to playing them. And the fans crowded the ball parks as never before.

It was another priest who carried—or should I say rolled— the bowling ball. That was about as silly a situation as one could imagine, but the American Bowling Congress (ABC) was as obstinate as it was illogical. Organized in 1895, it got a national charter from the state of Illinois to "promote and foster the interest in the bowling sport, and to have a general care, supervision and direction over the bowling game, and all bowling interests in the United States." This it set out to do, accepting all bowlers without concern about their race, religion or color. But in 1916, reacting to the growth of discriminatory attitudes and practices in the United States at that time, it inserted a clause limiting membership to city associations composed of teams having white male members only. But at this point, all logic deserted it. The restriction was to apply only within the United States. City associations affiliated to the ABC in places like Mexico and Hawaii might and did continue to accept members of other races.

Father Franklyn J. Kennedy, editor of the *Catholic Herald Citizen*, Milwaukee, Wisconsin, was the one who made this a national issue, starting shortly after World War II. The ABC tried to squirm out at first by insisting that it was a private social organization just like any other social club. But Father Kennedy wasn't appeased. He insisted that, on the contrary, it exercised an effective monopoly over the sport to such an extent that exclusion from membership represented a significant curtailment of an American's rights as a citizen. He persuaded so many people in Wisconsin that such was the case that the Attorney General ruled that the ABC was preventing citizens from enjoying rights upheld by the state laws, and he asked the courts to rule it "a public nuisance" and prevent it from doing any business in the state.

Catholic Interracial Councils and others had by now got working on the matter all over the country, and the Attorney General in New York took action similar to that of his colleague in Wisconsin. The Superintendent of Schools of New York City ruled that it was forcing a like discrimination on grade and high school students through the American Junior Bowling Congress, and he directed all public schools under his jurisdiction to withdraw from the Junior Congress. And so bit by bit, we closed in on them, illustrating once again that if only people can be got to look at a moral issue, enough of them will make a moral judgment and act on it.

Each such advance was music in our ears. But not even the public approval of a few bishops and the active participation of a small number of priests meant the end of the opposition of the general clerical body. This was brought home very forcibly in an incident that occurred in 1944, one that involved among others Father William Markoe, S.J., of St. Louis, my predecessor as editor of the *Interracial Review*. His colleagues and staunch supporters in St. Louis included Father Claude H. Heithaus, S.J., and Father Markoe's own brother John, also a Jesuit, a big powerful man and a former West Pointer. In fact, he had been the captain of the West Point football team of which Dwight D. Eisenhower was a member in 1914. This Father Markoe was assistant in St. Malachy's parish, and his pastor was also a Jesuit, Father Ralph Warner. Another member of the group was Father George H. Dunne, a professor at St. Louis University, who later wrote the play *Trial by Fire*. An equally dedicated colleague, Father John M. Lyons, S.J., who worked with Father William Markoe at St. Elizabeth's Church for many years and helped him to edit the publication that ultimately became the *Interracial Review,* had died in 1941, three years before the incident I am about to describe. I had got to know this small group of dedicated interracial workers well. Whenever I visited St. Louis, I would stay with one of them, and they would take me round to show the progress being made in the Negro areas. They were particularly proud of the fact that they had got some Catholic hospitals to admit Negro patients. Archbishop John Glennon of St. Louis, however, took a dim view of their activities. He did not want the Church in his diocese to be identified so openly with Negro rights.

The explosion occurred on February 11, 1944, on a curious occasion and in a curious place. It was the Feast of Our Lady of Lourdes, and Father Heithaus had been invited by the Jesuit authorities of St. Louis University to preach a sermon to the student body in the University chapel. By this time, with the war in its third year, the nation had made substantial progress toward recognizing the basic human rights of Negroes, even if there were still shocking anomalies to which I shall refer later. The opening of Catholic colleges to Negroes was proceeding gratifyingly. But here in St. Louis University, there was no sign of a start. And that was what Father Heithaus had on his mind.

"In what concerns justice for the Negro, the Mohammedans and the atheists are more Christlike than many Christians," he opened up. "The followers of Mohammed and of Lenin make no distinction of color; but to some followers of Christ, the color of a man's skin makes all the difference in the world. . . . Some people say that if Negroes are members of the Mystical Body, they are only nominal members. . . . Some people say that it is wrong to nurse a Negro in a Catholic hospital or educate a Negro in a Catholic university. . . . Some people say that Negroes have only those rights which the white men condescend to grant them. . . . Some people say that it is wrong to have a Negro play the organ in this University church. . . . Some people say that it is indelicate to kneel beside a Negro at a Communion railing. . . . Some people say that the Society of Jesus should connive at a wrong that cries out to heaven for vengeance. . . .

"I hang my head in shame when I see that some Catholics, who do not know the history of this country and have forgotten what terrible wrongs were endured by their ancestors in Ireland and Protestant England, have had the full strength of their Catholic convictions diluted by mingling with the descendants of their persecutors. I am horrified to find that some Catholics have been infected with this diabolical prejudice against the Negro. Self-deluded fools that they are, they cling with blind obstinacy to the idea that the time has not yet come to give justice to the colored children of God. . . . Some of the very people who disseminate this lie have themselves sent their sons to Harvard and Yale, where they were glad to sit in the same classrooms with Negroes. These people bow in reverence before Oxford and Cambridge, the University of London and Sorbonne, but if they ever attended these great universities, as I have, they would soon learn that in the world of scholarship there is neither white nor black, brown nor yellow. . . .

"To those who say our students will desert us, let me give a piece of good advice. Let them ask our students first before they tell us what is in their minds. They will learn something that will put them to shame. . . . And now I ask you Catholic students to look at the Blessed Sacrament and answer this question. Will you not do something positive right now to make reparation for the suffering which this prejudice has inflicted upon millions of your fellow Christians? . . . Will you rise, please? Now repeat this prayer after me. 'Lord Jesus, we are sorry and ashamed for all the wrongs that white men have done to your colored children. We are firmly resolved never again to have any part in them, and to do everything in our power to prevent them. Amen.'"

The entire student body accepted the invitation and repeated the act of contrition in tones that left no doubt as to the sincerity of their response. But the Church authorities in St. Louis lacked the humility to admit in public that they had failed to live the full message of Christ. They were as outraged as had been those of New York by Father Gillis's similar admission of Catholic sin at the Town Hall meeting on Pentecost Sunday in 1934. And they reacted even more violently. The entire team of "activists" was broken up, Father William Markoe banished to Denver, Colorado, Father John to Creighton University, Omaha, Nebraska, Father Dunne to Loyola University, Los Angeles, and subsequently to Georgetown University, and Father Heithaus to Marquette University, Milwaukee.

That was how the battle was fought in the 1930s and the 1940s. It was not all of a sudden in the late 1950s and the 1960s that good men found the courage to proclaim their beliefs and suffer for their rights. The difference in those earlier days was that those who protested did not even have the glory of headlines or the support of any significant body of public opinion. If I recorded their deeds in the obscure pages of the *Interracial Review*, it was more for the sake of the historical record than from hope of any quick public reaction. They suffered in silent isolation, yet not in vain. In fact, all of them lived to see in one way or another what plentiful harvests the Lord can bestow on small sowings.

In 1946, for example, Archbishop Joseph E. Ritter was transferred from Indianapolis to St. Louis. A survey of his archdiocese revealed, among other things, that policies of school segregation left some schools with empty places while others were overcrowded. He notified all concerned that all Catholic grade and high schools would be integrated with the start of the 1947 session. St. Louis University had already accepted the unanimous decision of the students and opened up for

Negroes in the fall of 1944. A group of parents made an issue and engaged legal counsel to fight the Archbishop in the courts. They were prudent men, men who understood prudence to mean complacent acquiescence in evil, silence in the face of the betrayal of Christianity. But their Archbishop knew no such prudence. Patiently, he explained to them in a pastoral letter that he was opening the schools to their Negro brothers because before Almighty God there is "equality of every soul." Then firmly he added that a continuance of their proposed action would mean their excommunication. To their honor, they not only desisted but they turned over to Catholic Charities the $2000 they had raised to fight their Archbishop.

One of the disgruntled pastors attempted a rearguard action. He put "for colored only" signs in some of the toilets, and he prevented the Negro pupils from going to the children's Mass on Sunday with their classmates, and from standing in line with them to enter or leave the school building. Some of the Negro parents talked to the nun in charge of the schools, and they got so sympathetic a hearing from her that they wrote to the Archbishop. In quick time, the marks of segregation disappeared.

The population of St. Louis was sixty per cent Catholic, and the impact of the new Archbishop's vigorous stand poured rapidly over into the entire community. "Are Catholics more Christian than Protestants in their practice of brotherhood," asked the interracial committee of the Metropolitan Federation of Protestant Churches. In an unprecedented gesture, the St. Louis *Globe Democrat* featured the wedding of a Negro couple. A Negro was elected to the board of the Greater St. Louis Community Chest, and the news was front-paged. Washington University, which a short time earlier had refused a $15,000 scholarship fund because of a non-discriminatory clause in the gift, admitted Negroes to two schools.

I remember that Thurgood Marshall was very excited by the potential ramifications of the Archbishop's action. "It opens up a new salient in the South," he told me. And a little later he went on the public record with a declaration that the St. Louis Catholic initiative had a far-reaching impact on public universities and school systems not only throughout Missouri, but in West Virginia and Kentucky also.

I have to thank another of the priests who actively supported the Catholic interracial movement in its early days for opening up for me another important means of reaching into Catholic education. This was Monsignor John J. Voight of New York, on whom (as I noted earlier) I relied for discreet and confidential guidance in my delicate dealings with the Chancery of the archdiocese of New York in the 1930s.

As superintendent of education for the archdiocese of New York, Monsignor Voight was familiar from the beginning with a movement which developed in the early 1950s among Sisters engaged in teaching, nursing and social work. It resulted from a recognition that in the world of today, all Sisters engaged in active works need a long and careful spiritual formation, a general intellectual training designed to equip them for a rich personal life and effective social leadership, and a precise professional preparation to make them equal or superior to lay people doing the same kind of work. It developed as a committee of the National Catholic Education Association charged with sponsoring annual meetings of higher superiors of Sisterhoods in the United States where suitable training and formation programs would be developed, and it adopted the name of Sister Formation. With a grant from the Ford Foundation for the Advancement of Education, it assembled a group of the most highly qualified Sisters in various academic fields to devise an "ideal" college curriculum for young Sisters in training to be teachers, nurses and social workers.

Monsignor Voight not only told me about this important development but arranged a meeting with Sister Mary Emil, professor of philosophy at Marygrove College, Detroit, and chairman for several years of the National Sister Formation Committee. From what Monsignor Voight had told me, I was not surprised to find that she was extremely conscious of the importance of a greater emphasis on the moral aspects of race relationships as a part of the teaching of social principles in Catholic schools. Out of this meeting came a long correspondence, in the course of which I was able to contribute the experience of the Catholic Interracial Councils as an enrichment of the reform of Catholic education which is a major goal of the Sister Formation movement.

Chapter 8

It will by now be abundantly clear to the reader that when the Catholic interracial movement began, things Negro were highly distasteful to the Catholic public and the Catholic press. The reverse was no less true. With far more justification, things Catholic were an abomination to the Negro public and the Negro press.

We were fully aware that this was precisely why we were in business, and in consequence I set out from the first day to establish what relations I could with anyone in the Negro community. In the process, I had to eat much humble pie. The Negro press, prejudiced as it was against all things Catholic, searched for an ulterior purpose in every initiative. Its references to Catholic affairs were usually garbled and preferably offensive. Still, there were many honorable and forgiving men among Negro thinkers, as we already knew in the Laymen's Union, and as Horace M. Bond showed in the letter to *Time* magazine commenting on Xavier University, New Orleans, which I reported earlier.

Curiously enough, I met two fine Negro editors for the first time on the same day on which I skirmished with *Time*. One was Elmer Carter, editor of *Opportunity*, the organ of the National Urban League. The other was Dr. William E. B. DuBois, the man for whom the DuBois Clubs, which in 1966 achieved a certain notoriety, were named. He was then editor of the organ of the National Association for the Advancement of Colored People, *The Crisis*. My reason for visiting them was

that I had brought back with me to New York from New
Orleans photographs of the new buildings of Xavier University
and of the dedication ceremonies, as well as some data about
the project, and I figured that these two magazines were logical
media in which to place a story. I had already offered the
photographs and information to the religion editor of *Time*,
but he was satisfied with his own sources and resources.

Elmer Carter greeted me like a brother that first day I walked
into his office, and brothers we will always remain. He was
about ten years younger than I, tall and well built, with close-
cropped hair and rather heavy features. He was a cultured man
and a fluent orator. Robert Moses said in 1939 that Elmer
Carter was the most eloquent speaker in all of New York. As
he grew older, he put on weight. But his character did not
change. He was always the soul of loyalty.

Elmer was not a Catholic, nor did he ever become one. But
of all the Protestant Negroes I dealt with in those early days,
he was the one with the most sympathetic understanding of
the Catholic Church. There was a reason for this difference, in
fact several, as he was happy to explain. Most Negroes had
either no contact with Catholics or a disagreeable one. He had
a different experience. First of all, as a child, he had seen an
understanding pastor at work. Elmer's mother was passing Saint
Mary's school yard one winter day, when a snowball thrown
by a mischievous or thoughtless child struck her in the face.
Her neighbors were incensed. A race riot threatened. Elmer's
father went to the Catholic priest, and he accepted responsibility and gave his word that while he lived no more snowballs
from Saint Mary's school yard would challenge interracial peace
in Auburn.

Later, Elmer had the further good fortune to live in St. Paul
and make the friendship of Father Stephen Theobald, the great
Negro priest protected by Archbishop Ireland, who has been
mentioned earlier. For the sake of Father Theobald and Archbishop Ireland, he could forgive many things. He knew that a

Church with such men was not wholly closed. In St. Paul, too, he knew Dr. John Markoe, father of the two Jesuits who were doing so much in St. Louis for Negroes precisely because their father had given them the example in their own home.

Not only did Elmer Carter carry the story about Xavier University, in *Opportunity,* but during the following years he was constantly available to help me in the activities of the Catholic Interracial Council. He spoke several times to the students of Manhattanville and became a good friend of Mother Grace Dammann. He frequently came to the weekly discussion sessions at the Council offices.

One of the things that most distressed him was the refusal of so many Catholic schools and colleges in the East to admit Negroes. "Out in St. Paul," he would say, "the Negro boys were welcomed in Catholic education at all levels. What is the difference between St. Paul and Boston?" He gladly accepted an invitation to participate in a team designed to change this situation, a team which in fact played a big part in the gradual opening up of the Catholic colleges and schools. The technique we developed was unique, and we were very proud of it. At that time, lectures tended to be more formal than today. Audiences were not accustomed to ask questions, and they seldom had the opportunity to do so. Even if they were invited, they felt that good taste forbade open disagreement. To combat this passive situation and encourage dialogue, we formed what we called trial courts. We set up the lecture room so that one member of the team went in the witness box and others pried him with leading questions, thus gradually opening up the audience to enter the lists as prosecuting counsel, and get them to speak their full mind.

Elmer became part of a team with Father LaFarge and myself. We traveled to Philadelphia, Providence, Rhode Island, and many colleges in the metropolitan New York area. His fame as an orator preceded him. Although we insisted that attendance must never be compulsory, the auditorium was always packed with students, nuns, priests, and lay professors. We would put Elmer on the stand and start with questions designed to clarify popular beliefs about the Negro. Elmer was never at a loss for historical references, comparisons, statistical analyses. Gradually, the things on the minds of the listeners came into the open, that the Negro is dishonest, that the Negro is lazy, that the Negro's intellectual capacity is inferior. Elmer knew how to play the audience, facetious when appropriate, condescending when necessary, but always effective.

The question Elmer best liked for a grand finale, and we always found a way to feed it to him, was this. "The last census showed that the United States has twelve million Negroes, Mr. Carter," the question would run, "and of these, seven million are listed as Protestants but only about a quarter of a million as Catholics. How do you explain this? Does the Negro perhaps have an antipathy for the Catholic Church?" Elmer would take it very cool. He would admit the facts. He would touch on historical factors. Then he would sneak up to his point. "Of course, you have to recognize," he would say, "that there are two sides to every situation. Here we are this evening in a Catholic college, but I see no Negro students in the audience. A Negro, as you know, can go to Harvard but not to Holy Cross. He can attend the University of Pennsylvania but not Villanova. He may enter Northwestern but is barred from Notre Dame. Have you checked your own records in this college recently? How many Negro graduates do they list? I suggest that perhaps you might like to rephrase your question slightly for a subsequent discussion."

For a special audience, we would set the scene more formally. I remember that in the summer of 1937, the opportunity developed to speak to the summer school, consisting in large part of teachers and administrators from across the country, at Fordham University. The magnificent auditorium of the new Keating Hall had recently been completed. We were confident we could fill it. The college authorities co-operated generously.

Advance notices appeared in the *News* of the summer session. Ade Bethune's striking cartoons adorned ten bulletin boards. We did fill the auditorium, and we gave them a worthy program. Dr. Hudson J. Oliver, the prominent Negro physician and then president of the Catholic Interracial Council presided. Beside him were Francis S. Moseley, a science teacher at John Adams High School, and Schuyler N. Warren. We had a string of witnesses, first Father LaFarge, then Dr. Edward E. Best, another Negro physician, Maceo A. Thomas, a Negro graduate of Cornell and general manager of a New York fuel company, Dr. Peter Murray, a Negro surgeon, and finally Elmer Carter. Attorney Gerard L. Carroll played the role of prosecuting attorney. The program was a success from start to finish, but as usual, none outshone Elmer. That was the day a member of the audience coined the description which stuck to him for the rest of his life: "A Negro Chesterton in appearance and manner."

Elmer Carter was always a peaceable man. In 1934, he was named a member of the New York State Commission Against Discrimination, the first such state organization to be set up in America. The text of the law called for emphasis on conciliation and persuasion, while using the courts only as a last resort. Elmer was constantly reminding his impatient colleagues of this clause in their terms of reference. But he would insist that his attitude of moderation was also dictated by practical politics. "If we set out right away to prosecute every offending employer," he would point out, "we'll have the entire New York business community in the dock. Remember what happened to Prohibition. It tried to catch the big and the small fish together, and it ended up by breaking the nets. Let's not do that." The event showed how wise he was. When they opened up a few doors, it turned out that many fair-minded employers were standing ready to pass through them. They just were afraid or didn't know how to begin. But when he found a bigot, he went after him relentlessly.

One example will illustrate how smoothly Elmer operated as

head of the New York State Commission. He was dealing with an employer who beyond all show of doubt had discriminated against an applicant for a job because of his color. Elmer suggested that the Commission would delay action until the next time a vacancy occurred for which this particular applicant was fitted. Then, almost inconsequentially, he noted that there appeared not only to be no Negroes but also no Jews on the man's staff, and that strangely enough the names suggested no foreign-born. "You are losing a lot of potential talent," said Elmer, "by your lack of contact with so many sources of skills, and today it's easy to contact such personnel through the Federation Employment Service or the Urban League."

The man's face grew redder and redder. It was quite obvious that Elmer was not making a friend. "It's only a suggestion on my part," he said, "and you are perfectly free to ignore it."

"And if I do ignore it," the man snapped.

"If you do," said Elmer in the same calm voice, "then I recommend a hearing before three Commissioners. They can request you to put the man to work, and they can request you to pay his salary from the date of discrimination."

"Will the public be at the hearing?"

"Yes," said Elmer, "the public will be at the hearing."

"I want no hearing. I'll hire the man."

My relations at the National Urban League were not only with Elmer Carter. I had also from the outset the full support of Lester Granger, for many years the League's executive secretary. The League dated its beginnings from 1910, the same year the NAACP was founded, though it took some years to get fully organized. It was interracial from the start. "Let us work not as colored people nor as white people for the narrow benefit of any group alone, but together, as American citizens, for the common good of our common city, our common country," was how Ruth Standish Baldwin, its first president, formulated its policy. Its function was a very specific one, namely, to provide for Negroes the job opportunity to which their training and education entitled them. They never went outside it into wider political or other issues, but they were always happy to cooperate with other agencies within the framework of their own purpose.

Like Elmer Carter, Lester Granger often talked at the meetings of the Catholic Interracial Council, and at meetings of other Catholic organizations to which we provided him an entree. He also contributed several important articles to the *Interracial Review*. He was a true community leader who understood that economic opportunity for the Negro had to be viewed in a broad context. "Full employment for the Negro," he once wrote, "is more than a question of mass picket lines, economic radicalism or CIO *vs.* AFL controversies. It is even more than a question of full stomachs for hungry Negro families. It is also a question of more secure property values in the Negro neighborhood, larger and better-distributed buying power in the whole community, cheaper police, fire and hospital services—in short, a safer, more beautiful and sounder community structure."

Because of this belief, he would lash out at real estate, banking and insurance companies who were so shortsighted that they could not recognize their own interest in maintaining good property values in Negro areas and in developing good residential areas for those Negroes who could afford the price. He marshaled all his forces against what he called "the notorious Stuyvesant Town project." The issue was whether public subsidies should be given to privately built housing while allowing the beneficiaries, in this instance the Metropolitan Life Insurance Company, to bar members of certain racial or religious groups. The New York State legislature, with the city's approval, passed a special law to permit this $90,000,000 project, without writing into it the safeguards demanded by the National Urban League and other interested parties, including the Catholic Interracial Council. It then exercised its right to exclude Negroes, as a sop to them constructing "a little Stuyvesant Town" in Harlem. But Lester Granger was not appeased, and in the end he and others like him had the last word. Under threat of special legislation introduced into the City Council as a result of the growth of moral indignation among decent New Yorkers, Metropolitan Life in 1950 announced a change of policy and admitted a token number of Negro families. The dike had started to leak.

Granger and Carter were typical of the National Urban League, gentle, courteous men who went about their work unobtrusively, so that few people realize what a big part the League has played in the interracial movement. Those familiar with the record of its achievements can tell a very different story. In 1950, for example, the year in which Metropolitan Life bowed to its insistence, it interviewed 52,575 persons for employment; placed 14,651 persons in jobs, many of them in new fields or in higher categories; found jobs for 261 Negroes in companies whose doors were formerly closed to them; conducted a campaign among 310,000 young people with advice on choosing their careers. Not bad for such quiet people.

Flamboyancy sat better in the offices of the NAACP. In this respect, they were a more appropriate setting for Dr. DuBois, the other editor I met in November 1933, the same day I first met Elmer Carter. Dr. DuBois also published for me a story and a photograph of the Xavier University function in his magazine, *The Crisis*. He was a man of extraordinary talent and culture, a graduate of the University of Berlin, a Ph.D. in sociology of Harvard. He was a very pleasant man to talk to, below medium height, looking a French diplomat with his mustache and goatee, and he spoke beautifully. His most important book, *The Souls of Black Folk*, first published in 1903, remains a basic document on the Negro in American Life.

DuBois was anything but the wild man he is sometimes represented. He was an intellectual for whom happiness consisted in propounding his theories on a shaded campus. That is in fact what he did for a long time as a highly regarded sociologist at Atlanta University, until his teaching proved more than his contemporaries could swallow. That teaching was actually very modest. He himself summed it up in one sentence. "The Negro race," he said, "like all races, is going to be saved by its exceptional men." This was a proclamation of intellectual equality of the races, which the white Northern philanthropists of the early twentieth century could not stomach. They let it be known that Atlanta University would cease to receive grants from certain foundations while DuBois remained on the faculty, and with typical disinterestedness he resigned rather than endanger the university.

But DuBois believed that God helps those who help themselves. In 1905 he assembled twenty-nine Negro professional men, ministers, editors and teachers, at Niagara. They met on the Canadian side because no hotel on the United States side would accept them. There they formed what became known as the Niagara Movement. Its objectives, as stated by DuBois at Harpers Ferry a year later, were simple. "We want full manhood suffrage and we want it now. . . . We want the Constitution of the country enforced. . . . We want our children educated. . . . And here on the scene of John Brown's martyrdom we reconsecrate ourselves, our honor, our property to the final emancipation of the race which John Brown died to make free. . . . We are men! We will be treated as men. And we shall win."

In 1909, the Niagara Movement joined with a group of whites, who included Mary White Ovington, Jane Addams and John Dewey, to form the first significant interracial organization in the United States, the National Association for the Advancement of Colored People. DuBois threw in his lot completely with the NAACP, giving to *The Crisis* his enormous erudition, his years of sociological training, and his gift of words. It started with 1000 copies, had 12,000 readers within a year, finally passed the 100,000 mark and became self-supporting. It was a magazine of culture and the arts as well as the organ of a cause. It was also the expression of a balanced mind, of one ready to put the good of the country before that of a group. "Let us, while this war lasts," DuBois wrote editorially in July 1917, "forget our special grievances and close our ranks shoulder to shoulder with our white fellow-citizens and the allied nations that are fighting for democracy."

Gradually, DuBois brooded more and more on the gap between pretense and delivery. He found his colleagues at the NAACP too gradualist for him. Already when I met him in 1932, he was expressing his doubts publicly. Two years later, he resigned over the issue of continuing co-operation of Negroes with whites. He insisted that he was forced by the duplicity of the white society to urge temporary withdrawal so that the Negro could build up the strength to be taken seriously as a partner. Although he was then speaking and writing of the Catholic Church with suspicion and bitterness, I paid a tribute to him in the *Interracial Review* as a man occupying a unique position among living Negroes, a dedicated leader and profound thinker. He continued to co-operate with the NAACP, and he was one of its three consultants at the San Francisco Conference in 1945 at which the United Nations was formally established. But year by year, his frustration grew until despair drove him into the ranks of the Communist party which he regarded as the one major organized force in the country and the world publicly committed to righting the wrongs of the Negro. He eventually left the country and ended his days in Africa at the age of ninety-seven.

Carter and DuBois represented two of the three leading Negro organizations at that time. The third was headed by A. Philip Randolph, also a Protestant of deep religious convictions and also (as I have already made clear) one of the great men I have known. I think I can call him the king of them all, regal even in his appearance, always on the right side, always selfless. And if I may seem to those with fewer Negro acquaintances than I have to go overboard in my comments, let me remind them that it wasn't as easy for a Negro as for a white to get to the top. To become a leader, a man had to be outstanding in a dozen ways. Randolph was outstanding in twenty.

He is, of course, universally known as head of the Brotherhood of Sleeping Car Porters. But that is simply the result of a bizarre necessity. He is an intellectual from away back, as DuBois was. Born in Florida, he went to school and segregated college there, later attended City College in New York. In 1915, he joined the staff of *The Messenger,* a journal of Negro life, and for thirteen years he kept on plugging economics to his readers as the basis for the solution of the racial problem, working his way up to become editor and publisher of the magazine. In the meantime, he also got himself into jail. Like other Negro editors, he expressed very strongly in 1919 the disillusionment of the 200,000 Negro soldiers who returned from overseas to find they had made the world safe for democracy but not the United States for one American in ten. Attorney General Mitchell Palmer labeled *The Messenger* subversive and arrested its editor.

They didn't hold him for long, and he went back to Harlem and gathered more talented writers around him, men like George S. Schuyler (later of the Pittsburgh *Courier*) and Theophilus Lewis, who became our most faithful contributor at the *Interracial Review.* Then in 1925, a man named Milton P. Webster, who had been trying to organize the sleeping-car porters in Chicago, realized that it needed a national figure to get anyone to take a Negro labor union seriously. So he went to Randolph and asked him to come into the labor movement as a front man. He recognized the need and the help he could provide. Quickly he got involved deeper and deeper, so that by 1928 he had to give up *The Messenger* and devote all his time to the Brotherhood of Sleeping Car Porters. It was a tough, tough fight, because then and for long afterwards a shameful conspiracy of employers and organized white labor sought to exploit the Negro to their mutual advantage, the white worker by keeping him out of good jobs, the employer by underpaying him in the menial jobs open to him. To maintain the conspiracy, it was necessary that the Negro should not organize his own strength. This was done in several ways: by forcing him into satellite unions controlled either by the company or by a white union, by excluding him from white unions that had a monopoly of certain categories of work, by co-operating in refusal to recognize a Negro union as a bargaining entity.

Randolph had to fight a company union for ten years before the National Mediation Board in 1935 held an election and accorded him recognition. By that time, his union was so important that the American Federation of Labor not only had accepted its affiliation but was forced to listen to a diatribe from him at its annual convention each year on the evils of discrimination inside labor. At first the delegates laughed at him or walked out on him, but he persisted, and soon the convention started passing the same resolution each year, and finally more and more of the affiliated unions began to read it and to live up to it. It is doubtful if Randolph's job is yet finished, any more than my own job, but I wish I could say I had made as much progress as has the man who is today a vice-president of the AFL-CIO and president of the Negro American Labor Council. An amazing thing is that the tough fight never affected his temperament. He remained always the man of peace and culture, editing the *Black Worker,* teaching economics and history at the Rand School of Social Science, garnering a handful of honorary degrees, receiving such awards as the NAACP's Spingarn Medal for outstanding achievement in the field of race relations and civil rights, and the Presidential Medal of Freedom, the nation's highest citizen award. He was a founder and first president of the Negro Labor Congress, but he did not hesitate to denounce it publicly and dissociate himself from it when he discovered two years later that the Communists had got control and were using him as a front.

Randolph never seemed to be interested in the rewards which normally accompany success for the union leader no less than for the company executive. When he could have reasonably claimed a country estate or a hotel suite, he was still in a four-room

apartment, where the visitor had to move an armful of magazines from a chair in order to sit down and feared to cough lest
an avalanche of books and magazines descend on him from the
pyramids cluttering the furniture or piled by the walls. Although his wife Lucille was a model of economy in her house-
keeping and personal habits, there were times when some of his
union members would pass the hat to buy him a new suit, simply because he lacked the money to buy one for himself. "Of
course, he was paid a salary by the union," Theophilus Lewis,
who knew him intimately, would explain, "but before he got
home, it had all gone towards the payment of debts incurred
by friends who took advantage of his good nature." There was
only one thing that he would yield to no man, no matter how
friendly, how important, or how importuning. That was his integrity. With anything else he parted easily.

Another Protestant Negro who was an invaluable ally in those
days was Floyd J. Calvin. A native of Hope, Arkansas, he was
one of Harlem's leading newsmen, and he built himself up a
unique news service which furnished articles to 130 Negro publications throughout the country. He wrote a syndicated column which expressed the most progressive Negro thought, noteworthy for its fairness and tolerance. At the start of the Council
I was often embarrassed by people like Floyd. The fact that
Cardinal Hayes had authorized the formation of the Catholic
Interracial Council and that we so quickly inherited a going
publication in the *Interracial Review* made them believe that
all the resources of the great Catholic Church were finally behind the movement, and they expected from us a kind of co-
operation we were in no position to give.

Floyd quickly got the hang of the situation, and I could count
on him to deal with us constructively and co-operatively. He
contributed several excellent articles to the *Interracial Review.*
He followed our activities closely, and he played a large part in
changing the idea of the Catholic Church previously universal
in the Negro press. He reported on the Manhattanville Resolu-

tions, and on the major steps in integration of Catholic colleges as recorded in the *Review*. He read not only *America* and *Commonweal* but even Catholic textbooks. I recall that he drew his readers' attention to a new emphasis on interracial justice injected into a college textbook on sociology, *Social Problems* by Murray and Flynn, and added graciously that the footnotes in the book credited the *Interracial Review* with having focused the attention of the authors on the issue. "The new spirit of the Catholic press generally in discussing frankly and fairly the problems of the Negroes, and their disposition to urge fair play on the part of their readers, is building new hope in the hearts of Negroes. This trend is evident not only in Catholic publications of the metropolis, but in lay publications throughout the land. The support given the Anti-Lynching Bill was most heartening."

The impact of such testimony from the man most highly respected by Negro editors was tremendous, and the Negro press itself was of decisive influence on Negro opinion, since in broad terms it was the only press that Negroes believed. And the Negro press was and is a greater force in this country than most of those who live on the other side of the cotton curtain realize. The first Negro publication started in 1827. Its editor was John B. Russwurm, who was also the first Negro college graduate in America. By the 1930s, there were about 150 Negro publications, nearly all weeklies except the Atlanta *Daily World*, started in Atlanta, Georgia, in 1932, by W. A. Scott. Fifteen of the weeklies were national, professionally produced in substantial plants, and giving major coverage to such events of special interest as Joe Louis, Negro college football and the Ethiopian War. Negroes needed this press, because the white press simply did not tell them what as a minority group they needed to know, or told it skimpily and in garbled fashion. For similar reasons, we had or have Spanish, German, Italian, Chinese, Russian, Ukrainian, Irish, and other group newspapers, surviving in the English lan-

guage even after the members of the group no longer com-
municate in their original tongue.

The Negro, like other Americans, thinks in terms of the beauty
of his women, the future of his children, and the social, cultural
and spiritual contacts afforded by his group. The Negro press
serves this need for him, and when he lived in a totally isolated
group, it did it more intensely than the general press needs to
do for the general public. But, for reasons already well explained, it did not include the Catholic Church within this cultural package; or if it did, it did so only in the same marginal
and garbled way as the white press touches on specifically Negro events. Floyd J. Calvin, a Protestant Negro, was largely instrumental in altering that situation. His untimely death on
September 1, 1939, was a heavy blow to me both professionally and personally. But he had done his work well. It lives on.

Roy Wilkins, who succeeded Dr. DuBois as editor of the
NAACP's *The Crisis* and later followed Walter White as executive secretary of the NAACP, was another of the early friends of
the Catholic Interracial Council. Like Elmer Carter, he had the
good fortune of having been exposed in his youth to a good
face of the Catholic Church. The son of a Methodist minister, he
was born in St. Louis in 1901. Four years later, his mother
died, and he was raised by an uncle and aunt in St. Paul, Minnesota, in a Negro community which respected and loved Archbishop Ireland. He attended journalism school in St. Paul and
majored in sociology at the University of Minnesota. His work
on the college newspaper won him a reporter's job on the Kansas
City Call, then and now the best Negro newspaper in the
United States.

Aminda Badeau, the beautiful girl he married in Missouri,
called Minnie by Roy and all their friends, was a devout Ro-
man Catholic. I must say for her that she took the pre-marriage
promises seriously and tried hard to show Roy that hers was
the true Church. I can recall a discussion of the subject with
Mother Grace Dammann of Manhattanville College, who ad-

mired him immensely and often got him to talk to her students. Roy's answer was always the same. "You people have no idea," he would say with a disarming smile, "how a Methodist resists being taken out of his own Church." So a good Methodist he remained, and a good Christian.

Roy Wilkins was a very useful friend for me to have at the NAACP in those days. In Catholic circles, there was a good deal of suspicion of the NAACP as being anti-Catholic and also Communist infiltrated. The second charge was always false, but there was some basis for the former, at least in the sense that the NAACP was a legitimate reflection of Negro opinion, and I have already made abundantly clear what the Negro community thought of Catholics. Some of the NAACP board members were outspokenly anti-Catholic, Dr. Algernon D. Black, for example. Walter White was prejudiced against Catholics, too, and he resented Roy being so friendly with us. But Roy did his work well, and there wasn't a thing White could do about it.

I was understandably anxious to avoid any kind of condemnation of the NAACP by responsible Catholic leaders. Not only would it have been unjust, but it would put the cause of interracial justice back a generation. I learned on one occasion that some of the things the NAACP was doing had been represented in a very unfavorable light to Cardinal Spellman. That was shortly after he had become Archbishop of New York. I was able to bring Roy Wilkins to give the new Archbishop a full briefing on the specific situation and on the general policies of the NAACP. Roy was completely loyal to his chief, Walter White. He did not attempt to deny his obvious bias, but he put it in a perspective that made it more intelligible to the Cardinal. This was only one of several conversations they had. They got on extremely well together. Once, Roy was going to an NAACP convention in St. Louis, and he was most anxious to have an interview with Archbishop Ritter (also later a Cardinal). Cardinal Spellman undertook to arrange it. "The only free minute I had was at two o'clock on the fourth day of the

Convention, and when Archbishop Ritter heard this, he adjusted his whole schedule to fit. They swept me in past a bevy of waiting bishops and monsignori."

Roy was always a demon for work, administrator, troubleshooter, wandering ambassador, speaker, writer, with a twelve-hour-a-day routine but always time to oblige someone, to give someone a hand, to straighten someone out. He does not drink and he stopped smoking cigars. He relaxes at home, gets to bed early.

One thing Roy never succeeded in doing was to change Walter White's ideas about Catholics, although I will say that White softened his views as we went along. He was a self-centered and self-opinionated man. "He could have been one of the great public relations men of all time," Arthur B. Spingarn, long-time president of the NAACP, once remarked of him; and he used some of that talent to keep himself in the limelight, as two autobiographies plus a biography by his second wife testify.

I had a clash with White the very first time I talked to him. It was very shortly after the founding of the Catholic Interracial Council, and my board had approved the idea of writing an editorial in the *Interracial Review* to support a federal anti-lynching bill then before Congress, one of many that would come and go before that blot on our civilization effectively disappeared. Having received some information from the NAACP to help me in preparing my editorial, I decided I'd take a copy of the text down to White for his comments, before publication. He read it and liked it. "It's a damn good editorial," he said, "but who the hell is the Catholic Interracial Council, and what weight does it think it can pull?"

I may as well admit I was ready to be nasty. I had not forgiven White for the part he played in ousting his predecessor in 1928, James Weldon Johnson, a man of great culture and charm who subsequently taught creative writing at Fisk University until his death in an automobile accident in 1938. So my answer was a little more aggressive than it otherwise might have been. "We are the newest, smallest, poorest, and at present least effective, of all organizations dedicated to interracial justice, Mr. White," I told him. "But don't forget this. There is no organization with a greater potential than ours, and you will live to see this potential being realized in action. The reason is simple. The Catholic Church teaches that all men are equal in dignity and rights, that all humanity participates in the fruits of Christ's Redemption. Catholics in the United States, with few exceptions, have not been conscious of this teaching of the Church. But we are going to make them. That is our job. And when we do, there will be an organized body of forty million white Americans, people who listen when their Church speaks, in there plugging for the cause to which we are both dedicated."

"I never thought of it like that," he admitted. "I am a Protestant and I know little about your Church. But if you really believe like that, then I can see why you are so confident of the future."

I think we respected each other a little more after that exchange. He even spoke at the Catholic Interracial Council. But we never really became friends. Time and again in the ensuing years, my name was proposed for membership of the board of the NAACP. It would have been good for that organization to have a man publicly identified with the Catholic interracial movement, and my board was happy to co-operate with a body which it regarded as doing an outstanding civic job. But White always blocked it. He told me so himself. "Philip Murray is a Catholic, George," he once said. "Isn't that as much representation as Catholics are entitled to on our board?" "Philip Murray is not on your board as a Catholic but in spite of his being a Catholic," I protested. "He is there as head of the CIO." But he held out as long as he could. It was only as he was starting on the sabbatical with which he ended his association with the NAACP in 1955 that he finally signed the letter inviting me to join the board. Roy Wilkins, his successor, presided at the first meeting in which I participated.

The great legal brain of the NAACP in those days was Thurgood Marshall. He appeared thirty-eight times before the Supreme Court in civil rights cases, and he won thirty-six of the cases he argued. They included such basic issues as the right of a Negro defendant not to have Negroes excluded from the jury that would try him, the right of a Negro to attend a state university, and the crucial decision that the doctrine of "separate but equal" has no place in the public education system of the United States.

Marshall was not just a good lawyer. He had a delightful sense of humor. He also had a sane understanding of the limited value of court decisions. He spoke many times at the forums of the Catholic Interracial Council, and he always insisted that only such organizations as ours could get the sympathetic understanding of the local community, without which even a Supreme Court decision is a dead letter. Needless to say, the Catholic Interracial Council was one of the many organizations which hailed his appointment to the U. S. Circuit Court in 1962 and to the office of Solicitor General of the United States two years later.

The program of the NAACP was a broad-spectrum one, but essentially a simple, straightforward one. We at the Catholic Interracial Council had no problem in supporting and promoting it from the outset. Its goals, as announced at its formation in 1910, were the abolition of enforced segregation, equal educational advantage for colored and white, enfranchisement for the Negro, and enforcement of the Fourteenth and Fifteenth amendments of the United States Constitution. These amendments clarify that all born in the United States are citizens, that all citizens have the right to vote, that no discrimination on the ground of race, color or previous servitude is legal, and that no state can legally restrict any of these federally protected rights.

One of the first big projects in which I became involved shoulder-to-shoulder with the NAACP was the Scottsboro Trial. It was a sordid business in itself, but it became important on the one hand as a test of human rights in a democracy, and on the other as a test of the ability of citizen groups to prevent their being misused by Communist infiltrators for subversive purposes.

The basic allegation in the case was that nine Negro itinerants, aged thirteen to twenty, had raped two white girls, admitted prostitutes, on a freight train. The first of several trials was held at Scottsboro, Alabama, in 1931, and it resulted in death sentences for several of the defendants. The trial had been held in an atmosphere of utmost tension and acrimony. Probably the boys were lucky to have escaped the then popular solution of verdict by lynching. In any case, the NAACP initiated efforts to test the validity of the legal decisions, particularly as the evidence finally rested on the testimony of one of the girls, and the jury agreed that she was perjuring herself in respect of some of the defendants.

Interested not in the fate of the boys but in the promotion of its own ends, the Communist party moved in, convinced the parents that the NAACP was in league with the "lyncher Bosses" and persuaded them to dismiss the NAACP-provided counsel, who included Clarence Darrow and Arthur Garfield Hays. Samuel S. Leibowitz was then retained and conducted several trials and appeals, but in 1934 the parents and Leibowitz decided they had had enough from the Communists, and Leibowitz became the representative of a new group, staunchly anti-Communist. Its members were both white and Negro, and they included Protestants, Jews and Catholics. Father LaFarge and I were the Catholic members, and I was named to the executive committee of an organization incorporated in New York as the American Scottsboro Committee in November 1934. Other members included Dr. George Edmund Haynes, head of the Race Relations Division of the Federal Council of the Churches of Christ in America, Reverend Fred L. Brownlee of the American Missionary Association, and William H. Davis, editor of the *Amsterdam News*.

One of the Committee's first decisions was to send me on a

fact-finding tour of the South, a commission I undertook immediately. I had earlier been in Louisiana, but this was my first venture into the heartland of segregation. Dr. Haynes, chairman of our executive committee, advised me to break my trip at Charlottesville, Virginia, and talk to Dr. James Hardy Dillard, a noted Southern educator.

It was good advice. My train reached Charlottesville early on a Sunday morning. I attended Mass, then telephoned the doctor, who sent his son—Major Hardy Dillard—to pick me up at my hotel and take me to his home. Dr. Dillard began by telling me of his great interest in Catholicism, stimulated in large part by reading the works of Hilaire Belloc and G. K. Chesterton, as well as pamphlets of Father Martin Scott, S.J. "I regard Father Scott," he said, "as a master of English style and an outstanding example of the gift of penetrating and enlightening exposition."

We then got down to our business, and Dr. Dillard had soon enriched me with a list offering a good cross-section of Southern opinion on the Scottsboro Case. From Charlottesville I went to Atlanta and talked to Dr. Jesse Thomas, secretary of the Atlanta Urban League; Dr. John Hope, Dean of Atlanta University, and Dr. Florence Reid, Dean of Spellman College, Atlanta University. They agreed on three things: (1) the boys were innocent; (2) a growing segment of enlightened Southern opinion was coming to recognize that there had been a gross miscarriage of justice; (3) in the face of the almost universal anti-Negro prejudice, it would be extremely difficult to get an acquittal.

The following day I had a long interview with a representative of the State Department of Education at the State Capitol in Montgomery, Alabama. I next talked with a judge of the U. S. District Court. Then I had an encounter with a white local lawyer, a Catholic and a graduate of Notre Dame University. The encounter, if brief, was enlightening. He made no effort to conceal his hostility and resentment at the idea that "a Catholic lawyer from the North should be so misguided as to come to the

South to seek the acquittal of some Negroes already judged by our Southern courts."

My next stop was the industrial city of Birmingham. There I made contact with two Protestant ministers and several social workers who were all involved in a quiet but well-ordered effort to win freedom for the boys. One of the two ministers, a Methodist, summed up the atmosphere of the South very succinctly for me. "Not one Southerner in a hundred would join a lynch mob," he said, "but at the same time, ninety-five jurors in a hundred would vote to acquit a man who brazenly admitted his part in a lynching." In Birmingham also, I met two important local Negro leaders, a white (Jewish) columnist on one of the important newspapers, and a prominent and extremely co-operative member of the Georgia Bar Association. In Tuskegee, I saw Dr. Monroe Work and W. T. B. Williams. In a period of about ten days, I was able not only to reach but to penetrate the thinking of a significant number of Southern whites and Negroes, educators, lawyers, editors, writers, and people active in interracial work. These white and Negro Southerners believed in the innocence of the boys and wanted them freed. They were outraged at what the Communists were doing to goad the South by inflammatory speeches, barrages of pamphlets and rabble rousing. My investigation convinced me of the innocence of all the accused. As I wrote later in the *Interracial Review*, "the nine Negro boys are innocent. They should be released. Alabama justice should be vindicated."

Ultimately, they were all released, but not thanks to Alabama justice. Our Committee supported Mr. Leibowitz in his appearance before the United States Supreme Court in February 1935, in behalf of three boys condemned to death. His attack on the exclusion of Negroes from both grand and petty juries drew nation-wide approval, and he succeeded in winning new trials for the accused. But new trials involved new expense, and the American Scottsboro Committee found itself being strained beyond its possibilities. This was the opportunity for which the Communists had been waiting, and they succeeded in joining with Morris Ernst, Norman Thomas and other liberals in a Scottsboro Joint Action Committee, which they hailed as the first major example of the "United Front," the new Party Line in the second half of the 1930s. They urged our committee to join this "United Front," but instead we voted in December 1935 to disband. We could not satisfy ourselves of the legitimacy of the Communist intentions. "They will use you for their partisan objectives," we warned the others. History was to vindicate us completely.

This experience served me in good stead when I was summoned before the Committee on Un-American Activities many years later, in 1949, and asked to testify on Communist infiltration of Negro groups. The Communists, I told the Committee in my sworn evidence, try to increase antagonism between different groups, and specifically between reactionary whites and the disadvantaged Negro groups, seeking to defeat constructive programs for social justice and turn the Negro from democratic processes to the relief promised by the Communist party.

"In my judgment, this sinister plot has failed completely," I then said. "There have been remarkable gains in interracial justice over the years. The Negro has not been drawn into the Communist party. . . . He remains completely loyal to his country."

I then illustrated my statement with a short history of the Scottsboro Case. I described how I had become involved and how I had investigated on the spot. I told them how my colleagues and I were convinced that the Communists "were willing to jeopardize the chances of those boys," that "they wanted them kept in jail, and so forth, to be held up as martyrs." After we pulled out, the Communists continued these tactics, as Roger Baldwin and Norman Thomas later admitted, exploiting the boys, goading the South, defying the courts and prosecutors, and making it impossible to secure freedom for the boys. These leaders, I told the Committee, informed us "that many times they had secured a tentative agreement of parole for some of the prisoners, and as soon as this was done, a group of Communists would come down and picket the courthouse and the negotiations would be called off. Today [1949] I think there are still two boys in jail, and I have no doubt but that if the Communists had their way, there would be seven others still in jail."

These two were subsequently released as a result of the perseverance of the NAACP, but they and two others never had the satisfaction of having their innocence vindicated. That was done for five defendants by a jury in Decatur, Alabama, in 1937, in a decision uniquely bizarre in that it used precisely the same evidence to convict four and acquit five. And even those five acquitted had been held nearly seven years in jail, the youngest a boy of thirteen when seized and now a dead-end twenty. Such was American justice for its own citizens in an era that it would take a rash man to say is entirely past.

What the Communists did achieve by all this was to increase the distrust regarding the loyalty of the Negro community among many sectors, a distrust to which certain conservative Catholic elements seemed particularly allergic. I was constantly getting inquiries from Catholic bishops, priests and laymen, most of them honestly concerned, some bitterly prejudiced, asking if the NAACP was not crypto-Communist. The Communists themselves, as I have indicated, were glad to encourage such rumors, but they were ably abetted by the White Citizens Councils, the Ku Klux Klan, and many others. I was fortunately always able to quote chapter and verse to support my conviction that such charges were baseless. Since I became an NAACP director and was consequently able to participate in the organization's innermost thinking and planning, I have further confirmed my views. The NAACP has always been faithful to its commitment to pursue its objectives through the orderly processes of American democracy, in the law courts and the legislatures. I have been credited with playing a part in enlisting two prominent life members of the NAACP, Francis Cardinal Spellman of New York, and Richard Cardinal Cushing of Boston. I am prepared to plead guilty as charged.

Mentioning life memberships in the NAACP inevitably brings to my mind the name of Kivie Kaplan, the man who solved the NAACP's financial problems at a time when it was faced with the immense cost of major court tests, all the way to the Supreme Court, on education and other issues. And the financial costs of justice in the United States are high. A 1925 trial in Detroit cost the NAACP $22,000, only to end in a hung jury. The second trial, which won an acquittal, raised the costs to $38,000. The NAACP paid more than $100,000 for its four of the five school desegregation cases which brought the Supreme Court decisions of 1954 and 1955.

Were it not for Kivie Kaplan, a Jewish industrialist from Boston, this might not have been possible. The 1925 case had created a real crisis. The NAACP was never tax-exempt, since its stated aims included efforts to mobilize public opinion in order to influence legislation in Washington. Accordingly, in 1939, it established the NAACP Legal Defense and Educational Fund as a separate corporation, and it was ruled tax-exempt for gifts.

With exemption, the Fund was able to call on big names to help in money-raising, people like Harry Emerson Fosdick, Archibald MacLeish, Jackie Robinson, Duke Ellington, Lena Horne, Marian Anderson, Nat King Cole. But Kivie Kaplan has been the biggest individual fund raiser, using a single gimmick. He sells life memberships. On one vacation abroad, he sold seventeen. On a beach where he goes swimming, he picked up six. Kivie has always taken a sympathetic interest in the Catholic interracial movement. He once told me that he didn't think he'd ever join a church, but that he had studied comparative religion widely and he considered the Catholic Church to be philosophically the most satisfying of all the religions about which he had read. "Your doctrines make sense to me," he commented. "What I do not understand is the failure of Catholics to live up to their professions."

On another occasion, Kivie explained to me his reasons for giving so much of his time to the NAACP. "My Jewish friends sometimes tell me," he said, "that we have our own discrimination problems still unsolved here in the United States, and that I'd be much better employed in helping those who are working on them. My only answer is that I quite agree that Jews are still discriminated against. But then I ask a question. 'When Hitler came along in Germany,' I say, 'who rallied to the support of the Jews? They had to go it alone because they had no friends outside their own tight circle. I want to see all the depressed groups in the United States working together. If we reach that point, do you think even a Hitler could take us on?'"

That's the kind of human being Kivie Kaplan is, and that's the spirit in which he goes around selling life subscriptions to the NAACP. Before he became interested in 1952, the life members numbered 300, and eight years later they were 5000 fully paid up, and that meant $500 out of each of those pockets. He signed up the young Aga Khan at Harvard. He signed up the late Prime Minister Nehru of India, Averell Harriman, Harry Golden, Harry Belafonte, Alan Paton, and G. Mennen Williams, which takes him just about all the way across the board.

Kivie Kaplan was not the only Jew who gave his time and influence generously to the NAACP. In 1914, just four years after its foundation, Dr. Joel E. Spingarn, professor of English at Columbia University, was elected chairman of its board of directors; and his brother, Arthur B. Spingarn, took over the supervision of the legal work of the Association. They were men of means, culture and dedication. Arthur served as chairman of legal defense without pay for twenty-seven years, and he got many other lawyers to act without pay. He was on what was probably the first interracial picket line in the South ever, a protest in Memphis in 1914 against the decision of the

National Council of Social Workers to withdraw Negro speakers from their program in deference to Southern prejudice. He became president of the NAACP in 1939 and retired from that office only in 1965 at the age of eighty-six. The Association appropriately chose Kivie Kaplan to succeed him. A great collector of books, he lives in Gramercy Park in the same building as James J. McGurrin, head of the American-Irish Historical Society, and the two are close friends. I shall have more to say later about Jim McGurrin's contributions to the Catholic interracial movement.

I'm afraid we never had a fund-raising genius like Kivie Kaplan at the Catholic Interracial Council, although, in his own unobtrusive way, Father LaFarge was always able to perform a miracle when nothing less would keep us in business. And we always have had support from Jewish and Protestant, as well as from Catholic sources. Our primary benefactors in our initial stages were Mother Katharine Drexel and her half sister, Mrs. Edward Morrell. They largely kept us going in our first office at 11 West Forty-second Street, facing the New York Public Library, and in the office to which we transferred at 220 West Forty-second Street, in May 1935. As those who know New York will appreciate, this was not then, as it is not today, the most exclusive address in the city, located as it is between Times Square and Eighth Avenue. Some, however, found a certain appropriateness in the fact that—as one of them put it—"the office of the Catholic Interracial Council is between two flea circuses directly facing Minsky's burlesque house."

We moved downtown to 20 Vesey Street in 1939. This is a historic part of the city. One looks out on the little cemetery of St. Paul's Chapel, which is in the parish of Trinity Episcopal Church, and whose treasures include the pew in which George Washington worshiped when he was President of the United States, and a magnificent collection of Waterford Glass chandeliers. By a curious coincidence, 20 Vesey Street had been the first home of the NAACP, when it was founded thirty years earlier. It was then the New York *Post* Building, and Oswald Garrison Villard of the *Post*, a founder of NAACP, had given the organization rent-free quarters there at a time when no respectable office building would lease space to an organization even partially staffed by Negroes. But the deciding factor for us was neither the view nor the NAACP neighbors, though their presence made it easier for another office with a racially mixed staff. The real reason for our going there was that 20 Vesey Street was in St. Peter's parish, and that the pastor was Monsignor Edward Roberts Moore.

Father Moore, a man just a few years my junior, had long been involved in a host of community activities in New York City. A graduate of Fordham, he had first been assigned to St. Peter's in 1919, went to the Social Action Division of the Catholic Charities of the archdiocese of New York in 1923, came back to St. Peter's as assistant in 1929 and became pastor in 1937. Simultaneously, he had taught at the school of social service at Fordham, published a couple of books, been a member of half a dozen city commissions and a member of the New York City Housing Authority appointed by Mayor LaGuardia in 1933, a post he retained until 1943.

It was in this post that I had come to know him. Housing was one of the areas in which Negroes were hardest hit. Not only were they gouged by private landlords, forced to pay far higher rents than whites for the same accommodations, but little public housing was available for them. A great advance was the first city housing project in Harlem, some units of which became available for occupancy in 1937. Immediately, an old issue was raised. Negroes and whites, many members of the Housing Authority insisted, should not share the same dwellings. Allocation should be on a basis of color, the odd-numbered buildings for Negroes, the even-numbered for whites.

Monsignor Moore phoned me and said it seemed to him that such a decision would in itself constitute discrimination and violate the spirit of the fair housing legislation. I expressed full agreement and undertook to use whatever influence I could marshal in favor of his stand. I called Elmer Carter of the Urban League, and the two of us went to see the Monsignor. By this time, some Authority members were willing to settle for segregation by floors, Negroes only on odd-numbered floors and whites on even-numbered, or the other way around. But it was precisely the principle in which Monsignor Moore was interested, and so were we. He stuck to his guns and won his point. And an error was avoided which might have set back seriously the process of integration in New York City.

We never regretted moving down to St. Peter's parish, old St. Peter's as it was known universally, for it was in fact the oldest Catholic church in New York City. It was on the same block as our office, almost directly behind it, and the first Mass had been celebrated in its still unfinished sanctuary, on the corner of Church and Barclay streets, in 1786. Monsignor Moore remained our friend until his death in 1952. Both he himself and his church were always available for any function we wished to hold, and his tradition was continued by his successor, Monsignor John S. Middleton.

Our first office at 20 Vesey Street was very tiny indeed. Members of the Clergy Conference on Negro Welfare, approached by Father LaFarge, paid for the furniture and equipment. But the space was quite inadequate. We had ambitious plans. We wanted a room for meetings, exhibits and a specialized library, and in fact such a unit was available on the tenth floor. Again Father LaFarge had an idea. An outstanding Catholic layman, John S. Burke, was head of the Altman department store and president of the Altman Foundation. Father LaFarge asked Mr. Burke to present his problem to his fellow trustees of the Foundation, all of whom were Jewish. They heard him sympathetically and undertook to pay the rent for at least a year. That was in 1929. The year extended to two and three and four. We remained in those quarters until 1962, and every year during all these good times and bad, we got our annual check for $2000 from this same Jewish foundation. The Council has since moved twice, first to the Woolworth Building close to City Hall, and subsequently to Liberty Street, closer to Trinity Church, Wall Street and the Battery.

We have had and have other faithful helpers, including the archdiocese of New York and the diocese of Brooklyn, as well as some educational foundations and three or four national labor unions. But simple justice forces me to record the critical contribution of a Jewish foundation, and that at a time when the liturgy of the Catholic Church still called us each year to pray for the perfidious Jews. Let us pray also for the generous ones.

We had contacts with other Jewish agencies, too. Of these, the one most specifically related to our work was the National Conference of Christians and Jews (NCCJ). It had its own troubles. In Catholic circles, in particular, there was much hesitation in those days before Pope John about public association with representatives of other religious bodies. In the early 1940s, the NCCJ sponsored a series of round tables in which Catholics, Protestants and Jews would sit down together and discuss in the presence of an audience issues that affected community relations and had a religious aspect or bearing. There was no problem in getting representative rabbis and Protestant ministers, but the Chancery of the archdiocese of New York persistently refused to approve the participation of a Catholic priest. It did not, however, go so far as to forbid a Catholic layman from attending in his individual capacity, and I was one who did so frequently. I believe I participated in about ten conferences over a period of some five years. We covered not only the Greater New York area but went as far afield as Atlantic City, New Jersey, and Reading, Pennsylvania.

While I found myself in full agreement with the broad positions on human rights sponsored by the NCCJ, both I and representatives of other interracial agencies were long highly critical of the Conference for its failure to condemn the moral wrong of prejudice based on color. Here, we used to say, is an organization which raises $3,000,000 a year to promote inter-group relations, yet it tries to stay neutral on this concrete acute issue.

Finally, at a meeting of the board of the Catholic Interracial Council some time in the winter of 1950–51, we decided that this had gone on long enough. The board instructed me to contact the officials of the NCCJ and see if we could not persuade them to take a definite stand on the issue. The first person I talked to was Mr. Allan Robinson. I found him most sympathetic, and together we drafted several possible formulas for a resolution in which the NCCJ would go on record as condemning the moral wrong of prejudice based on the accident of color.

A few days later, however, I got a telephone call from a Dr. Willard Johnson. He was several steps above Mr. Robinson in the hierarchy. He didn't like the idea and he said so in no uncertain terms. Neither the Catholic Interracial Council nor George Hunton nor any outsider would dictate the policy or actions of the NCCJ. "Our record is above reproach," he said. "We have condemned all and every type of prejudice, wherever it exists in America. You should be satisfied with that, and you may as well be satisfied with it, because that is all you are going to get."

Dr. Johnson obviously didn't know George Hunton, or his temperament. I blew my top. Completely overlooking the fact that it belonged to the editorial board and not to the editor personally to lay down a line of policy for the *Interracial Review*, and to the board of directors to lay down policy for the Catholic Interracial Council, I let him have it. "Very well, then, Dr. Johnson," I said. "If a resolution along the lines agreed between Mr. Robinson and me is not adopted and promulgated by the NCCJ at its upcoming conference, then the *Review* and the Council will publicly condemn your hypocrisy."

No sooner had I put down the phone than I realized what a fool I had made of myself. I had not only overstepped my authority but I had created a gulf that would not easily be bridged. Imagine my surprise and relief when within a few hours the telephone rang again and I found myself speaking to still a bigger wheel in the NCCJ hierarchy, Dr. Lewis Webster Jones. "If you are going to be in your office," he said quite affably, "I'd like to send you by special messenger a copy of the resolution we propose to submit at our convention."

It was a superb text, a text worthy of the NCCJ. It was one of those simple statements of integrity that stand the test of time and belong in anthologies. This is what it said:

"Although the primary purpose of the National Conference of Christians and Jews is to promote better relationships among Religions, we would point out that the just social order which we seek will depend upon good relationships among all the groups that compose our society.

"It is our common conviction that racial discrimination must be regarded as an evil which we cannot as religious people tolerate. We believe that the church and the synagogue must in word and in deed make clear the importance of racial justice. We are aware that racism has become a world issue deepening the urgency of its solution, but we are brought to judgment not by men but by God and we would underscore our common belief that the problem of race relations is a moral problem, and that those who believe in God must be concerned to see that the dignity of all whom God has created be recognized in our laws, in our institutions and in the daily conduct of our citizens.

"As members of different faiths we are cognizant of the divisions among us. Some of our differences are matters of conscience to which we must adhere; some are strong convictions from which we will not be lightly turned. We record our belief, however, that these differences need not be the source of conflict that sometimes they have occasioned and that as we work together on the basis of fundamental moral principles toward common civic goals, we shall gain in mutual respect and goodwill. In a day when moral values important to all of us are threatened, such cooperation becomes imperative."

Needless to say, we printed it in full in the *Interracial Review*, and we thanked the NCCJ for their generosity. The Urban League, the NAACP, and other agencies thanked the Conference for the statement and the Catholic Interracial Council for the part it played in obtaining it. It was congratulation day all around. Maybe, we should lose our tempers more often!

Another organization with which I established excellent and continuing contacts was the Jewish Labor Committee. The Interracial Clearing House was formed in 1943 by the Negro Labor Committee, the Jewish Labor Committee, the Presbyterian Institute of Industrial Relations and the Catholic Interracial Council, to work jointly in the pursuit of common goals. It was a pioneer effort, and it helped to develop standards for intergroup co-operation. Together we supported the movement led by A. Philip Randolph in the 1940s for the enactment of state laws to prohibit discrimination in employment and for the creation of a permanent federal Fair Employment Practices Commission (FEPC). I shall return to this important project later. We co-operated in setting up labor committees to combat intolerance in the major American industrial centers, and in the process we got many labor leaders to see for the first time the close relationship between the goals of labor and of those who fought racial and religious intolerance.

I was talking recently to Charles S. Zimmerman, who was a leader in this joint effort and who is today chairman of the Jewish Labor Committee's administrative board and also chairman of its National Trade Union Council for Human Rights. He recalled for me another of the "firsts" of the Interracial Clearing House. This was the first public condemnation of Soviet anti-Semitism. The occasion was a weekly forum at the Catholic Interracial Center. The Jewish Labor Committee presented there the first documentary proof that Soviet Russia had launched a campaign of discrimination and terror against Soviet Jews. Representatives of the Catholic, Protestant, Jewish, Negro, and labor press who were present gave the story national publicity.

It would, of course, have been absolutely impossible for anyone associated with Father LaFarge not to know many of the leading Jewish philosophers and theologians of our time. Not only did I meet such men, but I am proud to say that I came to count many of them as my own friends also. One who immediately comes to my mind is Rabbi Louis Finkelstein of the Jewish Theological Seminary of America. Another is Rabbi Marc H. Tannenbaum of the Institute of Human Relations of the American Jewish Committee. One of my most prized treasures is a letter in which Rabbi Tannenbaum wrote as follows: "In Jewish tradition, there is a maxim which holds that 'the righteous of the nations of the earth are assured a place in the world to come.' The 'righteous' are conceived of in Judaism as those who seek peace in their own place and pursue it in every place. By these definitions, George Hunton is certainly to be counted among the righteous and is vouchsafed a place in immortality." A good friend, surely, and a generous one.

Chapter 9

Irish Catholics played a major part in the growth of labor organizations in the United States. But from the outset, the attitudes of many of the leaders tended to be ambivalent. The hostility of the employers in the middle of the nineteenth century was such that organization had of necessity to be secret, and many Catholic bishops wanted to extend to the Knights of Labor the ban on oath-bound secret societies which was then regarded as one of the Church's main laws. The growth of socialistic influences in the ranks of labor in the twentieth century continued this gulf between labor thinking and Catholic thinking. Many on both sides knew it was mistaken, but it took much time to find a satisfactory emotional equilibrium.

Several factors forced me to become deeply involved. Many unions led by men publicly identified as Catholics excluded Negroes from their ranks, and some of them conspired with employers to keep Negroes in menial jobs. The Communists were trying hard in the 1930s to establish themselves as the sole champions of the Negro, and in particular to infiltrate organized Negro labor. And there were such further complications as Mike Quill, Catholic and Communist by turn according to whether he was speaking out of the right side of his mouth or the left.

Union issues were usually not cut and dried, but were factors in some broader conflict, as a short account of some events in Philadelphia will show. A major activity of the Catholic Interracial Council of New York from the outset was to promote the formation of similar councils in other cities, and I was constantly traveling throughout the United States, and occasionally north into Canada, to rally the wavering and explain to the converted how to move from decision to action. I was thus present in 1936 at the founding meeting of the West Philadelphia Interracial Forum, in the Negro parish of St. Ignatius served by Father William J. Walsh, and at the founding meeting of the Catholic Intercollegiate Interracial Council at St. Joseph's College, Philadelphia, the following year. Reverend Richard M. McKeon, S.J., Dean of Men, presided at that meeting. He was a close friend of Father LaFarge and shared his enthusiasms. He got the approval of Denis J. Cardinal Dougherty to organize units in all six Philadelphia Catholic colleges. Meetings were held in each college in turn, and close liaison was established with the West Philadelphia Interracial Forum.

The local Negro community was deeply involved in the effort then being made by the Communists to take control of the National Negro Congress, organized in 1936. A. Philip Randolph was active in this body (it was not until 1941 that he left it and denounced it), and while he was a member, it was understandably difficult to get any Negro to question it. What our two organizations did was to mobilize Catholic Negroes through their Holy Name and other societies to stay alert and attend meetings. And for eighteen months Mrs. William (Anna M.) McGarry carried on the fight in a weekly by-line column entitled "Interracial Justice" in the Philadelphia *Tribune*. Mrs. McGarry was the one who first contacted the New York Council for help in creating an interracial organization in Philadelphia. She later became Supervisor of Community Relations for Philadelphia's Commission on Human Rights. In that way, we kept the Communists in check in Philadelphia until A. Philip Randolph made his move at the conference of the National Negro Congress in Washington, D.C., in 1941, rejecting its offer to rename him president and declaring that the Congress was "being used as a tool by the Communists in America who were primarily concerned with the fight for the sovereignty of Soviet Russia." The Communists, he declared, "have no more genuine interest in any kind of equality for the Negro than they have in the advancement of the worker, whose cause they pretend to espouse. Their main concern is for the advancement of Communist propaganda in the various ranks of the people, especially among Negroes and labor groups. Their objective is to split the American community."

With the outbreak of war, Philadelphia experienced the bitter conflicts over Negro rights to work in defense industries which developed across the country, and which I shall describe shortly in their broader context. On these issues, our two Catholic interracial organizations co-operated faithfully in urging compliance with the executive order issued by President Roosevelt in 1941, and with the wider movement for legislation to promote fair employment practices.

A particularly sticky situation, however, developed in Philadelphia in 1944, when Mike Quill as head of the Transport Workers called a strike. Mike had always been a genius for confusing issues to his own advantage. In 1940, when New York City had taken over the two privately owned subway systems, the IRT and BMT, Mike had fought hard to prevent their Negro employees from graduating to the same job opportunities as Negroes already had on the city-owned Eighth Avenue system. At that time, the BMT excluded Negroes from the posts of motormen, conductors and platform men, allowing them work only as porters and sweepers. The IRT had the same de facto situation, except for two Negro conductors on the Lenox Avenue local, a section with a heavy Negro clientele. Mike wanted the union contract to be drawn up in such a way that existing personnel would be frozen at existing levels, and the union would dictate the intake of new workers. What that would mean had just been demonstrated by the experience of the Green Line buses, which had hired several hundred new employees with Quill's help, on taking over the Manhattan trolley lines, without including a single Negro.

The racial nature of the clash in Philadelphia was even clearer. The War Manpower Commission upgraded eight Negroes to the rank of motorman and conductor in the Philadelphia Transit Company, and six thousand employees walked out when the men were assigned to practice runs, halting the city's 3264 cars and buses. I wrote at the time that it was evident that race prejudice was the cause and central issue, and that the Transit Company, the CIO and Mike Quill were all guilty. What we in the interracial movement most feared was an aggravation of anti-Negro prejudice by the union leaders, who were—like Quill—identified as Irish, Catholic and anti-British.

The situation became really tense when the President used emergency powers to restore service, with an armed and uniformed National Guardsman on the platform of every car. Father LaFarge and I were in constant consultation with our interracial organizations in Philadelphia, and we succeeded in preventing any statement from local Catholic leaders which might be interpreted as justifying the Quill position. In this we were helped by close liaison with other interested agencies, which were brought together by the crisis into the Philadelphia Fellowship Commission, made up of the Jewish Community Relations Council, the NAACP, the Armstrong Association, the Urban League, the Friends Race Relations Committee, Fellowship House, and the NCCJ. Significantly, there was no Catholic organization in this body. The Catholic authorities of Philadelphia would not approve, and we were forced to cooperate informally and unofficially with it. But we achieved our purpose. The strike was settled without aggravation of racial tension, and on the basis of the principle involved. The Negro employees were upgraded. For us also, the crisis had a happy ending. Up to that time, the Archbishop had refused to authorize a Catholic Interracial Council for Philadelphia. All we had was the Forum, as it was called, in West Philadelphia, and an Interracial Council for the six Catholic colleges. Now, Monsignor Cletus J. Benjamin, impressed by our work during the strike, got Cardinal Dougherty's approval to name Father Edward F. Cunnie as chaplain of a diocesan unit. Father Cunnie was pastor of St. Elizabeth, a parish undergoing rapid racial change. With his help, the Philadelphia Catholic Interracial Council was formally inaugurated in October 1946. It was the seventh in a group of cells already scattered across the country, in New York, Los Angeles, Detroit, Brooklyn, Washington, and Chicago. And, as I promised the pioneers at the inaugural Communion breakfast, many more would soon follow in other cities with similar needs and aspirations.

The clash I have described in Philadelphia was not too different from what occurred a thousand times during the Second World War, and already during the build-up of the defense industries in the years preceding the conflict. Two issues were becoming concurrently critical. The return to barbarism in Europe under the totalitarian systems of Left and Right had forced the United States to reformulate its concepts of human rights, and the Negroes were properly demanding that they be included as human beings in the possession and exercise of all citizen rights. In addition, a job issue flowed from the issue of principle. The Negroes wanted an end to a traditional system which had kept them in menial jobs and at discriminatory pay scales for equal work. Most whites didn't want this, some from pure prejudice, some because as employers they benefited or thought they benefited from underpaid labor, some because as workers they saw a threat to their own security and living levels.

I became involved in 1941 in what became an important test case. Three major defense contractors in the New York metropolitan area—Grumann Aviation, Republic Aviation and Fairchild Aviation—were advertising in many parts of the country for high school graduates, offering to bring them to New

York and incorporate them in apprenticeship training programs for the manufacture of airplanes and airplane parts. At that time, New York had an integrated school, the School of Aviation Trades, which taught precisely the skills for which these manufacturers were advertising. Every white graduate of this school was snapped up by the first company to which he applied, but at this particular moment seventeen Negroes had been graduated as part of a class, and all three companies refused to take a single one of them.

After several discussions among ourselves at the Catholic Interracial Council we invited other agencies and individuals to a joint discussion. That meeting, held at our office, was attended by representatives of the Urban League and the NAACP, among others. I recall specifically Elmer Carter, Judge Stephen Jackson, and Harold P. Herman, a New York State assemblyman recently named chairman of a committee to study employment practices throughout the state and recommend means of reducing discrimination. We decided to form an ad hoc committee to deal with the case of the Seventeen Negroes, as it came to be called. I was named secretary and instructed to begin negotiations. I wrote to each of the companies, and not a single one did our organizations the courtesy of a reply.

So we took the matter to the public. The Catholic Interracial Council, for its part, adopted a strong resolution at its meeting, and the *Interracial Review* printed an equally strong editorial. These were distributed to the Catholic, the Negro and the labor press, and they were widely quoted and commented upon. The other organizations represented on our ad hoc committee took similar action through their respective organs. We worked out a program under which letters were written to Congressmen and Senators, a formal complaint was entered with the office of General Grunther, executive secretary to co-ordinate defense industries, and state and city officials were alerted. As can be imagined, the companies quickly recognized that the game wasn't worth the candle. They employed the seventeen

Negroes, and they reformulated their hiring practices to ensure that we would never again be tempted to come after them.

The success of this experiment played a significant part in encouraging the development of the March on Washington Movement, a proposal first made by A. Philip Randolph in 1941. Its purpose was to persuade the executive and legislative branches of the Federal government to put an end to all discriminations in bodies under their control and in firms enjoying government contracts. It quickly became a national issue; and to avoid a showdown, President Roosevelt in June 1941 issued Executive Order No. 8802 which banned employment discrimination in defense industries and in the government. As commander in chief, however, he did little at this time for the Negro in the armed forces. And that was indeed a sorry tale.

All armed service units were segregated and continued to be so throughout the war. In the Navy, prejudice was particularly bitter. As recently as 1937, the students of the Naval Academy at Annapolis, with the connivance of their superiors, had ostracized a Negro plebe, George J. Trivers, named by Congressman Arthur Mitchell, hazed him with refined cruelty, and hounded him in order to chalk up so many demerits against him that he would be flunked out. Trivers reached the breaking point and withdrew. An intelligent, hard-working student was thus sacrificed to the color of his skin. It was not until 1942 that a Negro got a commission in the Navy, Bernard Whitfield Robinson, a summa cum laude graduate of Boston College made an ensign in the U. S. Naval Reserve. If the other services were no worse, they were little better. The head of a project instituted by the Air Force at Tuskegee, Alabama, in 1940, to train Negro pursuit pilots, resigned in 1943, charging that the air command had "wholly unscientific notions that race somehow controls a man's capacity and aptitudes," with the result that they rejected every Negro applicant for pilot training and restricted Negro enlisted men mostly to labor work.

When Negroes went into the armed services, the discriminations they had known in civilian life went with them. For incomprehensible reasons, the segregated training camps were located mostly in the South, and Northern Negroes were expected to conform to patterns they had never known and which were grossly insulting to the uniform they wore. In these communities, white civilian policemen were not restrained in their repression of Negro soldiers. A Negro sergeant was shot dead by a policeman as he lay helpless on the sidewalk in an Arkansas town. Another soldier was killed in cold blood by a Baltimore policeman. According to a War Department statement, city and state police in Alexandria, Louisiana, shot and wounded more than a dozen Negro soldiers in a one-sided battle early in 1942. Negro soldiers were dragged off buses and kicked out of bars.

Rather than stretch out a grim litany, I can sum up the basic situation in a short extract from an article we published in the *Interracial Review*. It was entitled "He Fought for the Four Freedoms," and it was written by a Jesuit professor at Regis College, Denver, Colorado, Joseph P. Donnelly.

"This morning," it opened, "our college faculty attended the funeral of our first student to die wearing the uniform of our country. . . . The flag of our country decorated our departed. Yes, Walter was fittingly honored and he deserved to have been so treated. He was a near-great in the athletic world. In his studies he had done well. His fellow students had liked and respected him. He wasn't well fixed financially, but his companions held him in high esteem. He had many friends. They liked his wit, his humor, his unfailing good manners. And now he is dead. He died violently, suddenly, from gunshot wounds. A chaplain reached him in time to hear his confession and anoint him. Walter is probably still making merry, still causing mirth. But his death—that is something else again.

"You see, Walter didn't die from a bullet fired from an enemy gun. The Axis army neither in Libya nor in the South Seas saw our first casualty. He never got that far. Walter was a

Negro. He died from a bullet fired by an American citizen, on American soil. The Democracies killed Walter. The hand which struck him down is owned by a man with a white face, a man in whose favor the principles of democracy work to their fullest extent. But not for Walter."

This was the kind of thing which helped give the moral impetus for the March on Washington Movement. It defined its goals and revealed its strength at a monster rally in Madison Square Garden in June 1942, under the leadership of A. Philip Randolph. One of the interesting things about that rally is that it was denounced by both the Stalinist and the Trotskyite factions of the Communist party. We were off to a good start. The speakers were A. Philip Randolph, who had become the national director of the Movement, Dr. Channing H. Tobias, national director of the colored division of the YMCA (and later a member of the U.S. delegation to the United Nations), Walter White, executive secretary of the NAACP, Dr. Mary McLeod Bethune, director of the Negro Youth Division of the National Youth Administration, Lester Granger, executive director of the National Urban League, and Father LaFarge.

Addressing the Madison Square meeting, Mr. Randolph hailed President Roosevelt's Executive Order No. 8802 as a first step, while warning that it was not enough. "We are fighting to kill Jim Crow now, during the war," he insisted. "In Washington, D.C., the national capital, no Negro can exercise his constitutional and civil rights to attend a public theater, and he can starve to death with a thousand dollars in his pocket in downtown Washington in the midst of countless eating places. . . . If the President does not issue a war proclamation to abolish Jim Crow in Washington, the District of Columbia, and all government departments and the armed forces, Negroes are going to march, and we don't give a hang what happens. . . . The Negro is not challenged to prove his loyalty to the government and to democracy. The government is challenged to prove its loyalty to democracy and to the Negro."

Dr. Tobias echoed the same thought. "We are here," he ended his speech, "to remind the nation that the denial of fundamental citizenship rights under the Constitution of the United States and the Bill of Rights, and not the protest against that denial, is the real threat to successful prosecution of the war effort."

Father LaFarge for his part reaffirmed the principles enunciated in a statement of policy on employment of Negroes signed by leading Catholic industrialists, labor leaders and intellectuals, which the Catholic Interracial Council had issued the previous month, and which formed an integral part of the entire program toward which the Movement was working. "The policy of many of the defense industries in not employing Negroes is unjust, undemocratic, and constitutes a serious threat to our national unity," it said. "The Negro who is capable of going into industry must be absorbed into it just like any other capable worker. . . . Whether the denial of such opportunity proceeds from employer policies or union practices, or whether it may be chargeable to community attitudes does not alter the nature of the injustice, nor vary the harmfulness of its effects."

Long afterwards, A. Philip Randolph let me in on a curious secret about Father LaFarge's participation in this particular meeting. So many Negro organizations had been infiltrated by Communists, who were riding high in those days, that the March on Washington Committee decided the simplest way to keep them out was to adopt a policy of barring all white participation. However, they also saw that such a policy could raise objections that they were creating a Jim Crow in reverse situation. So by common consent, they decided to call on Father LaFarge as one white man whose anti-Communist credentials were impeccable.

All these activities brought no miraculous overnight change. A Labor Department report in mid-1943 revealed that in March, April and May of that year, three million man-hours were lost in strikes called by white workers protesting the employment or upgrading of Negroes and in riots resulting from the same cause. In October 1943, a Washington bureaucrat ruled that the order of President Roosevelt demanding non-discrimination clauses in government contracts was not "mandatory" but merely "a directive." But we kept the pressure up, and the President in November overruled his legalistic bureaucrat. And thus, step by step, we moved forward. By the end of the war, a million and a half Negroes were in essential industries, a third of them performing skilled or semiskilled operations. The aircraft industry's quota was up from practically nil to 150,000. Personnel in shipbuilding had doubled to 200,000. Of 250 plants surveyed by the National Urban League and reporting substantial Negro employment, more than half had no Negroes before the war.

But perhaps the most far-reaching of the outgrowths of the March on Washington Movement was the creation of a national council to urge legislation for a permanent federal Fair Employment Practices Commission. Original members of the council included Dr. Alan Knight Chalmers, A. Philip Randolph, Winifred Raushenbush (Mrs. James Rorty), Monsignor John A. Ryan of NCWC, and myself.

The FEPC idea had been developing for quite a time. It started at the state level, and the first state to vote such a law was New York, thanks in large part to the initiatives of Assemblyman Harold P. Herman, a Catholic and a staunch friend of the Catholic Interracial Council. Indiana followed the New York initiative and by the end of the war similar bills had been drafted in a dozen other states. At the federal level, the usefulness of legislation of this kind had been demonstrated by the working of the FEPC created by presidential order under emergency powers in 1941, but due to expire with the end of the emergency. In 1945, Senator Dennis Chavez introduced a bill in Congress, and it was immediately countered by a bill sponsored by Senator Robert A. Taft calling for a commission to "persuade" employers and unions to discontinue discriminatory practices. Immediately, we were launched on the second most popular of the arguments of the prejudiced (the first, of course, being the issue of marrying your daughter). Legislation, said Mr. Taft, correctly if quite impertinently, will not cure individual prejudices.

A. Philip Randolph gave a magnificent answer to that one in testimony before a Senate committee. "It is a fallacy to construe race prejudice as synonymous with racial discrimination. They are two different things. Race prejudice is an emotion or feeling. Racial discrimination is a practice. While we cannot by law make a white worker love a Negro worker, or a Protestant worker love a Jewish worker, or a worker in Boston love a worker in Atlanta, we can stop the worker from closing the shops and the unions at the same time. . . . The Bill does not seek to make white workers, black workers, or Jewish or Catholic workers, love each other, but to respect each other's right to work and live."

The Chavez bill was not enacted, nor the one that followed it, nor yet the one that followed that. But we kept on pressing, for each year we made gains. We held another big rally in Madison Square Garden, New York, in February 1946, and this time we had a turnout of 15,000 sympathizers. The banner behind the platform proclaimed "We Have Just Begun to Fight," and the spirit of the meeting thundered the same sentiment. By then, the country had lost President Roosevelt, but that caused no change in the administration's support of our cause. "I come here tonight clothed with full authority to speak on behalf of President Truman," Secretary of Labor Lewis B. Schwellenbach told us. "I come with authority to tell you that he is just as determined as was his predecessor that this fair employment practices principle be enacted into law by the Congress of the United States." Never had an interracial occasion been graced with such a galaxy of star speakers: Senator Dennis Chavez, Senator Wayne Morse, James V. Carey of the CIO, Matthew V. Wohl of the AFL, Mrs. Franklin D. Roosevelt, just back from the UN meeting in London, Rabbi William P. Rosenblum, president of the Institute for Democratic Education, Fiorello LaGuardia, former Mayor of New York, Judge Jacob Panken of the Jewish Labor Committee, Milton Webster of the Sleeping Car Porters, Roy Wilkins of the NAACP, Roger Baldwin of the American Civil Liberties Union, Orson Welles and Helen Hayes, and of course A. Philip Randolph.

It was my privilege to speak for the Catholic Interracial Council, and in accordance with our policy, I dwelt primarily on the moral issue involved. I remember that I used one phrase which, even if not original, struck a chord in every heart. "In a democracy," I said, "no issue is settled until it is settled right."

Victory did not come easy. The coalition of Northern reactionaries and Southern white supremacists had solid control of the Senate. It was not until 1957 that Congress enacted a civil rights measure, after an interval of eighty-two years of inaction in this area. But even Congress is unable to block the forward march of the nation. The groundwork laid by the dedicated individuals and small groups had by the middle of the century made such an impact on the American conscience that ways would be and had to be found to bring both law and practice steadily nearer the principles that hold us all together. Bishop Francis J. Haas was in large part responsible for a mobilization of Catholic opinion on a level never before realized. While Dean of the School of Social Science at the Catholic University in Washington, he was named in 1943 as chairman of President Roosevelt's Fair Employment Committee, a new high point in a lifetime of dedication to public work, with special stress on labor rights and the rights of the Negro as a citizen. His transfer in the same year to the diocese of Grand Rapids, Michigan, did not lessen his activity. "Shield of the exploited and sword against the exploiter" was how the official publication of the American Newspaper Guild, CIO, in Grand Rapids, hailed him three years later.

Within the Catholic community, he used his full authority

as a bishop to insist on justice, and justice now. In 1946, after World War II had just ended, he told a mass meeting in Grand Rapids: "Some influential employers took their obligations to Negro workers seriously, and enforced a policy of non-discriminatory employment throughout their plants, both in hiring and upgrading. I regret to say that of the cases that came to my notice, not more than two important Catholic employers took that stand." He constantly urged both the states and the Federal government to enact non-discriminatory (FEPC) legislation, to prevent an employer from denying a man a livelihood because of his color. "Both Christian ethics and common decency require government to put an end to such injustice and inhumanity." In 1947, he accepted appointment on President Truman's newly created Committee on Civil Rights, and his active part in this and other programs until his death in 1953 did much to shape the whole subsequent direction of the civil rights movement.

Other high-placed Catholics took up the challenge. "My reason for supporting this legislation is a very simple one," wrote Bishop Robert E. Lucey, of San Antonio, Texas, in a statement to a Senate subcommittee in favor of a federal FEPC law. "Negroes, Mexicans and other minority groups are human beings like ourselves, creatures of equal dignity and identical destiny. The Ten Commandments, threatening sanctions in the future, have not brought them justice. Only civil law, applying sanctions now, can compel unscrupulous employers to treat them fairly."

Nor had the years dimmed the voice or enthusiasms of my dear friend, Monsignor John A. Ryan, of NCWC's Social Action Department. As he had pleaded for the League of Nations, he now pleaded for the FEPC. Opponents of this legislation, he told the Senate subcommittee, say that "You cannot make men moral by legislation. If that argument were pushed to its logical conclusion, it would be equivalent to the assertion that we should abolish all the civil laws against murder, theft, extortion, and many other crimes."

By now, the moral voice was being heard across denominational lines. Congressman Charles M. LaFollette of Indiana, identifying himself as a Protestant lawyer, said that he found a striking similarity between his own thinking and that of "John Brophy, George Hunton, Father LaFarge, and other Catholics." In the course of a powerful statement, he said: "Fundamentally, the fight for a permanent federal FEPC, with enforcement powers, is not one of jobs for Negroes, nor is it even one of fair play with Negroes and other minorities. It is deeper than that. It is a soul-cleansing attempt to cleanse the nation of an anti-democratic and anti-Christian hypocrisy." And President Truman, who combined a moral sense with an unerring grip on the country's emotional pulse, also put himself clearly on the record. "The principle and policy of fair employment practice," he declared, "should be established permanently as part of our national law."

The total effect of the Senate's rearguard action was that the nation proceeded to bypass Congress and finally forced it to follow. By 1961, when the second federal civil rights legislation since 1875 was enacted, a law which laid special emphasis on the equal right to work of every citizen, seventeen states and many cities had their FEPC legislation, and the principle of fair employment practices had become a definite part of the American ethic.

The fact that our socio-political system is so flexible that it can find ways to circumvent the defects of congressional procedure does not in any way, it seems to me, absolve Congress for its failure to lead. The ability of the obstructionist minority bloc in the Senate to prevent passage year after year of anti-lynching laws will go down in history as a blot on our system, (4716 lynchings between 1882 and 1946), even if public opinion finally achieved what the legislators would not.

And, of course, the abdication by Congress of its responsibilities played no small part in the expansion of the activities of the Supreme Court, an expansion often criticized as an up-setting of the balance of powers on which our Constitution rests. If this had happened or is happening, then I suggest that Congress must itself carry a major share of the blame.

In the civil rights field, the most basic intervention of the Supreme Court was unquestionably the unanimous decision of May 17, 1954, that the "separate but equal" principle in race relations formulated by the same court in 1895 could no longer be sustained in public education, because in the United States of the mid-twentieth century, an imposed separation excluded the possibility of equality. As pioneers in the field of educational integration, the Catholic Interracial Councils had supported the NAACP, which was the protagonist in the protracted litiga-tion, and we utilized the victory to bring further pressure on Catholic schools, although the decision did not affect them directly. The history of this landmark has been told many times, so I shall confine myself to commenting on a few com-mon misconceptions.

Surveys of the progress of integration in the Southern states made periodically during the years following the decision some-times conveyed the impression that the Catholic school systems in some places showed less progress than the public schools. While it is abundantly clear from what I have said earlier that the Catholic record is far from spotless, I think that in most cases this impression was mistaken. The reason very often was that the Catholic systems had already been integrated and con-sequently did not show up in the figures. In a few Southern states, in addition, the Catholic population is very small and the white and Negro members are so distributed that de facto segregation continued simply because only white or only Negro children lived within the area served by a particular school.

The violence that later arose at such places as Little Rock in the implementation of the decision have caused many to assert that the Supreme Court was wrong in trying to foist on the

American public a situation for which the country was not ready. I think the blame for this violence lies elsewhere. The reaction of public opinion to the May 1954 decision was a very interesting one. Southern governors, attorney generals and senators agreed with the overwhelming majority of American lawyers that the issue was settled for all time. I joined at that time with other interracial leaders in urging President Eisenhower to take advantage of this unusual era of good feeling and move rapidly to implement the decision.

The President, unfortunately, did nothing. He would not even go on record in support of the Court's decision. Time and again, we called on him to move, warned him that his inaction was encouraging the opposition to organize. There is on the record, for example, a resolution adopted at a meeting of the Catholic Interracial Council of New York in 1956, deploring that after two years the nation still didn't know where its chief leader stood. "The President of the United States," it said, "should make his position clear and certain."

He did not do so. Instead, the Knights of the Ku Klux Klan, who had formally disbanded in 1944, began to reorganize and gather strength. The wartime decision to go out of business may have been primarily tactical, but there is no doubt that it reflected a decline in the influence of this group of hatemongers. It took time after the Supreme Court decision to stir up the bitterness anew and to make the Klans and the equally barbaric White Citizens Councils reach the strength which they were able to exert when the court finally forced an unwilling executive to implement its decisions. Little Rock need never have happened.

Another major form of integration which occurred during those same years was handled with decision and consequently reached its goal smoothly. In spite of the opposition of General Eisenhower, who was U. S. Army chief of staff up to February 1948, President Truman in July of that year issued Executive Order No. 9981, which declared that it was "the policy of the

President that there shall be equality of treatment and opportunity for all persons in the armed services without regard to race, color, religion or national origin." The President at the same time named a committee of seven civilians not in government service, and responsible directly to him, to advise on how the stated policy could be most rapidly implemented without impairing efficiency or morale. The chairman was my long-time friend Charles Fahy, now a judge of the U. S. Court of Appeals, a native of Georgia and graduate of Notre Dame and Georgetown, a man with a record of public service, including a period as president of the Catholic Association for International Peace.

After long discussions with the civilian heads of the services and with service personnel of all ranks, as well as with the President and his two assistants on minority problems (David Niles and Phileo Nash), the committee decided not simply to make broad recommendations but to present a concrete plan of action. By the time the committee had completed its report in May 1950, the service heads had already inaugurated the first steps of its recommendations and set up lines of policy which eliminated the need for further executive action. This was officially recognized in a public statement made by President Truman in the same month. It took note of the report and of the fact that programs had been introduced in all services to execute its recommendations "with a consequent improvement in military efficiency."

Back in December 1941, within days of the attack on Pearl Harbor, I wrote an editorial for the *Interracial Review* entitled "No Postponement." Unlike Dr. William DuBois, who in July 1917 had called on his fellow Negroes to forget their special grievances until after the victory of the democracies, I proclaimed that the issues underlying the war called for an acceleration of the rate of progress toward interracial justice. "It is essential that America should here and now demonstrate to the world that the rights and responsibilities of democracy are fully shared by Negro Americans." I was disappointed, at that time, at the slight response to my appeal. Today, on the contrary, whenever I reflect on the integration of our armed forces, I regain my faith in the power of the word, and I proclaim once more my slogan of "No Postponement." With decisive leadership, like that of President Truman and Judge Fahy in those circumstances, daring things can be accomplished rapidly and painlessly.

Chapter 10

All the external activities of the Catholic Interracial Council, which I have been describing for several chapters, ultimately depended on the survival and growth of the organization itself at its headquarters at 20 Vesey Street. The headquarters work was usually less dramatic but ultimately more important. It was there I spent the greatest part of my time.

When we moved to the tenth floor, through the generosity of a Jewish foundation, as I mentioned earlier, we had space to plan for the long term. Here we set up the De Porres Interracial Center, named for a Negro Dominican lay brother, one of the very few saints who was born and spent his entire life in the Western hemisphere.

The staff, as was proper, was always interracial. Although our level of payment was miserably low, there was very little turnover. Indeed, quite a lot of work was voluntary, including all contributions to the magazine. Our typical staff consisted of two Negroes, one Chinese, and one or two whites.

Shortly after we moved to Vesey Street, we inaugurated what I consider to have been the most fruitful of all the activities associated with the Council. This was a weekly forum, an opportunity for informal presentation of points of view and exchange of ideas. It was held every Thursday evening throughout the year, except on public and Catholic holidays, and it continued without interruption until the early 1960s.

The group was usually small. We were not disappointed if only a dozen or fifteen showed up. The speaker might be either white or colored, Catholic or non-Catholic, and the audience was spread all across the same categories. We started with a prayer and tea, then had usually a short formal exposition of the subject on which the speaker was an authority, followed by a frank general discussion. One person who was always present was Abigail E. Crawford, and she was almost invariably accompanied by her husband, Benjamin T. Crawford, a professor in Wadleigh High School. The Crawfords had joined the Council in the 1930s and, from the early 1940s, Abigail was in charge of the arrangements of the forum, including serving the tea. They were indefatigable in the interracial movement, writing, speaking, soliciting funds, looking for scholarship aid for talented Negro boys and girls, keeping open house for young people and adults of all colors and conditions. Only the other day Abigail was telling me that one of the most treasured memories of their lives is the part they played in getting Jennie Seabrook into the College of New Rochelle. Jennie was a Negro student of Ben at Seabrook, and they decided in 1943 that they would ask the College of New Rochelle to register her as its first Negro student. The faculty and students greeted her as a friend from the first day, and on graduation she entered the Order of St. Ursula as Mother Mary Vincent.

How many years of forums I attended, how many subjects, how many intellectual quests begun, how many friendships formed! Nobel prize-winning Norwegian novelist Sigrid Unset came to tell us that she felt literally sick the first time she entered a Southern railroad station and saw separate waiting rooms for white and colored. Father Urban Nagle and members of his Blackfriars Guild performed scenes from *Caukey*, a play by Father Thomas McGlynn, O.P., which reversed the social positions of Caucasians and Negroes in American society, presenting a conscience-pricking topsy-turvydom in which Negroes are the big shots and whites the underdogs. The play had its light touches, too, as when one culture-dripping Negro lady gushes: "Such unfortunate creatures, lazy, no education, no ambition, but you must admit that the darling white babies are the cutest things in the world."

If not precisely a paternal, we had at least an avuncular interest in *Caukey.* Shortly after Blackfriars was founded in 1940, the board of directors of the Catholic Interracial Council sent me to talk to its founders, Fathers Nagle and Carey, both Dominicans, to suggest that they experiment with interracial themes. *Caukey* was one of three or four they produced with considerable success. We publicized their efforts, and through us they sent invitations to prominent Negro leaders. We cooperated in a discussion of race relations from the stage of their theater with an invited interracial audience. The Blackfriars interracial presentations also included a dramatized biography of St. Martin de Porres.

Other memorable evenings brought Carey McWilliams, author of *Brothers under the Skin,* to urge that the United States remove all vestiges of racism from our immigration and naturalization laws; Thurgood Marshall, then legal counsel for the NAACP, to outline the legal strategy that won equal salaries for Negro teachers; Father Raymond Campion to describe how he got the Dodgers to sign Jackie Robinson.

We had a tremendous turnout the evening Cornelia Otis Skinner came to tell us about the progress of a long fight to desegregate the theater in Washington, D.C. The Daughters of the American Revolution (DAR), who have always had a genius for getting themselves bad publicity, were deeply involved in this operation. They owned Constitution Hall, one of the two live theaters in Washington, and they had outraged everyone worth outraging in 1939 when they refused to allow Marian Anderson to sing there. Mrs. Franklin D. Roosevelt promptly put them in their place by resigning from the DAR and asking Miss Anderson to sing at a concert for the King and Queen of England at the White House. She also sang for the people of Washington from the steps of the Lincoln Memorial. A truce was arranged for a concert in January 1943 for the United

China Relief. The terms were that Miss Anderson would sing in Constitution Hall to an audience not segregated by seating, but with the understanding that this "did not constitute a precedent."

Peace had hardly returned when the DAR demonstrated that indeed no precedent had been established. They denied Constitution Hall to pianist Hazel Scott, an action with which the United States Court of Appeals for the District of Columbia refused to interfere. The attempt to negate the advances made during the war raised a storm. Clare Boothe Luce, then a representative in Congress from Connecticut, led a group of DAR members who unsuccessfully urged an end to discrimination at the 1946 annual meeting.

Next, the actors began to get into the act. Ingrid Bergman said, when she was opening in *Joan of Lorraine* in Washington, that she would not act in a segregated theater, were it not for her contractual commitment. Dorothy Gish immediately took care of this by having a clause inserted in her contract excluding production "in any theater or auditorium in Washington, D.C., from which any persons are barred because of race, creed or color, or in which segregation is practiced on either side of the footlights." Eugene O'Neill gave a public commitment that no plays of his would in future be presented in a segregated Washington theater. Miss Skinner became chairman of an anti-discrimination committee of the Actors' Equity Guild, a committee in which Raymond Massey also played a leading role. In October 1947 it reached an agreement with the League of New York Theaters to keep its actors off the Washington stage if the anti-discrimination policy was not ended by June 1948.

During the discussions leading up to this ultimatum, I spoke twice at meetings of the Council of the Actors' Equity Guild, and Miss Skinner did me the courtesy of saying, when she talked at our Catholic Interracial Council meeting, that she believed that my second intervention at the Council was a determining factor in the favorable vote. Washington had now reached the absurd situation whereby a Negro might sit in the audience in Constitution Hall, home of most concerts, but could not appear on the stage, while a Negro could appear on the stage of the National Theater but might not sit in the audience. Well, the National Theater refused to budge, preferring to transform itself into a movie house and abandon the legitimate theater to the non-professional but excellent experimental theater of Catholic University. It took several years for reason to prevail. But in the end, Washington got a fully integrated live theater, and even the DAR capitulated.

Another famous actor who talked at a forum of the Catholic Interracial Council of New York was Frederick O'Neal, who came down one Thursday evening in early 1956. He was then vice-president of the Actors' Equity Guild, and the date is important in relation to his theme. "Negroes represent ten per cent of Americans," he said, "but only one half of one per cent of the performers seen on American television are Negroes. More than just a few jobs for Negro actors are at stake. If a person from childhood seldom sees a Negro on TV or the movies, seldom hears one on radio and knows few personally, why then should not that person be apathetic or even hostile to the Negro when he petitions for equality? He has been taught by the simple act of omission that the Negro has no place in American life."

Prophesying that the situation would change because Negroes in America constituted a fifteen-billion-dollar, and rapidly growing, annual consumer market, Mr. O'Neal said it was sad that the only way to justice seemed to be through the pocketbook. Americans, he said, "should do things because they are right and not because of promise of reward. All who are created in the image of God should want to walk together in his footsteps."

Ten years later, the American advertising and television industries were belatedly and reluctantly waking up to the validity of Mr. O'Neal's argument. The pressure of economics combined with that of equal rights legislation was forcing them to give token acknowledgment on the screen to the fact that one

American in ten is Negro. But I wonder how many in these fraternities have yet caught up to Mr. O'Neal's moral position. Incidentally, Mr. O'Neal developed a serious interest in our work and joined the Council board of directors in 1963.

A major asset of the De Porres Interracial Center was the Claver Index. It helped to bring our work to the notice of every educational and research center in the country interested in any aspect of race relations, and I believe that most of the significant studies of race relations in the past quarter century are directly indebted to it. The Index is a bibliography of race relations that constitutes the lifework of a Chicago Jesuit, Father Arnold J. Garvey. He spent forty years indexing both historical and current information from periodicals, journals, pamphlets, books, and university theses. When the Index was turned over to us in 1939, it contained 40,000 entries, and from that time onwards, it was continually updated. It is thus a unique reference source for sociologists and other students of Catholic principles and attitudes on race relations, constantly used by and always available to the researcher. To supplement it, we developed a library of books and magazines dealing with problems in our area.

As befits a professedly Catholic interracial organization, we have always given prominence in our library and in our promotional efforts to Negroes on whom the Catholic Church had set her official seal of sanctity. Those on whom we acquired concrete data included a St. Moses who performed apostolic work in Africa in the sixteenth century; St. Benedict the Moor, a member of the Order of St. Francis of Assisi, canonized in the sixteenth century; and the Uganda Martyrs, canonized in 1965. Our primary concern, however, has always been for Martin de Porres, born in Lima, Peru, in 1579, the son of a Spanish nobleman and a Negro mother. A Dominican lay brother, he helped to found Holy Cross College in Lima, one of the first Catholic institutions of higher learning in this hemisphere. He promoted social welfare initiatives in close collaboration with a white Dominican lay brother named John Masias, a detail we stressed as evidence of the long history of Catholic interracial brotherhood. Beatified in 1837, Brother Martin was canonized by Pope John in 1964.

Another holy Negro in whom we took a special interest was Pierre Toussaint, confidential adviser of New York's fashion leaders of his day, who worshiped for sixty-six years, until July 2, 1853, in the same church of St. Peter's in which we met for our religious ceremonies, occupying Pew No. 25. The discovery of his grave in 1941 by a student of Seton Hall University, New Jersey, now Father Charles McTigue, of Fairview, New Jersey, was a piece of detective work worthy of Dr. Watson. It can be read, along with the rest of Toussaint's fascinating career in a biography sponsored by the Catholic Interracial Council and authored by Arthur Thomas and Elizabeth O. Sheehan (New York: Candle Press, 1953). The John Boyle O'Reilly Committee for Interracial Justice, an offshoot of the Catholic Interracial Council to which I shall refer shortly, sponsored an annual pilgrimage to his grave for many years, and during the pilgrimage in July 1951, Cardinal Spellman dedicated a bronze tablet affixed to the old headstone. Two years later, a second bronze tablet was unveiled at the entrance to St. Peter's, Barclay Street, as a perpetual reminder of the devout Negro who had conversed with God in that holy place.

With the permission of Monsignor Moore, we were able to participate in a dialogue Mass in the lower chapel of St. Peter's Church one Sunday morning every two months, and the Mass was always followed by a Communion breakfast in a nearby restaurant, or perhaps in the cafeteria of the downtown division of Fordham University, which was within walking distance. At the Mass, we sought to express the spirit which had always characterized the Catholic Laymen's Guild. We were particularly happy when we could get a Negro priest as celebrant.

Whenever possible, we invited a group likely to benefit from informal exposure to an interracial situation, the Catholic Evidence Guild, the Catholic Teachers Association of New York or one of the neighboring dioceses, the Catholic Daughters of America, the Alumni Race Relations Council. There was always a speaker at the breakfast, and usually a spirited discussion. Copies of significant talks were distributed to the Catholic press through the NCWC news service. After we organized our own news service in 1941, we gave all such activities wide publicity in the Catholic and Negro press of the United States, and we also got publicity in the national press and overseas when the occasion warranted.

I could go on forever with an old man's reminiscences, but for the moment I'll content myself with trying to summarize one of the many inimitable stories told by an associate at the *Interracial Review,* Theophilus Lewis. How can I describe Theophilus? One of the finest writers of English in my fairly extensive literary experience, he is a Chicago-born Harlemite, a professional newsman and theater critic, a veteran of World War I, whose name appeared in the *Review* for the first time in April 1936. From that time onwards, he hardly ever missed an issue, and any issue he missed was the poorer for his absence. Sometimes he wrote about plays and sometimes he pretended that he was writing about a play. But more often, he just expressed his philosophy of life, kindly, charitable, realistic, with a weakness for the Irish and a corresponding distaste for the English, the basis for which I never clearly established but which was capable of popping up in the most unexpected and sometimes embarrassing situations.

The Theophilus Lewis story I want to recall appeared in the *Interracial Review*'s December 1947 issue. It was provoked (I think that is the precise word) by one Reverend Jesse W. Routte, a Lutheran minister. Four years earlier, Reverend Routte had visited Mobile, Alabama, wearing the conventional black dress and fedora; and—to quote Theophilus's own words— he "was pushed around like any other 'nigger.'" Reverend Routte may not have been a quick-thinking man, but his mind compensated in depth for what it may have lacked in agility. He finally came up with a plan. In 1947, he went back to Mobile, and to confirm the absolutely foolproof nature of his invention, he took on Montgomery, too. Both cities opened their arms to him and greeted him as the whitest of white men and the welcomest of welcome tourists. He ate in restaurants in which other Negroes entered only as servants, and the local brass gave him the honors due to VIPs.

When in due course, he got back to his home in Jamaica, Long Island, he announced to all willing to hear, and Theophilus Lewis was one of those most willing not only to hear but to draw the logical conclusions, that it was the fault of Negroes themselves if they had troubles in the South. The Reverend Routte had simply affected a Swedish accent, more or less, and wrapped a towel round his head. That was all that Mobile or Alabama needed to change a black man into a white man.

Others before him had got away with one half or the other of the transformation, Theophilus observed. James Weldon Johnson, the long-time executive director of the NAACP had recorded in his autobiography, *Along this Way,* that he frequently avoided riding in Jim Crow cars in the South by speaking Spanish. Dicky Welles, a prosperous New York night club proprietor, on the other hand, adopted the oriental hat trick. When desirous of enjoying the salubrious waters of Miami beach or tempted to squander some of the profits of his New York night spot in a Florida pleasure resort, he rented a Mystic Shriner's turban and described himself as the Maharajah of Hattan on hotel pads. The genius of the Reverend Routte was to combine the two methods.

"There are passages in *Sartor Resartus,* Carlyle's thoughtful treatise on fashions," Theophilus sums up as might one who had for the first time looked into Chapman's Homer or gazed with eagle eye on the Pacific, "where the author seems to suggest that a Bond or Weber & Heilbroner suit, or a Stetson Hat, is more important than the man who wears it. Mr. Carlyle, it seems, had something on the ball. When the Reverend Mr. Routte ventured into Alabama wearing an Adam hat, he was just another 'nigger' in town. When he visited the same state wearing a turban, he was accorded the civilities of a distinguished foreigner.

"Carlyle's thesis, as I vaguely remember it—I have not opened the book in the last quarter century—is that a man's garment expresses his true personality. If Carlyle's theory is sound, the crackers are right when they accept or reject a man as an equal according to his hat. The suit, especially the hat, makes the man. A dark-skinned man in a fedora is a Negro. The same man in a sombrero may be a Latin.

"One reason why it is so hard to solve the interracial problem is because it is so difficult to discover the basis of race prejudice and nail it down. Difference of color is not the answer, since Rev. Routte, when he was recently wined and dined in Alabama, was wearing the same skin he wore when he visited the state four years ago. He was the same person in 1943 that he is in 1947, except that he changed hats. Race prejudice has been denounced for its injustice, cruelty and stupidity. Rev. Routte has proved that it is also silly."

I rank Theophilus Lewis among the great intellectuals I have known. But he was not the greatest genius, the one to whom God gave the most remarkable talents and who used those talents in the way God intended them to be used. That was another Negro, this one born and raised in Harlem, the daughter of a journalist friend of Theophilus and a great newsman in his own right, George S. Schuyler, New York editor of the Pittsburgh *Courier*. I want to mention Philippa Duke Schuyler, not only because she was a charming person and not only because she was featured at our Center, but because she was and is a real problem for those who insist that Negroes are by nature or design of providence inferior to whites, or that their talents are concentrated in certain narrow bands of the intellectual spectrum, such as sports and music.

Philippa was indeed musical. It was the talent she developed most highly. But what she had left over was enough to give a swelled head to most parents of any race or condition. Her parents labeled her a child prodigy before she was three months old, but I took it with a pinch of salt. Parents are like that. She sat up at three months, stood at five and walked at eight. Still, it didn't seem catastrophic. She could always make a living in a circus.

Things looked more serious when she knew all her letters at eighteen months, and when at twenty-eight months she could read, write and spell accurately all the 500 words of her vocabulary. Soon after that, she started typing letters to tell her mother she wanted to go out. Her parents stopped calling her a prodigy. They got worried. About this time, the New York *Herald Tribune* heard about her, and they sent their ace reporter Lincoln Barnett to interview her. Barnett later became science editor of *Life* magazine and interpreter of the Einstein theories. His two-column story made headlines all round the world, and provoked the most outraged reactions from the "progressive" educators. Children shouldn't learn to read until ten or preferably later. Here was a clear example of word-oriented parents imposing their pattern on their child, and they would live to regret it. (The child's mother, Josephine, had the misfortune to be a talented writer in her own right, so there was a double fixation in the family.)

George and Josephine became properly guilt-obsessed. They decided they would expose their daughter to music, an art in which neither had the slightest talent. Before she was four, Philippa was setting her favorite nursery rhymes to music. Before she was five, Iri Allison, president of the National Piano Teachers Guild, told the press he had found a musical genius, with a perfect pitch and a phenomenal memory, and *Time* devoted its musical section to her.

The Schuylers were not Catholics, but a friend put them in touch with Mother Georgia Stevens at Manhattanville Convent, then located near their Harlem home, on Convent Avenue. As Philippa's mother once described her in an article in the *Interracial Review*, Mother Georgia "had a Chesterfieldian talent for paradox, a sixteenth-century wit, an eighteenth-century candor, a deep and touching piety, an unrivaled knowledge of early church music (she had been a concert violinist before taking the veil and since then had written a dozen works at least on Gregorian chant), and her devotion to God and music was inexhaustible."

Philippa made a hit at her first encounter. She played a piece she had composed at four and entitled "The Cockroach Ballet." Why cockroaches rather than angels as a subject, Mother Georgia asked gently. Philippa's answer showed that she knew more about Harlem than the nun. "I have seen many cockroaches, Mother Stevens," she explained, "but I have never seen any angels."

She started music study at the convent right away and entered school in the fourth grade at age seven, giving a half day to general studies and a half day to music. She kept grades of 95 and better, received the medal in English when she graduated from eighth grade at ten. From twelve, by special permission of the Board of Education, she concentrated on music, keeping up her general studies with a tutor in her spare time. At eighteen, when she spoke French and Spanish fluently, she got high grades in the state college entrance examinations.

By now, she was a famous concert artist. At five, she had been the first child to play her own original music over a national radio hookup. At fourteen, she made her debut to an audience of 15,000 with the New York Philharmonic Orchestra at the Lewisohn Stadium. At twenty-one, she gave her first Town Hall recital, and concert tours of Europe, South America and Africa followed. But that did not affect her scale of values in the slightest. She was and is still ready on request to give the members and friends of the Catholic Interracial Council the same outpouring of her talent as she lavishes on the choice audiences of world capitals. Harlem has its angels as well as its cockroaches.

An annual highlight of the work of the Catholic Interracial Council was the conferring of the James J. Hoey Award for Interracial Justice. The award was set up in 1942 to keep alive the memory of Jim Hoey, our first president, who had died in November 1941. It took the form of a bronze medal designed by Georg Lober, a member of the New York Art Commission (though the first medals were cast in silver because of wartime restrictions on the use of bronze). Two awards were made annually. One went to a Negro and the other to a white Catholic layman who during the previous year had made an outstanding contribution to the cause of interracial justice. Frank A. Hall and Edward LaSalle were the first recipients, in September 1942. Frank was head of the press department of NCWC, and his handling of news about Negroes throughout his long journalistic career distinguished him as a professional journalist and convinced Christian. Edward was, in 1942, president of the recently established Catholic Interracial Council of Kansas City, Kansas. Considerably earlier, he had been an associate editor under Father William Markoe of the *Interracial Review* under its original name of *The Chronicle*. The following year, the awards went to Philip Murray, president of the CIO, and Ralph Metcalfe, the famous athlete. Ralph was a graduate of Marquette University, who as director of athletics at Xavier University, New Orleans, had brought the young Negro university into the top rank of national athletics. He received his reward *in absentia*, because he was on active service as a private in the U. S. Army.

I want to linger a moment with the lady who shared the 1944 award with John L. Yancey, a distinguished Negro labor leader. She was Louise Drexel Morrell, widow since 1917 of Colonel Edward Morrell. She shared with her half sister, Mother Katharine Drexel, a unique place in the history of the Catholic Church's relations with the Negro in the United States. In 1889, she joined with her older sister, Elizabeth Drexel Smith, in establishing an orphanage for boys, the St. Francis Vocational School, at Eddington, Pennsylvania, an institution that was integrated at her insistence. Just a few years later, in 1895, she and her husband started the St. Emma Institute, which I have mentioned earlier, and it has been conducted continuously since that time as a training school in industrial trades and farming for Negro boys, thanks to an endowment from Mrs. Morrell. Recently integrated, it has currently an enrollment of over 300 students under the care of the Holy Ghost Fathers. The St. Francis School gives both scholastic and vocational training at the high school level for orphans and boys from broken homes. It also is endowed, and it is conducted by the Christian Brothers.

After her husband's death, Mrs. Morrell devoted an ever greater part of her substantial wealth to a variety of charities. I have already described how I first met her when I became associated with the Cardinal Gibbons Institute. During the Depression, when other wealthy people worried about the threat to their personal fortunes, she thought only of helping the desperate, setting up a warehouse on her estate to distribute the wholesale quantities of food, shoes and clothing for which there was a constant stream of applicants. She took a personal interest in every work to which she contributed, following closely the affairs of the St. Emma Institute and the St. Francis School.

Over the years she carried on a steady correspondence with Father LaFarge and me, to ensure that no detail of the progress of the Catholic Interracial Council escaped her. Almost up to her death, she would insist that I travel from New York to Philadelphia once every six or eight weeks to make a report. She always sent her car to meet me at the station, and I would arrive in time for lunch. Her intimate friend and constant companion for very many years, Miss A. Leona Colby, would also be present at the lunch. Mrs. Morrell would then take a siesta, and at three o'clock we would meet for the business session. She came with her stenographer's notebook in which she recorded everything that interested her, and the reference files of letters and other pertinent data would also be produced. One particular concern was the *Interracial Review*, and she kept a monthly record of subscriptions, listing separately the paid and the unpaid. Although circulation grew slowly, she was never discouraged. "We are getting there," she would say enthusiastically.

Emanuel Friedman, a Philadelphia lawyer who for many years conducted a large part of the business and legal affairs both of Mrs. Morrell and of Mother Katharine, recently told me a story which gives the true flavor of this amazing woman. As a boy before he studied law, Mr. Friedman had worked for Colonel Morrell, and Mrs. Morrell had subsequently followed his career with interest, even to the point of subsidizing him without being asked when he was struggling during the Depression. Among the papers which came into his possession as a trustee of the estate after Mrs. Morrell's death, Mr. Friedman told me, was a note written on the back of an envelope which read simply: "See Rabbi for boys." The story behind it was as follows. Mrs. Morrell was a very well-organized businesswoman, and she had a habit of making a note of any pending business. The Friedmans are Jewish, and Mrs. Morrell was concerned that the children should have a training in their faith which the circumstances of his upbringing had denied their father. The memo found among her papers was her reminder to herself to see that Mr. Friedman executed the plans they had discussed. "I am glad to think that I must finally have satisfied her," Mr. Friedman concluded the story, "for when the slip of paper came into my possession, a line was drawn through the writing to indicate that the matter had been disposed of."

It was to me a great personal satisfaction that we chose her for the Hoey Award in 1944, because she died only a year later, on November 5, 1945, aged eighty-two. Her half sister, Mother Katharine, though five years her senior, survived her by almost ten years. She died on March 3, 1955, in her ninety-seventh year. She used to say that the Lord delayed her departure for the sake of her convents and the many good works she supported. She had a life estate in a considerable part of the Drexel properties, and each additional year she lived represented a substantial income to those who depended on her.

What happy memories the Hoey awards bring back to me. It was no more than a gesture, but at least it was a different kind of gesture than that to which interracial pioneers were accustomed. The names crowd back into my memory. Many of them have been mentioned already or will be mentioned in the course of my story: Anna McGarry of Philadelphia, sculptor Richard Barthé of New York, Clarence T. Hunter, first president of the St. Louis Council, Mrs. Roger Lowell Putnam of Springfield, Massachusetts.

The story behind the award to Mrs. Putnam is an interesting one. An editorial in *America*, in 1945, urging Catholics to help finance the education of Negroes, set her to thinking on how she could contribute. After some discussion, she and her husband decided they could afford to establish a permanent scholarship for a Negro student at Regis College, Weston, Massachusetts. They talked to their bishop, Archbishop (later Cardinal) Cushing of Boston, and on his advice they incorporated under the name of Catholic Scholarships for Negroes, getting such well-known citizens as Mother Eleanor M. O'Byrne, R.S.C.J., Martin J. Quigley, Oren Root, Jr., and G. Howland Shaw to join the board of directors. The Catholic Interracial Councils naturally lent their moral support and encouragement, and soon the organization was getting not only monetary contributions but offers of full or partial scholarships from colleges. Within ten years, more than fifty colleges and universities were co-operating, and the number of students being actively aided at any given time was well over two hundred. The work has since continued to grow and prosper.

Though a resident of New England, Mrs. Putnam is a

Southerner. She was born and raised in Maryland, and she is a direct descendant of Charles Carroll of Carrollton, a signer of the Declaration of Independence. Many other Hoey award recipients were also from the South. I think immediately of Mrs. Gladys D. Woods, a teacher from Greensboro, North Carolina, the first Negro woman to win the award; Judge Collins J. Seitz, of Wilmington, Delaware, whose ruling in the so-called Delaware School Case influenced the 1954 Supreme Court decision to end segregated schooling in the United States; John P. Nelson, a lawyer from New Orleans, who courageously represented Negro victims of prejudice in spite of the insults and economic reprisals of his fellow whites; William Duffy, of Wilmington, Delaware, as well as others I shall mention later.

I think the South can also justly claim Dr. Francis M. Hammond. Although he was born in Nova Scotia, he was one of the early graduates of Xavier University, New Orleans, where he won his B.S. in 1937, before going on to garner two more degrees at Louvain University, Belgium, and a doctorate in Quebec, after which he taught philosophy for several years at Xavier and subsequently at Seton Hall University, New Jersey —Seton Hall's first Negro professor. And the South also has strong claims on Richard Reid, though he was born in Massachusetts and educated at Holy Cross. Like Dr. Hammond, he chose a Southern belle as his wife, and he won fame as a Catholic newsman in Georgia from 1920 to 1940, before coming to New York and further honors as editor of the *Catholic News* from 1940 to 1961.

Two other full-time newsmen were award winners, George Moore in 1960, and Gerard Sherry in 1965. George, who worked for the Cleveland *Press*, was one of the first Negroes ever hired by a metropolitan newspaper. Gerry came to this country from the *Catholic Herald* of London in 1950 and worked on Catholic newspapers in Baltimore, California, and Atlanta, Georgia. One of his major editorial innovations was to make newspapers that previously had concentrated on specifically denominational concerns expand their vision to the social and religious problems of the entire community.

A small but important group of Hoey award winners were businessmen whose enlightened personnel policies helped to open new economic opportunity for qualified Negroes and to set an example to their business colleagues. One who immediately comes to my mind is Joseph J. Morrow, director of personnel relations for Pitney-Bowes, of Stamford, Connecticut. Here was a man who was color-blind in his office at a time when most personnel people were afraid to give a Negro a good job, even if they themselves had no personal objection. He was honored in 1953, and he shared the award that year with John B. King of Brooklyn, the first Negro to be named assistant superintendent and later executive deputy superintendent of schools of the New York Board of Education. Three years later, we honored Frank M. Folsom, president of RCA, a man with a record similar to that of Mr. Morrow. Always an advocate of equal job opportunity, he was long on record by his testimony before congressional committees in support of federal fair employment practices legislation. When he accepted the award, he was able to make a statement which few American executives could match. Since its beginnings in 1919, he said, RCA has adhered strictly to a policy of non-discrimination. "Advancement is based on the individual's achievement and potential for promotion. . . . Not only are Negroes performing effectively in manufacturing, but they are doing a fine job in research and engineering too. . . . Negro engineers are carrying out professional functions both as trainees and as RCA specialists on a completely equal basis with their white colleagues."

I imagine that a recipient in 1958 could make a similar claim for the various important activities with which he has been connected. This was Robert Sargent Shriver, then president of the Chicago Board of Education, first president of Chicago's Catholic Interracial Council, and general manager of the Merchandise Mart Building, Chicago. His fellow recipient was

James T. Harris, Jr., assistant director of the American Society of African Culture. Sargent Shriver subsequently took a leading part in the formation of the National Catholic Conference for Interracial Justice, an organization to serve as liaison for existing Catholic Interracial Councils and to encourage the formation of new ones. I always remember a remark he made to me at one of the early meetings of this body. He had just become the first head of the Peace Corps, and I congratulated him on that inspired projection of American largeheartedness and enlightened self-interest. "You should congratulate yourself, George," he replied with typical generosity. "The Catholic interracial movement and similar grassroots activities in this country laid the emotional foundation on which it is now possible to build the Peace Corps."

Charles F. Vatterott, Jr., of St. Louis, was another winner of the Hoey Award who exercised his leadership in the business community. He was a builder and real estate developer, and when we selected him in 1952, he had already constructed 5000 homes and sold them without regard to the creed or color of the buyers. There was, however, a built-in discrimination in his work, one for which no group over challenged him. A higher than normal proportion of his houses were designed for occupancy by large families. Mr. Vatterott was also the owner of St. Ann's golf course, the only privately owned links in St. Louis at that time with an integrated membership. The other recipient in 1952 was Joseph J. Yancey of New York, a United States Treasury official and a famous athletic coach.

George Meany, president of the combined AFL-CIO received the award in 1957, a decision that reflected the gratifying progress organized labor had made in its treatment of the Negro as a worker. George Meany himself deserved personally no small share of the credit for that advance, and he continued to live up to the pledge that he gave, on behalf of the AFL-CIO, as he accepted the award, namely, that "our policy of interracial justice shall continue to be a major objective of our

Federation." Yet entrenched prejudices can take an awful long time to die. Four years later, at the AFL-CIO annual convention in Florida at the end of 1961, A. Philip Randolph was still repeating his complaint of twenty years, that not all the member unions had dropped discriminatory practices in admission of members and apprenticeship training. What was different, however, was that nobody publicly challenged Randolph's facts any more or attempted to justify the discrimination. At most, they begged for more time to put their house in order.

In retrospect, I think the Council's rule making members of our own group ineligible for the Hoey Award may have been a little too rigid. There is one, in particular, that I regret did not get it, and that is Harold A. Stevens, who was twice president of the Council. A native of South Carolina and stepson of a Methodist minister, Harold took the train for Boston one day with the intention of enrolling in the law school of Boston University. To his dismay, he found on arrival that enrollments had closed a few days earlier. The only suggestion the registrar could make was that he should try the law school of Boston College. The registrar at Boston College checked his educational background and agreed to accept him with the promise that he would have to maintain an average of eighty-five per cent. "If I can't do better than 85," was Harold's reply, "I wouldn't want to be a lawyer." Harold is no empty boaster. Both in law school and in his entire career, he will always be found up there in the nineties.

Most of his classmates were white Catholics, and personal friendships led to a favorable impression of their religion. In his third year, he took a course of instruction and joined the Catholic Church. After graduation with the highest honors in his class, he moved to New York and went to work for a law firm in Harlem, took his bar examination and was admitted to the New York bar. This was in the late 1930s. He was only a short time in New York when he met Father John LaFarge and through him attended some meetings of the Catholic Interracial Council, liked what he saw and heard, joined the Council, and in 1940 was elected a director. Both before and after that date, he was a member of a team that made presentations of race issues to college and other audiences in the form of a court trial. I have already described another team in which Elmer Carter was the star witness to the status of the Negro in the United States. Harold Stevens played a similar role. I recall a particularly brilliant performance at Fordham University, with Harold testifying on the facts of Negro life and Father LaFarge on the Church's teachings on race relations. On that occasion, I had the job of prosecuting attorney and conducted the direct examination of the witnesses, then turned them over to those in the audience who wished to cross-examine them. Harold became president of the Council in 1941 and held the position until he went on active military service in 1943. At the end of the war he returned to his law practice and ran successfully for the New York State Assembly in 1946. His election was particularly gratifying, because he triumphed over a white opponent in a predominantly white district. After two sessions in the Assembly, he was elected a judge of the Court of General Sessions, from which he moved up to the New York Supreme Court and subsequently to the Appellate Division of that court. Meanwhile, he continued his active participation in the work of the Catholic Interracial Council, serving as president the second time in 1952.

If we failed to give him an award, he garnered a goodly number from other directions. He has honorary degrees from Boston College, Fordham University, Creighton University, and Manhattan College. He is a trustee of the Church Peace Union and a governor of the Guild of Catholic lawyers. And in 1953, the Pope conferred on him and on Gerard Carroll, chairman of the board of directors of the Catholic Interracial Council, the cross *Pro Ecclesia et Pontifice.*

The Catholic Interracial Council was particularly gratified by these papal awards, because they brought to six the number of our board members so honored. Three years previously, in 1950, *Pro Ecclesia et Pontifice* medals had been given to Elmo M. Anderson, Emanuel A. Romero, Maceo A. Thomas, and also to myself. I need not say that I was deeply gratified at this expression of the Holy Father's approval of the work in which I was engaged, and my pleasure was greatly increased because of the caliber of the men with whom I shared the honor. All three could rightfully claim to be interracial pioneers, with the record for length of service going to Elmo Anderson. He was executive secretary of the Catholic Board for Mission Work among Colored People from 1922 until his death in 1951 at the age of sixty-three. He was first president of the Catholic Laymen's Union, and a founder and long-time vice-president of the Catholic Interracial Council. He was the first Negro ever to receive an honorary degree from a Catholic college in the United States. The college was St. Vincent, Latrobe, Pennsylvania, and the citation recorded that he had worked unceasingly for twenty-six years "to develop interracial harmony."

Emanuel Romero was, I imagine, the first employee of a Protestant seminary ever to receive papal recognition for his lifework. Born in Kingston, Jamaica, in 1887, he first studied in his home town and later at Columbia University and Fordham in New York. After service as a first lieutenant in World War I, he joined the staff of Union Theological Seminary. In addition to his official clerical duties, he quickly became unofficial guide and counselor to many generations of students. He was a founding member both of the Catholic Laymen's Union and of the Catholic Interracial Council, and his outstanding gifts for handling delicate human situations were always at my disposal for the asking. He was a truly astonishing man. When he reluctantly retired from Union Theological Seminary under the age rules of the institution in 1954, more than fifteen hundred former students, most of them pastors of Protestant flocks, wrote letters which testified to his lasting influence on their ideas and behavior. He was a man of boundless activity, many times president of the Catholic Laymen's Union, a board member of the Catholic Interracial Council, an official of the American Legion, president of the local tennis club, chairman of the education subcommittee of the Mayor's Committee on Harlem, the most important man in Negro scouting and one of the most important in the entire scout movement in the United States.

Maceo Thomas belonged to what was then a very small group indeed. He was a successful business executive at a time when many Negroes with college degrees worked as elevator operators in New York. The business skills that brought him that unusual distinction were matched by his moral and spiritual qualities. He never yielded to the temptation to which successful members of deprived groups often succumb, namely, to turn his back on his own. He was a dedicated member of the Catholic Laymen's Union and the Catholic Interracial Council, a president of the former and a board member of the latter. His civic spirit was matched by that of his wife. I knew them well when they lived in St. Charles Borromeo's parish, and she put her heart and soul into development of the interracial school and community center Monsignor Drew started there. She fully deserved the honor she received when the National Catholic Conference on Family Life chose her as Catholic Mother of the Year in 1952.

God knows I have little stomach for telling the next story that comes up in my record of how we occupied our time at 20 Vesey Street, but truth is truth, no matter how it hurts. I can put the problem in the terms used by Father Charles Keenan, S.J., a Belfast-born associate of Father LaFarge on the editorial staff of *America* magazine. On his return from a two-month visit to his native Ireland, he reported as follows. "One Irish journalist told me, with pained indignation, about the prejudiced attitude he had encountered in a returning Irish-American. People in Ireland find it hard to understand how anyone with a Christian and Irish background could condone the injustice of discrimination and segregation."

Now, I yield to no one in my pride for the race from which I derive three fourths of my genes and a hundred per cent of my ideals. And from the outset, the Catholic Interracial Council had the support of distinguished Irish-Americans, Jim Hoey, Gerard Carroll, and Nicholas Donnelly and Thomas Diviney. But one would have to be as partisan as Theophilus Lewis not to see that the Irish were failing to pull their weight in the interracial movement, that on the contrary as a group they opposed the granting to Negroes of the same citizen rights their parents and grandparents had struggled to win for them. There were, in fact, very few of them willing to have their names associated with an organization called a Catholic Interracial Council. Yet we needed their active support. More than that, those of us who were Irish knew that the honor of our race was no less at stake than the benefit of the American Negro.

After a lot of discussion, we decided to try out the technique that had worked so often for Father LaFarge, the creation of a small specialized body with simply defined aims and a name neutral enough not to frighten anyone away at first glance. We worked up to it gradually. The first shots were fired by an Irish-born newsman who had providentially arrived in New York by way of Argentina. His name was Thomas Doyle, and he has since made himself a reputation in the Catholic press of the United States for his work on the editorial staff of the NCWC News Service and on that of Religious News Service.

Tom wrote a magnificent article in the November 1940 issue of the *Interracial Review*. He described the emotions with which he first saw New York, the traditional haven of Irishmen seeking justice and liberty, how he became an American and pledged his allegiance to the Constitution and Bill of Rights, and how he lost some of his illusions. For he discovered that the racism he had left behind in Europe was flourishing in

America, and that his own American cousins were actively supporting it.

It was a body blow to the Irish-Americans, precisely because of the truth it contained, and we did everything in our power to see that it was brought to the attention of as many of those to whom it applied as possible. Some were offended, but others had the humility to be impressed. Tom Doyle stuck to the job. He issued a challenge and an appeal to the Knights of Columbus. The top brass ignored it but others examined their consciences. He wrote a story about John Boyle O'Reilly, an Irish newsman born a century earlier, transported as a felon to Australia, from where he escaped to become editor of the Boston *Pilot* and to dedicate a great soul and a flaming pen to the double cause of justice for the Irish and for the Negro. The Negro, he once wrote, "is the most spiritual of Americans, for he worships with his soul and not with a narrow mind." When his adopted city of Boston in 1888 dedicated a monument to the Negro Crispus Attucks, the first American killed by an English bullet in the Revolution, he wrote the poem delivered at the dedicatory exercises. He was a good poet, and this is how he ended:

> Indian and Negro, Saxon and Celt,
>   Teuton and Latin and Gaul—
> Mere surface shadow and sunshine,
>   while the sounding unifies all!
> One love, one hope, one duty theirs!
>   no matter the time or ken,
> There never was separate heart-beat
>   In all the races of men!

James McGurrin, president of the Irish-American Historical Society, was one of those impressed by Tom Doyle's pleadings, and he wrote to the *Interracial Review* to say so. The upshot was the creation of the Irish-American Committee for Interracial Justice, a name later changed to the John Boyle O'Reilly Committee for Interracial Justice. We had some very distinguished members. In addition to Jim McGurrin, the roster included the late Chief Justice Joseph T. Ryan of the City Court of New York, the first chairman, William J. McNulty, Thomas J. Whalen, and Matthew J. Troy, all judges, State Senator John L. Buckley, John F. X. McGohey, now judge of the U. S. District Court, John P. O'Brien, Richard Reid, editor of the *Catholic News* and John J. O'Connor, former editor of the *Commonweal.* Its name and purpose confined it to those of Irish birth or extraction but the members showed their chauvinism in 1946. "Anyone who is that good has to be Irish," they said, and they incorporated Elmer Carter as an honorary member. I have never understood why they failed to do as much for that persistent rooter for the Irish, Theophilus Lewis, unless perhaps it was that Theophilus complicated things by becoming a Catholic, while Elmer Carter stuck steadfastly to the Methodist faith received from his parents.

The John Boyle O'Reilly Committee made a definite contribution to the interracial movement. A biography of O'Reilly, *Seek for a Hero,* which it sponsored, was a contribution equally to the history of the Irish in America and to the development of race relations during and after the Civil War. It exposed many leaders of Irish groups and associations to Catholic teaching on race relations. Many of its members were available to use their personal influence in a crisis. But I fear that, as a group, it has not yet succeeded in penetrating too deeply into the thinking of the great mass of middle-class Irish-Americans, one of the most resistant masses in today's America to the principles of fairplay and human dignity proclaimed by the Church to which they profess allegiance, and accepted in large part by the consensus of American opinion. John Boyle O'Reilly is still far from fully vindicated.

Chapter 11

The Second World War constitutes a clear dividing line in the history of the interracial movement, as in so many aspects of the life of the United States. Labor shortages in the industrial North brought great masses of Negroes out of the South into the ghettos of our big cities. The movement of troops caused Northern Negroes to be subjected for the first time to the rigid barriers of discrimination by means of which white Southerners sought to preserve their racial privileges.

As a result of this experience, the nation developed a greater awareness of the seriousness of the continuing problems and of the urgent need for basic solutions. It became fashionable to direct all attention to the South, where the offense against human dignity was most apparent, and to urge what would in effect be a new crusade by the North against the South.

Many Catholics developed such attitudes in step with the rest of the citizenry. I must confess, however, that I never felt tempted to go along. Deeply as I deplored the injustices in the South, I could never see a solution by the means proposed. The original founders of the Catholic Interracial Council of New York had always felt that the biggest impetus we could give to the cause of interracial justice in other parts of the United States, including the South, was to put our own house in order. The new factors introduced by the Second World War did not seem to me to invalidate that judgment in the least.

A small incident, which occurred in April 1945, confirmed me further in my judgment. I happened to be invited to speak on the same platform in the auditorium of Hunter College, New York, with Lillian Smith, the author of *Strange Fruit* and other successful novels. Lillian was not a Catholic, but she was an ardent advocate of interracial justice and a great admirer of Father LaFarge. When the original manuscript of Father La-Farge's autobiography, *The Manner Is Ordinary,* was sold at auction in New York, she outbid the two most persistent competitors, Kivie Kaplan of the NAACP and Roger Baldwin of the American Civil Liberties Union.

"You are a Southerner," I said to Miss Smith at the Hunter College meeting, "and I'd like to ask you what help can a group like our Catholic Interracial Council of New York give to your fellow workers and yourself in your efforts to secure justice for the Negro in the South."

"The greatest kindness you can do us," she replied forthrightly, "is to keep your advice, suggestions and criticisms to yourselves. Accelerate and extend your programs in your own neighborhood, thus demonstrating that progress in race relations is concretely possible in the United States. We are not stupid in the South. If we like what we see on the other side of the Mason-Dixon line, we can take the hint."

Acting on this advice, we continued to avoid a militant offensive against the Southland while our home defenses were in such poor shape. Nevertheless, we did what we could for those who asked our help, especially by encouraging them to form Councils similar to ours but adapted in name and function to the conditions of each city and region. We developed a simple formula, which we recommended to all enquirers. The original founding group should consist of five to ten, and it should include Negroes and whites. It should meet twice a month to study a basic course of race relations and problems, for which we prepared a reading list, and to train speakers for later appearances before local Catholic organizations. Often I would visit the group during this training course, or some of the members would come to New York and observe our methods

in action. From all this would grow a concrete program geared
to the needs of the particular city, and this would be submitted
to the local bishop with a request to approve the creation of a
Catholic Interracial Council and to designate a priest as its
chaplain and spiritual adviser.

Our attitude toward Washington, D.C., was perhaps a little
different from our feeling for the rest of the South. Regardless
of its geographic position, it was the national capital, set apart
from the surrounding states. As the home of diplomats from
every corner of the globe, it was exposed and it exposed the
United States to the ruthless spotlight of a world opinion in
which a nation's race practices were a test of the sincerity of
its commitment to the principles we were all proclaiming in
the newly founded United Nations. Every American, we felt,
had a right to participate in the fight for interracial justice in
Washington.

As it happened, however, we were able to get a native Wash-
ingtonian to lead the struggle. He was John J. O'Connor, a one-
time editor of *Commonweal* and subsequently head of the department of history of St. John's University, Brooklyn. He was
a founder-member in 1942 of the group which became the
John Boyle O'Reilly Committee for Interracial Justice. The following year, he joined the armed forces, and since that time
he has lived in his native city of Washington, D.C., teaching at
both Catholic University and Georgetown, and engaged in an
infinity of extracurricular activities. He was a founder member
of the Catholic Interracial Council of Washington, which held
an organization meeting in December 1944, at which I was
present and explained how our New York Council operated.
The highlight of the inaugural meeting on January 20, 1945,
was an address from moral theologian Father Francis Connell,
C.Ss.R., of Catholic University. The teachings of the Catholic
Church, Father Connell said, stand for "the full, unqualified
equality of the Negro with every other human being," and all

Catholics "should work for the day when the Negro will be granted the fullness of his natural and civil rights in our land."

John O'Connor took him seriously, and from that day forward he was a one-man tornado in his efforts to make his home town worthy of its position as the first city in the land. It was a man-size job. A committee on race relations of the Council of Social Agencies reported in 1946 that its study had "revealed a systematic pattern of gross denial and deprivation to the Negro population of the District of Columbia. We do not believe that healthy and mutually helpful relations between races can develop from a pattern no less degrading to those who impose it than to those who suffer under it."

The committee recommended drastic changes in the pattern of Washington's community life, laying stress on "four factors in respect of which the Negro citizens of this community are now grossly handicapped: health, housing, employment opportunities, and education. These are the keys to advancement. Adequate medical care, decent living conditions, a fair chance to work, and a fair chance to learn are a birthright of all Americans. They cannot be attained under a system of segregation. We cannot palter with practices and customs offensive to the most elementary instincts of human decency. We cannot set before the conscience of this community, the national capital of the United States, less than the ideal. We cannot in good faith recommend less than what seems just. We cannot offer anything less than full freedom to men and women born to the promise of freedom. And for this we tender no defense save that which may be found in Christian ethics and in the postulates that animated the formation of the American Union."

The Catholic Interracial Council immediately endorsed the report, and John O'Connor began to use his journalistic as well as his oratorical talents to put and keep Catholics in the forefront of the reform movement. As a member of the faculty of Georgetown University, he publicly ridiculed the university's policy of excluding Negroes from all its faculties, including its law and medical schools and its famous school of foreign service. He deplored equally the exclusion of Negro doctors from the staffs of Georgetown and other voluntary hospitals under Catholic control. I, for my part, welcomed a powerful new ally in a struggle in which I had been long engaged, and I gladly gave him a tribune from which to express his ideas in the form of a monthly column in the *Interracial Review*, a contribution which he still continues today. "We hear a lot about the brotherhood of science, the great fraternity of science," he wrote in one of his early columns in 1947. "Yet in the medical profession, neither the spirit of Christianity nor the spirit of science seems strong enough, either singly or in combination, to demand and insist on a change."

He became involved in the then flaming issue of segregation of Washington theaters, which I described earlier, even leading a picket line, and with his colleagues in the Catholic Interracial Council he got Eugene O'Neill to undertake that no play of his would ever again be shown in Washington to a segregated audience. He rejoiced without gloating when in the fall of 1948, Georgetown broke its self-imposed ban and enrolled a Negro in its law school, and Trinity College also admitted a Negro student, thereby completing the formal integration of the four major Catholic institutions of higher education in the capital. Catholic University had led the way in the late 1930s, and in September 1947, Dumbarton College admitted Mable Patricia Goins, of Charlottesville, Virginia, on a four-year scholarship awarded her by Archbishop (now Cardinal) Cushing of Boston.

But the Catholic Interracial Council in Washington had to fight on many other fronts as well. In 1953, a Negro could still hardly get a meal outside Union Station, except in government cafeterias and a few private cafeterias. Nearly all downtown hotels became suddenly booked out when a Negro appeared in the lobby. A white cab seldom stopped to pick up a Negro, and Negro cabs were hard to find in the center of town. No private hospital had a Negro physician on its staff, and anyone wishing to be buried in Washington had to be satisfied with a segregated grave. But in that year, the Supreme Court ended a long legal fight by ruling that a civil rights law enacted in the 1870s had never been repealed, and that in consequence no restaurant could exclude a Negro client. The Catholic Interracial Council had been one of the most active organizations in carrying this issue through the courts. They had found top-flight lawyers willing to serve without fee, and they shared with other organizations the cost of printing the legal documents. The Council played a similar role in the Bolling Case, designed to abolish segregation in the public school system, a case which similarly was carried all the way to the Supreme Court in 1953.

Among the organizations with which the Washington Council co-operated was the Leadership Conference on Civil Rights. Established in 1950 with Roy Wilkins as chairman and Arnold Aronson as secretary, the Conference sponsored a meeting attended by 2000 persons at the Auditorium of the Department of Labor in 1956. The focus of the meeting was on the need for federal legislation to protect the right to vote, and the problem was made concrete by holding "mock hearings" with three victims of intimidation. I was invited to act as counsel for one of the three, John Blackman of Elloree, South Carolina. The evidence established that the White Citizens Council had enforced a boycott of Mr. Blackman, a builder, on the ground that he was openly supporting school integration. Although he always paid cash for supplies, he was cut off from his sources of cement, lumber and shingles. The Ku Klux Klan burned crosses on his lawn several times. "Did they tell you to get out of town?" I asked him. "Yes," he answered, "but I refuse to be intimidated. I am going to stay in Elloree despite their threats."

We didn't achieve much for Mr. Blackman. Shortly afterwards, he was forced to close his business. But he didn't give up. His two sons and he started an agency to sell subscriptions to Negro magazines and newspapers. And we had an impact on the national scene. The hearings played a significant role in the campaign which ultimately secured the passage of the Civil Rights Act of 1957.

It was in Washington also that the first steps were taken in an operation that helped to project the Catholic interracial movement dramatically onto the national Catholic scene. A major existing organization, the St. Benedict the Moor Apostolate, asked us—in effect—to infiltrate it. Needless to say, we were most happy to do so.

The action started in a warm-yellow brick building in Washington, D.C. It is an unconventional-looking building, even if it is technically a convent, the home of a Franciscan community and the theology seminary of the Franciscans of Holy Name province. Holy Name College, located in the "Little Vatican" (Brookland) section of Washington, is built on trapezoidal lines rather than the conventional rectangular. It is buttressed every few yards by a brownstone pillar that culminates in a large bust of one of the numerous Franciscan saints. The building gives the distinct impression of New World Aztec overlaying Old World Franciscan.

It was here that the seeds of what Father LaFarge termed "the second stage of the Catholic interracial movement" were planted; it was here a talk of mine set in motion the forces that would result within a few years in a grand alliance between the Catholic Interracial Council and the Third Order of St. Francis.

I first became aware of the Franciscans at Holy Name College in the late 1940s when I learned that the seminarians had started a movement to make the life of St. Benedict the Moor more widely known. My first contacts with the seminarians were casual. In line with our policy of accumulating all information about Negro saints, I wrote to ask what they could contribute to the St. Peter Claver file. Getting a positive response, I wrote once more to encourage the seminarians. I pointed out to them that St. Benedict could become an important symbol for Americans. At that time, he was the only formally canonized Negro saint, and he had been canonized for almost 150 years.

The St. Benedict the Moor Apostolate was started in 1947 by Frater Dominic Coscia, O.F.M. (now a Bishop in Jataí, Brazil), as an informational apostolate in response to the lack of knowledge among Washington's Negro population about Negro Catholics and Negro sanctity. Frater Dominic and his fellow seminarians managed within a short time to produce biographical pamphlets, novena booklets, prayer and holy cards, twelve-inch statues and medals. In 1949 they launched the first issue of a quarterly, *St. Benedict the Moor Newsletter*. By 1951, their publicity had become nationwide and every American bishop at least knew of their work.

The almost instant growth of the apostolate convinced me that here was a potentially strong ally at a time when Catholic allies were scarce, and I encouraged and helped the seminarians as much as I could. I had given talks at Holy Name College on a number of occasions. After one of these talks, not long after the Supreme Court desegregation decision in 1954, discussion with those involved in the apostolate centered around the almost total lack of impact of their work on the civil rights movement. The students felt that merely promoting devotion to a Negro saint fell short of exhausting the organization's potential contribution to the quest for interracial justice. As a result of these discussions, the seminarians, then under the leadership of Frater DePaul Genska, O.F.M., decided to make interracial justice in American society a formal goal of their movement. The apostolate had become interracial as well as informational.

I gave my most important talk at Holy Name College in the fall of 1957. This talk was important not so much because of what I said as because of the response of one seminarian newly arrived at the College. As he later confided to me, he had up to that time no involvement and no interest in the civil rights movement. His name was Frater Roy Gasnick, O.F.M., and he was to be the key figure in the establishment of Action for Interracial Understanding as a nationwide movement in the Third Order of St. Francis.

In the change of leadership in the St. Benedict the Moor Apostolate the next year, Frater Roy became the editor of the *Newsletter*. He and the others working with him decided to make a complete review of the whole apostolate and to inaugurate any changes necessary to make it a truly effective contribution to the interracial movement. The review resulted in two conclusions: (1) that the Franciscans had been making capital of the race problem as a means of spreading devotion to St. Benedict the Moor, and, unintentional as it was, this was pure exploitation; (2) to correct this, means and goals of the apostolate had to be switched around, that is, the solution to the race problem had to become the goal while St. Benedict the Moor, as an intercessor and symbol of the Franciscan social philosophy, would become the means.

Frater Roy, beginning at this time, kept a steady contact with the New York Council and myself. One early letter posed the problem of approach for the apostolate. Frater Roy strongly believed that the most important contribution the Franciscans had to offer the interracial movement was the concept of social charity envisioned by St. Francis and formulated by St. Bonaventure and Duns Scotus. He saw St. Benedict the Moor as a concrete symbol of the practicality of this approach: "He was a Negro accepted without question into an all-white community and, even more than this, was chosen by his white confreres in two different friaries to be their superior. The concept and commandment of Christian love not only prevented a race problem in the life of St. Benedict the Moor, but even went so far as to raise him to that raceless class of people we call saints." Frater Roy queried then whether an approach of interracial charity and understanding would look as if the Franciscans were challenging the approach of interracial justice as promoted by the Catholic Interracial Council, or if it would possibly lead to confusion in the ranks of the still rather small Catholic interracial movement.

As a reply, I sent Frater Roy a copy of Father LaFarge's book, *No Postponement*. The book hit its mark. In an early history of the movement published in the *Interracial Review*, Frater Roy noted: "It was here that the Jesuit influence entered in. In one of his books, *No Postponement*, Father John LaFarge, S.J., devoted a chapter to arguing the necessity for developing the concept of social charity in relation to the race field. In the course of the chapter, he remarked: 'Hitler . . . raged against the priests and brothers of the three Franciscan Orders precisely because these men were close to the people. The Franciscans were armed with a tremendous weapon . . . the power of God-inspired social love.'" The young Franciscans at Holy Name College had taken this as their challenge, and the challenge gave them their approach.

Reaction to this new approach was far greater than Frater Roy and his co-workers had expected. A number of the strong, clear and dynamic articles written for the *St. Benedict the Moor Newsletter* were reprinted in national newspapers and magazines. Bishop Thomas Gorman of Dallas-Fort Worth ordered Frater Roy's "Prayer for Interracial Charity to St. Benedict the Moor" to be said after Mass every Sunday. Correspondence became so great that the seminarians of Holy Name College realized they had something on their hands too big for them to handle. Working through their Provincial, they arranged to have the apostolate adopted by the lay Franciscans of the North American Federation of the Third Order of St. Francis, as an educational, public relations and Catholic Action project. The Central Office of the Third Order in Chicago accepted the apostolate in October 1959, and the official transfer took place in February of the following year.

Between October and February, I helped Frater Roy in publicizing the transfer of the apostolate through my good friend Frank Hall of the NCWC News Service. We were both anxious to get as much publicity as possible since at this time news about Catholic involvement in the civil rights movement was still inadequate.

Frater Roy was ordained to the priesthood that year, and I attended his first Mass in East Paterson, New Jersey. When he was temporarily assigned that summer to the busy Franciscan Church of St. Francis on West Thirty-first Street, New York, we had ample opportunity to discuss the potentialities of the new apostolate and to discuss its first projects with Third Order officials.

At the invitation of Father Philip Marquardt, O.F.M., the Executive Secretary of the National Third Order, Father Roy made the first formal introduction of the apostolate to the Third Order at a Youth Congress held at Notre Dame University in July. Besides helping him draft his speech, I also suggested that the Congress should end with a solid set of resolutions. These "Notre Dame Resolutions" were drawn up at the Congress and released immediately as a prime news story by Frank Hall who had been advised to expect them.

The Cathedral Rallies held throughout the country during the fall of 1960 constituted the first big venture. There were gatherings of Third Order members in the major cities of the country, with "Interracial Charity" as their theme. I felt that this was the time to cement relations between the Catholic Interracial Council movement and the Third Order of St. Francis. I had my good friend Bob Krouskoff draw up an editorial cartoon showing the Catholic Interracial Council as a football team welcoming the Third Order of St. Francis players as "new reserves for the winning team." I also got officials of both organizations to issue pledges of mutual support and co-operation. Dr. John O'Connor, speaking for the National Catholic Conference for Interracial Justice, called the Franciscan action "a major contribution to the cause of interracial justice and world peace," and urged Catholic Interracial Council support for the Cathedral Rallies. Father John McGuirk, T.O.R., speaking on behalf of the Third Order, noted that the "work of the Catholic Interracial Councils is excellent and we pledge to do all in our powers as Tertiaries to co-operate in their program."

Father Roy, in the meantime, had gone to St. Anthony's Shrine, a worker's chapel in downtown Boston for his Pastoral Theology program. Here he set up the pilot project of the new movement in the local Third Order Fraternity. It was at this time, for the sake of better emphasizing the nature of the Third Order movement, that the name was changed to Action for Interracial Understanding (A.I.U.).

Out of this pilot project came the man who was to emerge as A.I.U.'s National Director: Ralph Fenton of Norwood, Massachusetts. Mr. Fenton, his wife and daughter were all members of the Third Order and among the first volunteers for establishing A.I.U. as a pilot project. He was the Office and Methods Director of Factory Mutual Fire Insurance Companies, and as such, he contributed an essential element to the movement: dynamic, modern and efficient organization.

Both Father Roy and Mr. Fenton joined the Boston Catholic Interracial Council, working together with Monsignor Francis J. Lally, editor of the Boston *Pilot* and then president of the Council. At my suggestion, Father Roy was named a director. Later Mr. Fenton became Council president, infusing new vigor and strengthening the lines of co-operation with A.I.U.

Action for Interracial Understanding initiated a series of pilot projects in Boston. It formed a task force of speakers and panelists who appeared before numerous parish and civic organizations, inaugurated a school for adult Negro education in the Roxbury section of the city, and made a survey of the racial attitudes of the Boston parishes. These projects worked so well that I suggested to Father Roy that the time had come for a full statement of the movement's purpose and methods.

The statement was made at the quarterly Communion breakfast of the New York Catholic Interracial Council on April 16, 1961. It poured rain that day and few members were able to attend. The talk, however, was later reprinted in *Interracial Review* and it received very wide coverage in other publications. Father LaFarge noted its significance in an editorial in *America:* "Certainly it must have been the intercession of Assisi's great saint which inspired the directors of the Third Order in this country to embark upon the dynamic program announced by its chief promoter, Father Roy Gasnick, O.F.M., at a Catholic Interracial Council communion breakfast in New York on April 16. This step taken by the Third Order, said Fr. Gasnick, opens up unlimited possibilities for the Catholic interracial movement. It means that 106,000 lay Catholics, organized in 1,200 fraternities throughout the United States, have been committed to work actively in helping to solve racial problems. A thoroughly practical five-point program has been adopted: for the parish, the school and the community. Every effort will be made to impregnate the civic community with Christian life and spirit in order to prevent racial tensions and strife."

In the early summer of that year, I was invited to a meeting of the national leaders of the Third Order held at St. Francis Church on West Thirty-first Street, New York, and at that meeting I was appointed a consultant for the Third Order's interracial movement. Unknown to me at the time, the main reason why the Third Order officials invited me to attend was to sound out my views and to look me over. After I left, they nominated and elected me to receive the 1961 St. Francis Peace Medal, one of the great honors of my life. The ceremony took place on September 21 at the Statler-Hilton hotel in New York. Auxiliary Bishop John M. Fearns of New York, in making the presentation address, gave a forthright declaration of diocesan approval of the New York Catholic Interracial Council. The medal was conferred on me by Father Philip Marquardt, O.F.M.

One more step was needed to cement the grand alliance. On the Feast of Christ the King that year, the New York Council gave the James J. Hoey Award to Ralph Fenton, the National Director of A.I.U.

Since those first days at Holy Name College, Action for Interracial Understanding has blossomed and become established. Today it exists in Third Order fraternities throughout the country. Quietly, persistently and effectively, the members are working over backyard fences, in offices and factories, in schools and in churches, to bring the message of interracial understanding. It has set up schools for adult education, organized interracial home visits, worked with fair housing committees, but most importantly has sent forth laymen and women to preach and live the word to a racially torn America. And in the spirit of St. Francis and of the Catholic Interracial Council, it has sought to recognize justice and praise merit wherever it found them. It is proud, for example, that it was the first Catholic organization to honor Dr. Martin Luther King, who was the recipient of the St. Francis Peace Medal in 1963.

By chance it was also in Washington that I first met Paul D. Williams, the Southerner who did more than any other to spread the principles and techniques of the Catholic interracial movement in the Southland itself, recipient in 1945 of the Hoey Award. "Courageous always, embarrassing himself but saving the embarrassment of others, battling injustice wherever he finds it, hopeful of the future, thoughtful, tactful, cultured, this is Paul Williams, the real Catholic and the real American." Such were the words used to describe him on that occasion by Bishop Vincent S. Waters of Raleigh, North Carolina.

Born in Richmond, Virginia, Paul won a football scholarship from high school to Georgetown University. His father's business was hit so hard by the Depression, however, that he had to leave college for work on a Philadelphia newspaper. From there he moved to a part-time job with a publishing house in Boston, and put himself through Boston College, forming friendships in the college with several Southern Negroes, one or two of them from Richmond. A chance meeting with Monsignor John A. Ryan of the Social Action Department of NCWC blossomed into a close friendship. When Monsignor Ryan was organizing a Catholic social action conference at Cleveland, he asked Paul to assemble some Catholics from the South, to constitute a delegation and make a contribution. The ad hoc group became the Catholic Committee of the South, which under his guidance contributed significantly to the promotion of religious and racial understanding. In 1944, for example, it gave its award for distinguished service to the South to a Methodist sociologist and educator, Dr. Howard W. Odum.

I still recall vividly that first meeting with Paul Williams. It was in Union Station, Washington, in 1942. He was a man of medium height and build, with a pleasant but very strong face, a prominent chin, and dark hair brushed straight back from a high forehead. He was one of a group of fifty or sixty who had come from all over the country to urge Paul V. McNutt, chairman of the War Manpower Commission, to resume the interrupted hearings on the Fair Employment Practices Committee. We were led by A. Philip Randolph, and he informed us that McNutt would see our spokesmen but not the entire group. "Who would the spokesmen be?" Williams asked. "Walter White of the NAACP, George Hunton of the Catholic Interracial Council, and myself," Randolph answered. "They represent the full spectrum of our opinion," someone commented, and it looked for a moment as if that would be the decision. "It may be representative," I interrupted, "but I don't think it's fair to the rest of our people who have at great expense and sacrifice come here to support this cause. They have a right to a little more courtesy. If McNutt won't see all of us, I vote we go home." There was a long discussion, and we went home again without calling on McNutt. We may have achieved more than if we had seen him. McNutt was shortly replaced as chairman by Monsignor (later Bishop) Francis J. Haas, Dean of the School of Social Science of the Catholic University, and an open friend of the position we espoused.

Paul Williams worked in civic as dedicatedly as in Catholic organizations. He hailed the Atlanta Statement issued in 1943 by a group of white Southern leaders headed by crusading editor Ralph McGill, of the Atlanta *Constitution*. The Statement accepted the challenge made by Negro leaders at Durham, North Carolina, the previous year. Its signers undertook to work constructively to give Negroes the civil rights and economic opportunities to which as American citizens they had equal claim. Paul was also director of the Virginia Interracial Commission. In a region predominantly Protestant, he was elected president of the Interracial Southern Regional Council dedicated to promoting equal opportunity and other human rights for all citizens.

During all this time, the number of Councils was growing steadily. Thirty-five local and regional councils were represented at the observance of our twenty-fifth anniversary in 1959, without including other interracial activities we had inspired, such as the St. Benedict the Moor Apostolate of Interracial Charity, and a social action workshop in Cleveland, conducted by the Sisters of Notre Dame. The Councils had spread from New York not only north and west, but also southwards, to Philadelphia, Baltimore, Washington, Wilmington, Delaware, St. Louis, Greensboro, North Carolina, Richmond, Rock Hill, South Carolina, New Orleans, and San Antonio, Texas. In this way we—and when I say we, I most emphatically include Paul Williams and his pioneering colleagues—had by the early 1950s created a situation in the South that was the opposite to that prevalent in the North when we started our movement there in the early 1930s. Thurgood Marshall was able to tell a conference on human relations at Central State College, Wilberforce, Ohio, in 1956 that the Catholic Church was "in the forefront of the struggle for racial integration in the South," whereas the participation of Protestants—with the exception of the Friends and some individual ministers—was "very spotty." This opinion was confirmed in 1957 by *Ebony* magazine. In many sectors of the South, it said editorially, "Catholics can rightly claim to have led desegregation."

I do not pretend that all Catholics had been fully converted. The scandalous resistance to Archbishop Joseph F. Rummel's belated integration of Catholic facilities in New Orleans, in the early 1960s, is still fresh in all memories. But at least very solid groundwork had been laid in advance of the historic decision of the United States Supreme Court of May 17, 1954, declaring unconstitutional laws imposing racial segregation in public schools. In a pastoral issued in March 1953, Archbishop Rummel ordered that there should be "no further discrimination or segregation in the pews, at the Communion rail, at the confessional, and in parish meetings, just as there will be no segregation in the kingdom of heaven." Two months later, Bishop Waters of Raleigh similarly ordered that "there is no segregation of races to be tolerated in any Catholic church in the diocese of Raleigh. The pastors are charged with the carrying out of this teaching and shall tolerate nothing to the contrary. . . . All special churches for Negroes will be abolished immediately." And in April 1954, Archbishop Robert E. Lucey of San Antonio, Texas, declared that the day of racial injustice had passed and that of Christ's charity had arrived. "Henceforth, no Catholic child may be refused admittance to any school maintained by the Archdiocese merely for reasons of color, race or poverty."

The emotional impact of the Supreme Court decision was consequently much less severe on the Catholic than on the general community in the South, and even though Catholic schools were not directly affected, the process of integration was speeded up quickly and as a rule painlessly. Even before that time, all or almost all Catholic higher education had been integrated, and there was more integration than is sometimes realized at the grade level. In the St. Louis area of Missouri, Archbishop Ritter completed integration at all levels in 1948, and the beneficial effect for the entire community became gradually evident by creating a climate of understanding. By 1951, St. Louis University had 351 Negro students and four

Negro faculty members. The result was that St. Louis obeyed the 1954 Supreme Court order without the slightest incident and has continued to lead the South in reshaping its living patterns. Catholic schools at all levels in the District of Columbia ended segregation before 1954. Those in the Greater Baltimore area were integrated in 1954, and those in the Greater Washington area (including southern Maryland) in 1955. Also before 1954, Negro pupils were admitted to Catholic white schools in Arkansas, if there was no separate Negro Catholic school. Kentucky, South Carolina and Tennessee integrated at least in principle either before or shortly after the Supreme Court decree, although the smallness of the number of Catholics in these states, combined with the neighborhood patterns, meant that the change had not too much practical effect. In Texas, also, the Catholic authorities proclaimed the principle of integration, although the practical results were often delayed in areas where the public schools fought delaying actions. Incidentally, Xavier University began to admit whites in the early 1950s and thus became the first integrated institution in the Gulf South Coast.

All the world is familiar with the tragedies that have marked the struggle for human rights in the South during the past decade—Little Rock and Selma, and the barbaric gunning down of James Meredith on a public highway as I write these very lines. But the one thing that dominates the scene, as I view it, is the strength of public opinion in every part of the country behind the moral stand of such great Americans as Nobel Prize Winner Dr. Martin Luther King. Today there is still suffering, but it is not a sectional war of North and South or a racial war of Negro and white. It is, as Father LaFarge always insisted, the moral clash between good and evil, and it is being fought where it should be fought, on the field of human rights. That so broad a section of white Southern opinion sees the issue in its proper terms I attribute to Paul Williams more than to any other single individual.

I think I can consequently say that the South in the 1960s is going through the process already substantially completed in the North, and it is going through it at the accelerated pace characteristic of life in the nuclear era. The North today has accepted the principle that one citizen has the same public rights as another, the right to use the political, educational, cultural, recreational, business, commercial, and travel facilities of the community to the extent to which his personal qualities enable him, without taking into account the color of his skin or other arbitrary distinction. It has accepted the principle not only at the rational level, but to a large extent emotionally. The South still fights it, because it involves so profound a social, economic and political upset of its static pattern of living.

The North, nevertheless, is far from the end of the road. We always insisted in the Catholic interracial movement that the issues were not only legal but moral. We said the community must recognize the rights of individuals not only as citizens but also as human beings. And in this area of strictly human rights, the North has a long way to go. What I think is important to note, however, is the continuing relationship between the two kinds of rights. When the whites in the North today insist that they recognize the rights of the Negro as a citizen, they often are deceiving themselves, because their denial of his human rights frequently involves not only injustice but covert violation of law as well.

Let me take a fact that practically every American observes for himself every day in the week, regardless of where he lives, which has failed to impinge on the consciousness or the conscience of most of those who observe it. Negroes represent ten per cent of Americans, but—apart from stereotyped situations— one sees few Negroes on television. Frederick O'Neal reported some years ago at a forum of the Catholic Interracial Council that only one half of one per cent of the performers seen on American television were Negroes. The situation has since improved slightly, but even today Negroes have scarcely reached one full percentage point.

For once, no die-hard could plead lack of ability or preparation on the part of Negroes. They excel in the world of entertainment as in the world of sport, not—let me add—because of some racial characteristic which makes them particularly suited to be entertainers or athletes, but simply because these are areas where prejudice was less successful in holding them back. In 1966, they excel also as soldiers, although as recently as 1948 General (later President) Eisenhower was warning that the armed forces of the United States would suffer gravely if Negroes were given equal opportunity as fighting men. Figures released in 1966 showed that 18.3 per cent of the Army's combat dead in four years in Vietnam were Negroes, that Negroes constituted 18 per cent of the combat units in Vietnam, and that an even higher proportion of the volunteer paratroopers and "Green Berets" training to go to Vietnam were Negroes.

Do these facts, or the further fact that Negro re-enlistments when their term of duty expires are three times as high proportionately as those of whites, mean that Negroes enjoy risking their lives? Of course not. They risk their lives because President Truman, by Executive Order No. 9981 issued in 1948, opened up for them a new area of the American economy in which they have a chance to get a break on their merits. Victor Hall is risking his life to make the money to complete his biology degree in Tougaloo College, Jackson, Mississippi; Lee Ward Jackson, because his divorced mother is ill and he has to support her; William Peterson, because the alternative is "to go back to Birmingham, Alabama."

The threat to America's social stability inherent in the efforts by the white community to halt at an arbitrary point the implementation of the rights it had agreed in principle to admit for Negro citizens has been a concern of the Catholic interracial movement, as of other social agencies, since the early 1940s. The many outbreaks of violence in the 1960s and the steady growth of influence of extremist leaders on both sides have more than confirmed the legitimacy of our concern.

I think I can fairly claim that the Catholic Interracial Council of New York was the first organization not only to make a formal analysis of the problem, but to draw up a concrete program for its solution. This program, in the implementation of which I was to become deeply involved over a long period of years, became known as the New York Plan.

As we approached the tenth anniversary of the founding of the Catholic Interracial Council, we devoted several meetings of the directors to an evaluation of what had been achieved and what new directions we might now profitably take. These discussions were held in the fall of 1943, under the shadow of the race riots which had occurred in Detroit in June and July of that year, the reactions to which presaged further violence and terror in many parts of the country.

Our first conclusion was a very positive one. We were satisfied that we had made gratifying progress in arousing the interest and support of Catholic leaders for the principles on which we stood. The ideological fight had been won. Catholic editors, educators, sociologists, lecturers, and writers no longer questioned the principles of the Catholic interracial program.

Our second conclusion was less comforting. Little progress could be recorded for our efforts to project the intellectual conclusions into the emotional reality of the American community. The rank and file of Catholics continued to think and behave as they had done before at the community and neighborhood level, where people lived and worked together.

Our concrete decision was that we ought to work for the creation of neighborhood councils in those parts of New York in which race tension existed or threatened, and we set out our plan in the April 1944 issue of the *Interracial Review*. In the light of subsequent events, our presentation of the issues can hardly fail to sound prophetic. Racial clashes, the statement warned, will increase after the war unless the discriminations and antagonisms that have caused them are removed. The mobilization of force to prevent conflicts and riots will not suffice, unless the causes are removed. Legislation to end employment discrimination is desirable, but it must be supported by public opinion, and public opinion in turn must be implemented in concrete programs of action at the community level.

The specific program we then proposed was to encourage the religious leaders of the community, the priests, ministers and rabbis, to take the initiative in forming community councils which could "achieve for the well-being of the neighborhood what political district clubs had long accomplished on behalf of political parties." They should enroll social welfare leaders, educators and local teachers, the police, attendance officers, probation workers, representatives of the minor courts, leaders in business industry and labor, and representatives of racial and ethnic groups.

"As the council brings together peoples of different races, nationalities and cultures, common understanding and mutual respect will develop; conflicts and misunderstandings will be prevented and resolved; problems of discrimination and denial of essential opportunities will be seen as grave violations of human rights, as contrary to democratic ideals and disruptive of the common good."

Reprinted as a pamphlet, thousands of copies of this program were distributed throughout the country. One Jewish agency took 500 copies for its own members. A pilot project in the Rockaways section of Queens was so successful that in February 1945 I was asked to head a subcommittee on community programs of the advisory committee on human relations of New York City's Board of Education. The plan on which the subcommittee quickly agreed followed in broad outline the one we had proposed the previous April in the *Interracial Review,* the applicability of which to New York's conditions had already been established by our pilot project in the Rockaways.

The Superintendent of Schools agreed to start with three neighborhoods. The most complicated of these was South Jamaica, and we knew that if we could succeed there, we could succeed anywhere. The area had been urbanized in the eighties and nineties of the last century when home-hungry Irish and Jewish refugees from Manhattan slums had built solid one-family and two-family homes. A generation later, Italians and Poles followed them. By World War II, however, it had degenerated into a formless brick-and-asphalt jungle bestriding the tracks of the Long Island Railroad from Van Wyck Boulevard to Belt Parkway. Negroes and Puerto Ricans were moving in. Teenage gangs of the many ethnic groups roamed the streets and muggers lurked in the shadows of the railroad underpass. There was no proper shopping center, no branch public library, not even a movie house. It took more time to ride across the area by bus than to go by subway to Manhattan.

As the Board of Education had sponsored the study, it fell to one of its employees, Mrs. Herman W. (Betty) Kammin, principal of P.S. 116 in South Jamaica, to get the project on the road. After a host of jurisdictional problems had been resolved, she called an organizing meeting at her school in May 1945 to form a committee that would serve an area embracing four public schools, an area already seventy per cent colored and faced with the proximate loss of the remaining thirty per cent of Italians, Jews, Poles, Irish and other whites.

Attendance included white and Negro teachers, social workers, lawyers, labor organizers, priests, ministers, rabbis, storekeepers, realtors, a tailor, a beautician, the presidents of various organizations of parents and several housewives with views of their own. The group called itself the Advisory Council of South Jamaica. It started off by organizing an informal survey of the area's problems, then set up a series of subcommittees, each charged with working on a major problem. Issues of tolerance, bias or discrimination were left to one side. It was agreed that the entire community lacked certain basic services, and that these should constitute the first order of business. By September, when school reopened, major progress had been registered. The Board of Education had agreed to establish a full-time community center in a junior high school, to open all schools either afternoon or evening for recreational purposes, to provide evening classes for adults in a wide range of practical subjects and the arts, to equip a games room to keep the kids off the streets at night. Needed medical and dental facilities were secured. Programs were introduced to encourage civic pride and improve sanitary conditions. Police protection improved significantly after the police captain was brought in as a member of the Council. In the following years came a child care center, and a better schedule of crosstown buses.

Intangible but priceless indirect benefits were an almost complete ending to discrimination in restaurants, hotels, and places of public entertainment and recreation, a lessening of racial tensions, improved school-community relations, a sharp decline in truancy, juvenile delinquency and vandalism, and a relative stabilization of property values which had been dropping disastrously because of panic selling. Classroom discipline and classroom performance rose strikingly. More graduates of the junior high school not only finished high school but went to college, some winning scholarships in open competition. I remember Mrs. Kammin telling me that previously she and the other principals in South Jamaica used to have no end of trouble trying to get teachers, but that when word got around of the new atmosphere, they quickly had long lists of highly qualified applicants.

Another unanticipated result of the New York Plan in South Jamaica was integration of religious worship. When the Council was established, only a handful of the seventy per cent Negroes and Puerto Ricans attended the Catholic, Episcopal, Lutheran, Presbyterian, Congregational, Baptist, and Unitarian churches located in the area. In 1945, some Negroes asked the regional Presbyterian Board for help in building a church. The Board worked out an arrangement with the existing "white" church for a service for Negroes following the regular service. Soon, both groups recognized the absurdity of the arrangement and joined in one service. Other religious groups followed suit, so that in a few years the congregations were fully integrated. Attendance of Negro children in the Catholic parochial school rose from about a dozen to over a hundred.

Although as an outsider I had no official standing in the South Jamaica Community Council once it got under way, I followed its activities closely and was always welcomed at policy discussions. The non-white population of South Jamaica had grown to so big a proportion of the total before the Council started to function that it was unrealistic to hope for stabilization as a balanced interracial community. We were concerned, nevertheless, to prevent the fringe areas from becoming slums and racial ghettos, and we accordingly embarked on a positive intercommunity policy. One of the most acute issues quickly resolved itself. With the improvement of recreational facilities and community sense, the Negro youth quickly stopped the border raids into neighboring white districts, in which they had previously indulged. And in 1950, the Council was able to convince a delegation from the nearby community of Hollis that they could absorb an influx of non-white homeseekers by taking a firm stand against panic selling.

I had also the good fortune to get the opportunity to prove that integrated housing was possible in a wealthy suburban community, and that the way to go about it was to start with the New York Plan. The pilot community in this instance was Manhasset, Long Island. In January 1945, some of the citizens met in the home of Mrs. Dorothy Fremont Grant, the author and lecturer, to see if some way could be worked out to help the white and Negro residents of a slum area known as "The Valley." Four men and eight women attended that meeting.

The group was mixed racially and religiously—two of the women were Jewish, and two were Negroes.

Somebody in the group had heard or read about my involvement in the New York Plan, and I was invited to the next meeting to explain more fully how it worked. On my recommendation, the group formed a community council similar to those already functioning in South Jamaica and the other areas in which the Board of Education had taken the initiative. The Board of Education was not officially involved in Manhasset, but we did have the co-operation of the teachers as citizens, alongside the clergy, social workers, housewives, and business and professional men. The community council decided to undertake a major housing project, but because the town was not incorporated, the state of New York had to pass legislation to create a Manhasset Housing Authority. This Authority made a survey in 1947 of housing needs, and on the basis of its findings, the State Housing Commission made a loan of $2,000,000 for 70 housing units in Port Washington and 100 in the Manhasset Valley area. By 1952, the Spinney Hill and Harbor Homes, two-level garden apartments, were ready to receive the white and Negro population of the Valley, and the shacks were eliminated from the Manhasset scene. Rents charged, although not significantly higher than those for the shacks, made the project self-financing. Other Long Island suburban communities soon followed the lead given by Manhasset.

In 1953, the New York Board of Education made a decision which I then opposed and which I still think was mistaken. It decided that bureaucrats could do more for the citizens than they could do for themselves. It accordingly withdrew its support from community-controlled Councils and introduced a group of functionaries to be known as community co-ordinators, who would run the show. We had seen this coming for a considerable time, because the city had stopped expansion of the autonomous Council program into new areas, in spite of its success in the pilot areas where it had been introduced between 1944 and

1948. I appeared before the Mayor's Committee on Unity in December 1951 and I insisted that local autonomy was essential to success. "The trouble with an appointed Council," I then testified, "is that the appointive power always appoints to these committees the people who are causing the least trouble. That, of course, is precisely the way not to get anything done. What you need is a committee that will go down to Borough Hall and say: 'If you don't do something about this, we will fix you at the next election.' The government always takes care of nuisances."

By 1953, however, an internal dynamism had been generated by the Councils in South Jamaica and in several of the other pilot areas. In spite of the Board of Education's withdrawal of support, they continued to function. With Mrs. Count Basie, wife of the band leader, as president, the South Jamaica Council proceeded to develop its own program and simultaneously to co-operate with and influence through public opinion the functioning of the new "community co-ordinator." Its subsequent accomplishments include the organization of the South Queens Mental Clinic, operated by volunteers, in 1954; and the opening of the Queens Guidance Center in 1957. As I write, the Council is still a vital element in South Jamaica. Although Mrs. Kammin has retired from the school system, she keeps in touch with the old neighborhood. She told me in August 1966 that a short time previously she had talked to Mrs. Ruby Couch of the South Jamaica Human Relations Unit of the Board of Education, and that Mrs. Couch assured her that the community council is still controlled by the ordinary people of the community, and that it is doing "an outstanding job" and is a model for other communities.

I had yet another opportunity to plead the cause of the community councils not very long after the Board of Education withdrew from the program. After the Supreme Court had ordered the desegregation of public schools in 1954, the Board created an Integration Commission to implement the decision, and I was invited to serve as chairman on one of its six sub-commissions, that on community relations and information.

Our report was completed early in 1957 and was in due course approved by the Integration Commission and adopted by the Board of Education. It started from the premise that residential segregation rather than any policy of the school authorities had created school segregation in New York, but the school authorities were nevertheless involved because experience had demonstrated that good educational standards could not be maintained in schools located in trouble areas. The mal-adjustment of the community inevitably spilled over into the schools. Even if the schools were integrated, the situation would not normalize itself. An unorganized community lacks satis-factory intergroup relations. It lacks machinery to deal with real or imagined grievances, for example, to stop a wave of panic selling.

While we did not challenge the value of the "community co-ordinator" program to which the Board of Education was committed, we insisted that it was inadequate to do what the community required. In addition to those district-wide and school-inspired organizations, we called for neighborhood coun-cils under the policy control of local community leaders, each serving a small area and concentrating on the social, cultural, economic, and educational needs of that area. The activities of these councils should be confined to local community problems. They should remain free of all political affiliation. They should not represent the city in any city-wide campaign or movement. They should concentrate on the most urgent problems of their own area, housing, employment, delinquency, recreation, sanitation, transportation or whatever the particular area re-quired.

"We repeat," the report concluded, "our conviction that our schools alone cannot provide all the solutions to the problems of the changing neighborhoods, of group tensions. . . . The most effective community programs are carried out in local communities by leaders of the communities, including rabbis, ministers, priests and other representative leaders. Any plan to rely on the school alone for the development of intergroup relations is impractical, unrealistic, and bureaucratic. . . . What is indispensable is a climate of opinion in local areas favorable to residential and educational integration. This can be provided through the deliberations of neighbors working together on problems of their neighborhoods."

Chapter 12

It was in 1958, my seventieth year, that my eyesight began to interfere seriously with my ability to work. Two years earlier, I had undergone a successful operation for removal of cataracts from both eyes. An unpleasant experience, it had slowed me down temporarily. But cataract removal seldom creates complications any more. The doctors had given me every assurance of success, and the event proved them correct. I was quickly back in my office, able to function as well as a man of my age could reasonably expect.

Apparently the new trouble, which developed shortly afterwards, had no connection with that earlier experience. In 1958, the doctors diagnosed a detached retina of the left eye. In due course, they operated, and again the first reports after I returned from the theater indicated that all was normal. It is essential, however, that the patient remain perfectly still for a considerable period after the operation, and a totally unanticipated and unrelated development made that impossible. I had a lightning attack of stomach ulcers that caused such loss of blood that I had to be removed to another hospital for transfusions and appropriate treatment.

The ulcers were stilled, but the movement had caused the retina to become detached again. A second eye operation not only proved unsuccessful but created a condition which forced the doctors to decide that nothing more could be done for that eye. It had become permanently sightless.

This time, the period of recuperation was longer and the toll on my physical strength was greater. But I was far from ready to give up. My right eye was still reasonably good. I could travel with confidence, could usually read for extended periods without ill effects. Soon I was not only back at my desk but moving around the country to lecture, to attend conventions, to help in the formation of councils, to promote the co-ordination of national effort through the National Catholic Conference for Interracial Justice established in 1959, an organization of which I was chosen an executive committee member.

Nevertheless, when Father LaFarge would show up for a Thursday evening forum at our offices, as he still did with amazing regularity, he and I would look at each other and recognize that neither of us was getting any younger. Father LaFarge was eight years my senior, and he had become very stooped and feeble. But his health was extraordinarily good and his spirit still soared dauntlessly over every obstacle.

We were both sufficiently realistic to know that we could not continue on forever. Besides, we had in our thirty-year association, with the help of our good friends, built an institution that we were confident could take care of itself. We finally reached the conclusion, after many discussions with our board of directors and others, that we should both retire together while we still had the physical and mental strength to advise and encourage the new chaplain who would replace Father LaFarge and the new executive secretary who would replace me. Father LaFarge would assume the title of chaplain emeritus, and I would continue as a member of the board of directors and be given the new title of consultant.

The decision was announced at the annual Communion breakfast and membership meeting of the Catholic Interracial Council of New York on February 11, 1962. Father Philip S. Hurley, S.J., was inducted as chaplain, and Dennis Clark as executive secretary. Though still quite young, Dennis was extremely well known in interracial circles. He had taught sociology at St. Joseph's College, Philadelphia, subsequently worked for the

Commission on Human Relations of the City of Philadelphia. He had published two books dealing with intergroup problems and contributed many articles to the *Interracial Review* and other periodicals.

One of the first acts of the new administration was to arrange a testimonial farewell dinner for the two old men, to be held at the Roosevelt Hotel, New York, on June 4. But even before that date, other long-time friends showered us with kindnesses. The American Jewish Committee and the Anti-Defamation League of B'nai B'rith arranged luncheons in our honor. The National Catholic Social Action Conference chose me for its annual Social Action Award.

At the June 4 ceremony, Lawrence Pierce and Judge Harold Stevens, two of our associates for many years, were respectively general chairman and dinner chairman. The principal speaker was Mayor Robert F. Wagner of New York. He presented citations from the city to both of us for our efforts to make New York a better place for people to live in. Other speakers included James A. Farley, Rabbi Tannenbaum, and George Fowler of the New York State Commission Against Discrimination.

The highlight of the evening, however, was a telegram carrying a message which subsequent events have further enriched. With pride, I quote the entire text.

"Father John LaFarge, S.J., and George Kelly Hunton, honored by friends of justice upon the occasion of their retirement tonight, are remarkable examples of the power of free men to do good. Beloved priest and dedicated lawyer, these men have for three decades worked together to secure justice amid difficulties caused by prejudice and misunderstanding. Their inspiring careers have led thousands of citizens to work for the advancement of civil rights and the achievement of interracial justice. The teaching, writing and zeal of these dedicated men have kept fresh America's promise of freedom and opportunity for men of all creeds, colors and conditions. In a nation blessed with high ideals of justice and human dignity, citizens of all backgrounds are grateful for the selfless work of Father John LaFarge and George Hunton. Their service and spirit encourage us to devote ourselves more fully to the life of our democracy. With all best wishes. John F. Kennedy."

I welcomed the freedom from a daily office routine which I now enjoyed principally because it permitted me to devote more time to the care of a maiden sister who had long lived with me. Early in 1962, the doctors ordered her into hospital for treatment of a tumor, which after a considerable delay they decided to remove, and which unhappily proved to be malignant.

I also found time, nevertheless, to retain contact with my friends and their concerns. I had several discussions in the early part of 1963 with A. Philip Randolph concerning the civil rights program which President Kennedy was promoting. We were all happy at the President's commitment, but we knew from long experience that massive opposition could be expected. Two things seemed particularly important, namely, the widest possible agreement among supporters of civil rights on what legislation they wanted and what they would be willing to accept, and the clearest possible public demonstration of the extent of the groundswell in the country in favor of the President's program.

A. Philip Randolph was the man most widely trusted by all civil rights workers, and he led a group of forty representatives invited by the President to discuss the issues with him in Washington in June 1963. I had the honor of being included, and we were received most courteously by the President, who was accompanied by Vice-President Johnson and Attorney General Robert Kennedy. Among the things we told him was that we were planning a mass demonstration in Washington to put Congress and the nation on notice that there could be no further postponement.

The meeting was held on Wednesday, August 28, at the most

appropriate place in the capital, in front of the Lincoln Memorial. There had been doubters. Some feared the letdown of a small turnout. Others feared counter-demonstrations and violence. Neither catastrophe occurred. With scarcely a boo or a hate slogan, 240,000 Americans converged from all over the nation for what was one of the most impressive sights of my long life. The Catholic Interracial Council of New York alone chartered and filled five buses. Along with Council members, they carried Young Christian Workers and Catholic Trade Unionists.

Father LaFarge was there. He was eighty-three, and like myself, he couldn't march very far any more. But we both were determined to march, if only a token step. A. Philip Randolph, the chairman, recalled that it had taken twenty-two years to stage the March on Washington. "We held a mass rally in New York in 1941 to start the idea, and Father LaFarge was the only white man invited to speak then," he noted. "He was the one Catholic clergyman in the group, and here today we have six hundred." It was indeed a sign of the times. Priests and seminarians, Protestant clergymen and Jewish rabbis joined in carrying placards that proclaimed that all faiths marched together in the demand for equal rights.

That was the year we lost three great men, Pope John XXIII in June, President John F. Kennedy in November, and Father John LaFarge a few days later in November. It would be to stray from my purpose to do more than record the sense of personal loss which I shared with everyone I knew and countless millions I did not know around the world at the deaths of the first two. As for the third, it is hardly necessary to add to what I have recorded about one who was my father, my brother, my confidant, my friend, my encourager. I can, however, sum up in a few words, his own words, the spirit of the man, the message he would want remembered and which I too most want remembered.

The words were written after the March on Washington in

August, and they appeared after their author had died, in the December 1963 issue of a little-known publication, the *Jesuit Seminary News*. The final words of Father LaFarge's article summing up his impression of the March on Washington were these:

"Of one thing we can, I think, be certain. Through this demonstration the voice of the American Negro has broken through a great silence that had smothered its authentic expression. And the true voice of the Catholic Church, too, was heard in most compelling form on that August 28 day: a voice which forty-two American bishops have sounded from coast to coast of this country. Quite a bit of the rest, dear brothers in Christ, is up to you and me."

During 1964, much of my time and energy was concentrated on the care of my sister. It became progressively more obvious that the operation had failed to resolve her trouble, and finally the day came in early 1965 when the doctors said hospitalization was indicated to provide the constant attention she needed. She was scheduled to leave the third week of March. On Saturday, March 13, the date recorded in the first paragraph of this book, I was in the kitchen emptying a carton of groceries. Just as I picked up a bottle of milk, it seemed to transform itself in my hand into a series of vivid lines, blue, green, the entirety of the spectrum, then to sparkle like a diadem of precious stones. The illusion lasted no more than a few seconds, and it was followed by total darkness. "What have you done to the lights," I called to my sister. "Now the place is black as night." "What's the matter with you," she called back. "The lights are the same as they always are. Besides, it's still broad daylight."

Whether it was the emotion of the situation, or a total coincidence, or perhaps the hastening of a developing condition because of the crisis of my sister's illness, not even the specialists could tell me. But of one thing they were certain, and they were right—my second eye had deserted me. I would never see again. As for my poor sister, she never returned. A merciful death claimed her two months later.

Since then I have lived alone. My friends, as I said, help me all they can, especially my lifelong friend Schuyler Warren, the one I have to thank for first putting me in contact with Father LaFarge, and the one I now thank each day for being my eyes, my ears, my hands, and my feet.

I have long hours for thought. I will not deny that sometimes they are depressing, when I think of my extreme dependence, the burden I am on others. But generally speaking, they are pleasant thoughts, the kind of thoughts that must come naturally to one who has seen the great events I have been privileged to witness, to know the wonderful people I have been privileged to address and treat as friends.

I am satisfied that the Catholic interracial movement was well worth all the efforts and all the sacrifices. I am satisfied that the Catholic Interracial Councils were a sound idea, an idea that is still far from being exploited to the point of exhaustion. As Monsignor John J. Voight, for many years secretary of education of the archdiocese of New York, once said, they have demonstrated "the effectiveness of an organization conducted by the Catholic laity, and the fruitful co-operation of a priest and laymen." The viability of the idea is confirmed by the fact that, after thirty-two years of effort, these lay-controlled organizations working for interracial justice have received the approval of the authorities of 150 Catholic dioceses across the United States.

The potential of the Catholic Interracial Councils is, accordingly, far from exhausted. I am satisfied that Arthur D. Wright, who succeeded Dennis Clark as executive secretary of the New York Council in 1963, will carry on the lines of policy we initiated and will lead the Council to ever deeper and more important service to the community. I am confident that much more is going to be heard in the years to come about the community council concept which we developed at the Catholic

Interracial Council of New York in 1943, and which I described in the last chapter. Indeed, I believe that this is the most important unfinished business bequeathed by my generation to the hands that now guide the movement.

Just as the Catholic Interracial Councils have changed in the light of experience and developments, so we can expect them to continue to change. It was in the nature of the situation when we first started them, for example, that they should be unobtrusive free-lance operations. They had to be free lance, because the official Catholic leaders—with the few exceptions I have noted—were not ready or did not judge it timely to give them official status within the institutional structures of the parish or diocese. Today, this situation no longer prevails, and I know that some people are arguing that the unfinished business can be expedited by integration of the councils into the diocesan structure. Already, in fact, some dioceses have set up commissions to deal with racial issues in the same way as the Chancery normally has a structure to deal with education, with health, with welfare, with housing, or whatever the concrete social problems of the Catholics of the diocese may be.

The advantage of such a commission is obvious. Race policy cannot be handled in isolation from the total social situation. It needs co-ordination with policy on education, on housing, on welfare, on juvenile delinquency, and the rest. What I am far from sure is that such commissions make interracial councils redundant. On the contrary, it seems to me that the lesson of our experience with the New York Plan is the very opposite. The district-wide programs of community co-ordination operated by the Board of Education supplemented the neighborhood councils which channeled the internal dynamism of the smaller communities, each adding a strength to the other. A diocesan commission can make policy with a greater knowledge of the concrete attitudes and assumptions of the Catholic public, if it is influenced by local councils representing the racial groups in each neighborhood. The councils for their part can be more effective, if a commission exists in the Chancery with the authority and contacts needed to ensure that the policies they advocate are not being unwittingly undermined by contrary policies in other areas, such as education or housing, for example, the responsibility for which lies with other chancery officials.

The other major change I anticipate, and which is already taking place, is a closer co-operation and more specific co-ordination of policy between Catholic interracial councils and other community organizations working in the same field. This, of course, will involve no change of direction for the councils but at most a change of emphasis. As all I have written indicates, we sought from the first day to enlist the help of other workers in the field, both religious and neutral, and to support their initiatives to the fullest extent to which their purposes and ours ran parallel. In the nature of our situation, nevertheless, our primary concern had to be with Catholics as Catholics. Now I think the councils will be progressively concerned with the Catholics as citizens and members of the community in which they live. This follows in part from the evolution of Catholicism in the United States. We are no longer an underprivileged minority but a part of the mainstream of the nation's culture. It also, I suppose, follows from the evolution of Catholic thinking which has been going on for at least half a century but which came dramatically to the surface during the pontificate of Pope John XXIII and during the deliberations of the Second Vatican Council. But it also follows from the evolution of the race situation in the United States.

That we are involved in a radically new phase of race relations in the United States in the mid-1960s is perhaps the one statement about what is currently happening on which all will agree. Perhaps not all will agree with me that it is a logical evolution from what has gone before, but I have deliberately chosen this word to describe my own belief. If today we have violence, if today extremists threaten to take charge, if today the signs portend hatred and bloodshed, all of these things follow logically from the events of the previous quarter century. Before the First World War, the NAACP and the National Urban League were already presenting their modest demands, namely, that the American Negro is an American citizen and is entitled under the Constitution of the United States to equal rights and opportunities with other citizens. By the 1930s, other small voices were heard in support, each arguing from a slightly different but convergent position. The Catholic Interracial Council's basic premise was that the American Negro was a human being made in the image and likeness of God and called to the same eternal destiny as other human beings, and that this fact entitled him to equal rights and opportunities with other children of God.

By World War II, the consensus of American society, both lay and religious, had accepted the logic of these arguments, and it started out slowly and reluctantly, to implement the practical conclusions. The paradox of today's situation is that it represents the success as much as the failure of that implementation. The success is found in the vastly increased number of Negro grade-school graduates, high-school graduates, college graduates, engineers, scientists, professional men. It is found in the token acceptance of Negroes in banking, the stock market, industrial and business management, fraternal organizations. It is found in the more than token acceptance, sometimes approaching true equality of opportunity, in a few areas, such as the armed forces, the trades unions, the field of education, and various areas of public service at the federal, state and local levels.

All of this adds up to "Black Power," an expression I deplore and dislike intensely, because of the danger of abuse and implication of divisiveness, but a reality which is not only desirable but existent. Negroes today do have power, vastly greater power than they had a century ago, for the simple reason that more of them are better educated, more of them are earning more money, more of them are strategically placed in positions of confidence and authority in every area of our religious and civil life, and more of them understand the techniques of organization and manipulation of individuals with a common grievance in the pressure groups which are a basic constituent of the American way of life.

Today's tension is the measure of the conflict between this power and the reluctance of American white society to implement, at a speed acceptable to those who wield this power, the principles fully accepted by the consensus of American white society. One such area is education, an issue not only in the South because of unwillingness to accept the letter of the Supreme Court rulings on educational integration, but an issue in the North, where the spirit of the rulings is violated by de facto segregation in substandard slums. Many whites today criticize Negroes for "pushing too hard," claiming that the high level of school dropouts, delinquency, drug addiction, and the other indices of retarded social development is the fault of the Negroes themselves and must be eliminated before they can expect acceptance. The Negroes know that these factors result from the deprived conditions in which they live, that the vicious circle of underprivilege is the sociological cause of the all too manifest inadequacies of the social behavior of many Negroes.

The Negroes are accordingly right in their insistence that the white community is unjustified in its attempt to continue the segregation of all Negroes so long as there are some Negroes whose social behavior makes them undesirable neighbors. Today, a significant proportion of Northern Negroes have all the indices which entitle them to live in decent neighborhoods. The 83,000 members of the National Association of Real Estate Brokers, an organization which continues to put its own sectional interests before moral right or the good of the nation, may succeed in the efforts in which it is engaged as I write these lines "to generate an immediate wave of indignation" against the proposal of the civil rights legislation currently before Congress to prevent them from discriminating in home sales. If it does, it will be to blame for the bigger wave of indignation that will inevitably result among the moderate Negroes who can only conclude that demonstrated right will not win them justice unless it is backed up by power.

When I express myself in these terms, I voice not only my own personal view but that of the entire Catholic interracial movement. It was spelled out by the Catholic Interracial Council of New York in the most explicit terms in the summer of 1966, just after James Meredith had been shot and wounded while engaged in a peaceful demonstration to encourage voter registration in his native South. That dastardly invocation of violence to prevent justice, the Council said, brought closer the breaking point of the Negro elements who had sought to win racial justice by non-violent methods. Tensions are built up across the country, it said, and "the mood of the ghetto is sullen—it is quiet, it is struggling to contain its anger." Physical attacks against Negroes participating in freedom marches or other peaceful demonstrations will make it "increasingly difficult for the voices of decency, moderation and non-violence to be heard and listened to. . . . We have reached the point in time when the Negro is prepared to defend himself to the very end. It is to be expected that violent assaults will be met by violent defense. It is not unwise to anticipate that we may now be beyond the breaking point."

As I see it, one of the most inspiring things about the Negro struggle for equality has been the moderation of its leadership. I speak from a lifetime of deep and intimate friendship with many of the great men of that movement, Elmer Carter, Lester Granger, Thurgood Marshall, A. Philip Randolph, Roy Wilkins. These men were no less convinced than I was that interracial justice was a winning cause. They were no less convinced than I was that there could be no postponement. But they were also convinced, as I was, that the cause would have to win by peaceful means. They were so convinced not as a matter of expediency, but because they had peace in their hearts. The stronger they became by the progress of events, the more they were concerned to avoid force. Even among the new leaders, who could claim that James Meredith lacks power, or that Dr. Martin Luther King lacks it? Yet they have continued to preach a doctrine in total conformity with the tenets of the heroic exponents of non-violence in our violent century, Mahatma Gandhi and Chief A. J. Luthuli. I am honored to have known such men and proud to have been able to assist their efforts to fulfill their dream of a world of justice. It is one of the blessings of age that the eyes of the mind grow sharp as those of the body dim. For they permit me to see through the dark storm clouds of today a proximate tomorrow in which we in the United States, of all creeds and color, will have completed that dream in the harmony of an interracial society.